EASY MARC

A Simplified Guide to Creating Catalog Records for Library Automation Systems Incorporating Format Integration

Third edition

Scott Piepenburg

1999
F & W Associates, Inc.
San Jose, California

Dedication

This book is dedicted to Jack Kaye and Gay Patrick.
Two people who rise far above the mediocrity in the world.

Orders to:
LMC Source
PO Box 720400
San Jose, CA 95172-0400
800-873-3043 or
831-630-0589
831-634-1456 FAX

Correspondence to:
F & W Associates
PO Box 720268
San Jose, CA 95172-0268

Library of Congress Cataloging-in-Publication Data

Piepenburg, Scott
    Easy MARC: A simplified guide to creating catalog records for library automation systems incorporating Format Integration / Scott Piepenburg – 3rd ed. - San Jose, Calif.: F & W Associates, 1999.

    ISBN: 0-9652126-2-9
    1. MARC formatting – United States – Handbooks, manuals, etc. 2. Cataloging – United States– Handbooks, manuals, etc. I. Title.
    Z693   025.3'16 dc20

CONTENTS

PREFACE

Scott Piepenburg has accomplished a difficult task in preparing this work, **Easy MARC**. He has selected those MARC fields and subfields most likely to be used by those cataloging for school and small public libraries and carefully explained each, giving numerous examples.

There have been so many changes in every aspect of cataloging in recent years, with more changes to come. Cataloging rules have changed considerably since the original **Anglo-American Cataloging Rules** was published in 1978 – we had the 1988 edition and now the 1998 edition, with periodic changes between editions. We have Library of Congress rules interpretations for many of these rules and rule changes.

The MARC format, developed originally at the Library of Congress during 1966-68, became the communications format that designated codes and tags for every piece of the bibliographic record created using AACR2. Developed originally for books and serials, it was expanded during the early 1970s for most types of media housed in/circulated by libraries. In the 1980s a new format was developed for computer files, making a total of seven formats that were mostly alike, but differed significantly one from another. In the late 1980s discussion began on integrating formats into one. The first group of changes was implemented in late 1991, with other changes implemented in mid-1994, early 1995, and early 1996. This format integration process continues internationally, with differences being resolved between USMARC and those versions used by other countries.

The USMARC format is changed periodically by the Library of Congress in consultation with the cataloging community through MARBI, a committee of the American Library Association. **Bibliographic Formats and Standards** is the version of the MARC format used by members of OCLC, and is probably the most commonly used MARC document in the world. That impressive document contains a description of every code, tag, indicator, field, and subfield available to OCLC/MARC users, with detailed explanations and extensive examples; it is the document I use daily.

Scott has, I believe, made wise selections in choosing those portions of the format most likely to be used by school and small public libraries catalogers. I especially like his pages on what to include and what not to include in MARC field 246. He gives a clear explanation of each field chosen and supplies examples. He wisely refers his users to their system manuals for explanation of MARC field 007 for each type of material -- there is no simpler way to document that information.

There are many MARC-based systems in use in schools, small public libraries, and small libraries of other types. Each has its own design, workforms, and limitations. The user of this book must be aware of the needs of the system for which they catalog while deciding on the appropriate codes and tags.

Nancy B. Olson, Professor
Minnesota State University Mankato

INTRODUCTION

The MARC format has undergone significant changes in the last three years, some of the most dramatic changes since its inception in the 1960's. This change is known as *Format Integration* or *FI*. FI has been developed with significant input from librarians around the world, not just in the United States. The purpose of FI was to create a consistent, uniform data-coding format. Instead of having one format for books, another for sound recordings, and another for videorecordings, all a librarian need do is understand the basic format to be able to fully use the rest. This "downsizing" of USMARC has resulted in the printed documentation shrinking from a three volume 3-ring bound set to a two volume 3-ring bound set and changes are being implemented more quickly.

Since the serial format was the most comprehensive, it was chosen as the "base" for FI. Some tags were added, some removed, and some redefined. Among the greatest changes was the increased use of the 246 tag and the addition of the 024 and 028 tags to all formats. While some automated systems may not be able to fully utilize these tags initially, those that can are reporting significant benefits in access and usage. By using the 024 to store the UPC code, new items are searched by simply scanning the item's barcode instead of typing it out. Some changes, like moving variant titles from 740 to 246 will be transparent to users, while others like the "detail" coding of the 505 and 520 could have significant impact. As with all changes, it remains to be seen if the user will react with the same excitement as many catalogers have. In short, the market and our patrons, will drive future development of the system. At least let us hope so. A major concern is to allow the format to be driven by "theoreticians" who know what is "philosophically" good, but the wisdom of such changes has yet to be born out in actual user experience. An example is the subfield **v** in the 6XX tags.

The Internet has also drastically changed the way many patrons view the library. What is important is that the library and its resources now serve as the starting point for the search for knowledge. Today's users are more computer experienced and demand more information be made available to them, oftentimes with less work. The challenge to the cataloger still remains, to anticipate how the users of a specific library will search for the information contained in the library. It is for this reason that this book still stresses the fact that the cataloger has the latitude through cataloging and tagging rules, as well as a professional obligation, to fine tune the cataloging and records in the database to meet the needs of the user. While there are some standards and rules that must be followed, automation has enhanced our ability to better serve our local customers. No longer do the pre-printed cards or records from a jobber or vendor limit us. Each record can be custom-tailored for our customers. That is the goal and obligation of the cataloger.

Because of FI, it has been possible to expand the cataloging of AV items in this book. What has been done with this work is to incorporate AV examples along with book samples where appropriate. Where necessary, specific tag information has been added to accommodate AV cataloging obligations. The user is reminded that cataloging AV items is more similar to cataloging print items than it is different from them. The same basic rules apply, the same basic concepts and ideas still work, and most means of execution are the same. Where they are different, that difference has been noted. This book has also been waiting until more of FI was stabilized in the March 1996 updates to *USMARC bibliographic*. Now that most of the major items have been settled, the time appears right for a book explaining how to use FI in the typical school and small public library, as well as any library which is operated and staffed by a single person. While some topics and issues are still being debated, most notably the cataloging of Internet resources and legal publications, most users will find that the information contained in this book will be relevant and sufficient for their needs.

Another thing that has not changed is the emphasis on quality. Good spelling, authority work - which is becoming even more critical as even PC based systems incorporate some type of authority control system - and a detailed analysis of the physical description and subjects of the item, are the heart of the record. Also, this book is <u>not</u> intended to take the place of AACR2 or formal coursework in cataloging. For information on courses available in your area, you may wish to contact ALA or your vendor to find out if they offer some type of MARC or cataloging training. Many state associations and networks also offer cataloging seminars. Past experience working with librarians around the country has reaffirmed my hypothesis that any librarian can create good records if they are willing to devote the time and effort to it.

This book builds on the strengths of earlier works. It has a liberal inclusion of examples and samples, explanations on the implications on the use or non-use of certain pieces of information, and explanations and samples on the cataloging of curriculum and interest information. Sample records are at the back so that the librarian has a guide that they can use to compare to the records being obtained from vendors and decide if they wish to continue using that vendor as a supplier. This book does not include information on the 007 tags. Because of their detailed nature, space does not permit the thorough coverage they deserve. While their use is strongly encouraged for possible future access and retrieval of records, it is not absolutely critical that they be included in records. If the user desires more information on these tags, you may wish to consult *USMARC Bibliographic Concise* for a listing of them.

Can this book make you the "perfect" cataloger? No, it is not intended to do so. Its intention is to enable you to create thorough records using an automated system. Records designed with an eye to the power of the computer and to the needs of your users. While there are tools available which provide a template and allow you to "fill-in-the-blank" to create records. These do not teach cataloging principles and bibliographic interpretation of items and can result in a haphazard collection and fragmented indexing structure. While you may be creating good records, you do not know why those records are good, and how to use them effectively in your system. The aim of this book is to enable you to create better than average records in a minimum amount of time. The references to *AACR2*, *LCRI* and *USMARC Bibliographic* are designed to serve as a reference point toward enhancing your understanding of these tools. Those in a cataloging class will find them particularly useful, as well as the real-world examples taken from readily available items. Conversations with users of the book have been positive, with a frequent comment that after a year of cataloging using the book, the librarian felt comfortable enough to "solo" without looking at the printed page. If the librarian achieves this, then this writer has succeeded. This book is intended to be a teaching, hands on, practical tool, and not a scholarly tome on cataloging. There are far more detailed works written to that end. Accordingly, while not every cataloging scenario has been addressed, I trust that enough examples and possibilities have been presented to advance your knowledge of cataloging and bibliographic control, and, hopefully to encourage your pursuit of further study in this area.

Scott Piepenburg, 1999

Byrne, Deborah J. *MARC Manual*, 2nd ed. Englewood, Colorado: Libraries Unlimited, 1998

Drazniowsky, Roman. *Map Librarianship*, Metuchen, N.J.; Scarecrow Press, 1975

Joint Steering Committee for Revision of AACR. *Anglo-American Cataloging Rules*, 2nd ed.1998 revision, Chicago: American Library Association, 1968.

*Library of Congress. Cataloging Policy and Support Office. *Free-Floating Subdivisions*, 8th ed. Washington, D.C.: Library of Congress Cataloging Distribution Service, 1996.

*Library of Congress. Cataloging Policy and Support Office. *Subject Headings*, 17th ed. Washington, D.C.: Library of Congress Cataloging Distribution Service, 1994.

Library of Congress. Network Development and MARC Standards Office. *USMARC Format for Authority Data*. Washington, D.C.: Library of Congress, 1993-

*Library of Congress. Network Development and MARC Standards Office. *USMARC Format for Bibliographic Data*. Washington, D.C.: Library of Congress, 1994-

*Library of Congress. Network Development and MARC Standards Office, *USMARC Format for Holdings Data*. Washington, D.C.: Library of Congress, 1991-

*Library of Congress, Network Development and MARC Standards Office, *USMARC Code list for Countries*. Washington, D. C.: Library of Congress, 1993-

*Library of Congress. Office for Descriptive Cataloging Policy. *Library of Congress Rule Interpretations*. Washington, D.C.: Library of Congress, 1990-

*Library of Congress. Office for Subject Cataloging Policy. *Subject Cataloging Manual*. Washington, D.C.: Library of Congress, 1991-

Sears, Minnie Earl. *Sears List of Subject Headings*. New York: H.W. Wilson Company, 1991.

NOTE: Items with an asterisk (*) are available on either Cataloger's Desktop or Classification Plus, two CD-ROM products available from the Library of Congress.

TAG LAYOUT

Below is a sample of how each tag is structured, including terms used in the descriptions, nomenclature, and the significance of each area. It should serve as a guideline for you as you work through each tag.

TAG NUMBER AND NAME

This area contains the number and name of the tag. For the most part, tags are arranged in numerical order, although some have been rearranged to locate similar ideas together.

REPEATABLE: This denotes if the tag is repeatable. Some tags can be repeated in the MARC Bibliographic format, but some can only be used once. Some automation systems will not allow you to repeat non-repeatable tags, while some others will. Note that this denotes only if the <u>tag</u> is repeatable, not if individual <u>subfields</u> in the tag are repeatable.

MANDATORY: This area denotes if the tag is required under the rules of *USMARC Bibliographic* in the record. Some systems will not allow you save a record without the mandatory tags filled out and completed. Note that while some tags may not be mandatory, they may be advisable. That is, if you have the information, you should enter it into the record.

RELATES TO: Some of the tags have a direct relationship to other areas of the MARC record. This area will help you form those linkages. It can also aid you in checking the accuracy of your work.

AUTHORITY: If the information in a tag is under authority control, it is noted here.

1st Indicator

The value and what it stands for in the first indicator position are recorded here.

2nd Indicator

The value and what it stands for in the second indicator position are recorded here.

It is very important to accurately record the information for the indicator positions. Every tag has two possible indicator positions, but both positions may not be used for every tag. Some tags will use only the first position, some only the second, some will use both, and some will not use any. The values in the positions are independent of each other, that is, the value 10 in the **245** should be read as "one-zero" not "ten." While the values may be the same in different tags, they often mean different things.

Accurately entering these values is critical to how your system will process the information. These values are used for indexing, storage, and retrieval of the information in the tags. Incorrectly entering these values could cause the record or the tag to be improperly indexed, thus making it unretrievable, or the information may not be displayed on the screen since the indicator has told the computer to suppress the display of the information. This could keep record data from serving as an access point for retrieval.

SUBFIELD CODES

a   First subfield

The individual subfield codes and what the value stands for are recorded here. There may just be one subfield for a given tag, but most will have more than one.

Subfields are used to separate information in the tags into smaller pieces so that the system can store and access them. Perhaps the most significant thing to remember here is that the subfields are not necessarily in alphabetical order, and that they must be separated by the correct forms of punctuation so that they system can properly index and sort the information. Most of the information in a MARC record will be stored in subfields.

After the heading for the contents of the subfield, there will often be the letters **R** or **NR**. **R** denotes if the particular subfield is repeatable. If **NR** is listed, that means that the subfield is not repeatable.

Most tags must have a **$a**, but there are some exceptions. Some tags will have many subfields, but some will have only a few. What information is contained in the tag is determined by AACR2. How that information is organized and separated is defined by *USMARC Bibliographic*.

EXAMPLES

This area contains sample entries of the information for the relevant tag being discussed. They are taken from AACR2, Library of Congress USMARC documentation and examples, samples of items in selected libraries, or are constructed specifically to highlight problem areas in the tag.

The examples provide the single best way to examine how information is organized. While every scenario may not be covered, the examples provided are based on areas that seem to generate the most problems or are ones that the librarian will encounter most of the time. Write in any other examples that you think are useful for quick reference.

LOCATION

This area will aid you in locating the information in the book or item being cataloged. Most of the time, the information will be recorded on the title page, but at other times you will need to look elsewhere in the book. AV and electronic media usually have the equivalent of a title page, but each will be slightly different. Do not hesitate to devote the time to going through the item looking for the correct information. While you may need more time to catalog the item, you will find that this time is well invested in improved access and retrieval by your patrons. It is far easier to create the record completely when initially entered than having to go back and re-do incomplete records. Those librarians who have had to update records from a shared cataloging utility will heartily agree with this statement.

NOTES

This area discusses how the particular tag and subfields function in an online environment. They also give hints on how the librarian can use them to better serve patrons. Many times the librarian will be presented with options and choices for entering the information. Also, you will find justification for entering non-required areas, most notably notes and summary information.

A very good way to determine if you are entering a record correctly or a record that will be accessible is to enter the record and then see if it is readily accessible in your online system. If it is not, go back in and change or update the record. Since automation systems index items electronically, there are no cards to type or pull, so you can do "what-if" scenarios as much as possible. To the computer, it is just another exercise in indexing. Do not hesitate to try to see what works best in your library. It is through this experimentation that you will be able to determine what works best for your patrons, and what is unnecessary or redundant.

The suggestions given here are exactly that; suggestions. You should interpret them in light of what would be the most useful for your particular library based on your personal experience.

THE SUBFIELDS IN DETAIL

a   **Subfield a's description and narrative**
Each of the subfields in a record is recorded here, along with a brief description of its contents and function. Some areas will have very extensive information, while others will have very little information. Note that they are listed in the order that they should appear in the record. Again, the repeatability of the subfield may be indicated directly after the name of the subfield. To assist the reader, examples listed in this section are italicized to draw attention to the subfield in question. The Italics would not be used in the actual record.

PUNCTUATION

The punctuation for each tag is listed here. Note that punctuation is defined as what <u>precedes</u> each subfield, not by what <u>follows</u> it. The punctuation for each subfield is listed in subfield order.

You may come across the notation *terminal mark of punctuation*. These are marks of punctuation, except where noted, that can end a tag. The terminal marks of punctuation are:

Period	{.}
Exclamation point	{!}
Question mark	{?}
Parenthesis	{)}
Square bracket	{]}
Dash	{-}

Unless noted otherwise, these marks of punctuation can end a tag.

IN GENERAL

Subfields are indicated by **$**
Tag numbers will be **bold** whenever they are mentioned.
Italics are used to draw attention to rules being illustrated.

0XX TAGS

The **0XX** tags contain information that your system will use for routine processing of the records. Very rarely is it used directly by patrons or library staff. Rather, it is usually used during inventory, weeding, report generation, and re-ordering of replacement materials. While many of the tags should be system-generated, they are included here so that if you can view them, you will be able to use the information which they contain to evaluate union or shared records, or when you last made changes to the record. For those items that serve as control numbers, their importance cannot be emphasized enough. For those that are system generated, check with your vendor to see if, and how, the system uses them. Some of the tags, most notably the **024** and **028**, are relatively new to many librarians, although they have been used for specific forms for quite some time. You should check with your software vendor to determine how your system handles them, and if they are indexed or searched.

The **0XX** tags covered in this book are:

000   **Leader**
001   **Control number**
003   **Control number identifier**
005   **Date and time of latest transaction**
008   **Fixed Length Data Field (combined with 006)**
010   **Library of Congress Control Number (LCCN)**
020   **International Standard Book Number (ISBN)**
022   **International Standard Serial Number (ISSN)**
024   **Other standard identifier**
028   **Publisher number**
040   **Cataloging source**

000

000   LEADER

REPEATABLE: NO
MANDATORY: YES
RELATES TO: --
AUTHORITY: NO

The Leader is the first field of a bibliographic record. It is fixed in length at 24 character positions (**00-23**). The Leader consists of data elements that contain numbers or coded values that define the parameters for the processing of the record

1st Indicator
There is no 1st indicator for this tag.

2nd Indicator
There is no 2nd indicator for this tag.

SUBFIELD CODES

There are no subfield codes for this tag. Rather, there are data elements. There are 24 possible positions for this tag (**00-23**) that provide coded information about the record as a whole or about special elements of particular tags.

EXAMPLES

Due to the wide variety of possible ways of displaying this information among the various automation systems, no examples are given. You are encouraged to review the manual for your system regarding how the information for this tag is displayed and edited.

LOCATION

Because of the nature of the information in this tag, it is not possible to give a location to find each piece of information necessary. You will need to scan various areas of the item, as well as review what you have entered in the individual tags in the rest of the record so that this information can be coded correctly. The information you enter here should agree with what you enter in the individual tags in the record. Because of their nature, you will not enter information into some of the element positions, as they are system generated.

NOTES

Many systems will use the information in this tag in screen displays, sorting routines and, limiting criteria, (such as serial or not, type of media, or bibliographic level.) While this information may be contained in narrative form elsewhere in the record, here it is positionally defined. This makes it easier for programmers to write software to limit searches and reject or accept necessary pieces of data.

Because of their dependence on the information in this tag, both now and in the future, it is very important that you enter it correctly. While the particular automation system you are currently using may not use this information now, it may in the future. Also, you may migrate to another system that does use this information. If you have not entered it, you will need to go back and do so, a very costly and time-consuming proposition.

DOCUMENTATION CONVENTIONS

Character positions are positionally defined. Character positions that are not defined contain a **blank** [b] or a **fill character** [l]. All defined character positions must contain either a defined code, or a fill character. **Code** [n] (not applicable), when it is defined for a data element, indicates that the character definition does not apply to the record.

Your particular system may automatically generate some values, while some are defaulted in by the designers. Anytime an alphabetic character is entered, it must be lowercase.

The character position(s) of each element will be listed first, followed by the element name. Below each element will be a statement of Mandatory or Optional. Each element will also contain information regarding the acceptability of the use of the fill character and blank values. Depending on your system, you may only have the character position numbers displayed, or you may have a narrative phrase for a single position or group of positions.

Many vendors will use some type of editing aid, like pop-up boxes, hot keys, or mnemonic aids. Again, check the manual that came with your system to determine how your particular editing aid is designed.

000/00-04   Logical record length
Mandatory   These five character positions contain a number that is equal to the length of the entire record, including itself and the record terminator. The number is right justified and unused positions contain zeros. As a rule, this information is system generated and cannot be edited by the user. In some systems it is "hidden" or not displayed.

000/05   Record status
Mandatory   This position contains a one-character alphabetic code that indicates the relationship of the record to a file for file maintenance purposes.

CODE VALUES AND THEIR APPLICATIONS

a   **Increase in encoding level.**
This value indicates that the encoding level in **000/17** has been increased to a higher encoding level. This value is used when a preliminary cataloging record is raised to full cataloging level. Unless you are editing preliminary records from a database, you will not use this value.

c   **Corrected or revised value.**
This value indicates that an addition or change has been made to the record. This change, however, does not constitute an increase in the encoding level of the record. You will only use it if you are updating or correcting records from a union database.

d   **Deleted.**
This value indicates that the record has been deleted. You will never enter this value. It is only used by the system.

n   **New.**
This value indicates that the record is a newly input record. When you are creating an original or new record, you should use this value.

p   **Increase in encoding level from prepublication.**
This value indicates that the prepublication record has had a change in cataloging level resulting from the availability of the published item and has been upgraded to a full record. You should use this value if you have imported or created a record in your system based on CIP data. When you get the item and you complete the record, you should change this value from **n** to **p**.

000

Type of record

This position contains a one-character letter that specifies the characteristics and defines the components of the record. Use the code appropriate to the type of material. Many systems will automatically enter the correct value here based on the template selected when creating the record.

CODE VALUES AND THEIR APPLICATIONS

a   **Language material.**
This code is used for most printed items, namely books. This code is also used for large print items. Microforms of language material also use this code.

c   **Printed music.**
This code indicates that the content of the record is for printed music or a microform of printed music. This would include items like sheet music.

e   **Printed map.**
This code indicates that the content of the record is for a printed map or a microform of a printed map. This would include sheet maps, folded road maps, and wall maps.

g   **Projected medium.**
This code indicates that the record is for a motion picture, videorecording, filmstrip, slide or transparency. All of these media are intended for projection, either directly or indirectly. Material specifically designed for overhead projection (transparencies) are also included here. Items that contain a projected item and a sound recording may be coded for Kits (**o**) or for Projected medium (**g**) depending on your library's policy.

i   **Nonmusical sound recording.**
Use this code to indicate that the record is for a nonmusical sound recording. This would include such items as talking books and speeches, as well as the author reading his or her own works.

j   **Musical sound recording.**
This code is used for sound recordings that are predominantly musical as opposed to spoken.

k   **Two-dimensional nonprojectable graphic.**
This code indicates that the content of the record is for a two-dimensional nonprojectable graphic such as activity cards, charts, collages, computer graphics (such as the output of computer software graphics programs, but not computer software in general), drawings, duplication masters, flash cards, paintings, photonegatives, photoprints, pictures, postcards, posters, prints, spirit masters, study prints, technical drawings, transparency masters, photomechanical reproductions, and reproductions of any of these.

m   **Computer file.**
Use this code when the record is for a body of information encoded in a manner that allows it to be processed by a computer. The information in the computer file may be numeric or textual data, computer software, or a combination of these types. Although a file may be stored on a variety of media (such as magnetic tape or disk, punched cards or optical character recognition font documents), the file itself is independent of the medium on which it is stored. CD-ROM material would be coded here, as would Interactive video discs and CD-Graphics. This value includes interactive multimedia.

o   **Kit.**
Use this code to indicate that the content of the record is for a mixture of components from two or more types of media when none of the items are identifiable as the predominant component. This category includes packages of material called laboratory kits, and packages of assorted materials, such as a set of K-12 social studies curriculum material (books, workbooks, guides, activities, etc.). Items that contain a projected graphic and a sound recording may be considered kits, projected graphics, or sound recordings depending on your library's policies.

p   **Mixed material.**
This code indicates that there are multiple types of materials together in a unifying whole, none of which has precedence. This will be primarily used for AV or electronic pieces of information. It will be up to the individual library how they wish to interpret this value as opposed to kits.

r   **Three-dimensional artifact or naturally occurring object.**
This code indicates that the content of the record is for a three-dimensional item or a naturally occurring object. This includes man-made objects such as models, dioramas, games, puzzles, simulations, sculptures and other three-dimensional art works, exhibits, machines, clothing, toys, and stitchery. It also includes naturally occurring objects such as microscope specimens (or representations of them) and other specimens mounted for viewing.

000/07   **Bibliographic level**
Mandatory   This position contains a single character indicating the bibliographic level of the record.

CODE VALUES AND THEIR APPLICATIONS

a   **Monographic component part.**
This code indicates a monographic bibliographic unit that is physically attached to or contained in another monographic unit such that the retrieval of the component part is dependent on the physical identification and location of the host item or carrier. For single items, you will not use this value.

b   **Serial component part.**
This code indicates a serial bibliographic unit that is physically attached to or contained in another serial unit such that the retrieval of the component part is dependent on the physical identification and location of the host item or carrier. For single items, you will not use this value.

c   **Collection.**
This value is used to indicate a made-up multipart group of items that were not originally published, distributed, or produced together. This would be used if you created artificially collected items. As a rule, this is not a good policy to follow as it can reduce access to particular items in your collection.

m   **Monograph/item.**
This value indicates an item either complete in one part or intended to be completed in a finite number of parts. You will use this value when cataloging most books.

s   **Serial.**
This code indicates a bibliographic item issued in successive parts bearing numerical or chronological designations and intended to be continued indefinitely. This would include such items as periodicals, newspapers, annuals, yearbooks, etc. These items are outside the scope of this book.

000/09
Mandatory

Undefined character position
This character position is undefined and should be left blank.

000/10
Mandatory

Indicator count
This position contains a one-character number equal to the number of indicators occurring in each field. By *USMARC Bibliographic* conventions, this value must always be 2. Most systems will automatically supply this value and cannot be edited by the user.

000/11
Mandatory

Subfield code count
This position contains a one-character number equal to the number of character positions used for a subfield code in variable data fields. By *USMARC Bibliographic* conventions, this value must always be **2**. Most systems will automatically supply this value and cannot be edited by the user.

000/12-16
Mandatory

Base address of data
These positions contain a five-character number that specifies the first character position of the first variable control field in the record. This value is used only by the system and is usually system generated. Generally, it cannot be edited by the user. Numbers are right justified and unused positions contain zeroes.

000/17
Mandatory

Encoding level
This position contains a one-character code that indicates the fullness of the bibliographic information and/or content designation in the bibliographic record.

<u>CODE VALUES AND THEIR APPLICATIONS</u>

blank   **Full level.**
This indicates the most complete USMARC record. It signifies that the information used in creating the record is derived from an inspection of the physical item.

1   **Full level, material not examined.**
This is the next most complete USMARC record. The information used in creating the record is derived from an extant description of the item, but the item has not been physically inspected. This code is used primarily in retrospective conversion of records.

2   **Less-than-full level, material not examined.**
This value indicates a less-than-full level record that has been created from an extant description of the material without inspection of the physical item. Generally, this is used in retrospective conversion of records when some of the information from a catalog record has not been entered into the electronic format, or there is not enough information on the record to permit the creation of a complete MARC record.

3   **Abbreviate level**

This value indicates a brief record that does not meet the National Leve
Bibliogaphic Record minimal level cataloging specifictions.

4   **Core level.**

5   **Partial (preliminary) level.**

This value indicates a preliminary cataloging level record that is in the
process of being created. Generally, you should not use this record
unless you have the physical item in hand and are willing to upgrade
the entire record.

7   **Minimal level.**

This value indicates a minimal level cataloging record that meets
National Level Bibliographic Record minimal level cataloging
specifications. Such a record is considered a final record by the final
agency. You should use this record only after verifying the
information, and adding any missing information, based on a direct
physical examination of the item.

8   **Prepublication level.**

This value indicates a prepublication level record. This indicates that
the record is a CIP record. You can use the record if you have the
physical item in hand and update the record as needed. Remember, you
will need to change the value in **000/05** from **n** to **p**.

000/18 **Descriptive cataloging form**
Mandatory This code indicates whether the record was formulated according *the Anglo-American
Cataloging Rules*, 2nd ed. (AACR2). Records that you create using this book follow
AACR2, therefore you will code this position accordingly.

CODE VALUES AND THEIR APPLICATIONS

a   **AACR2**

This code indicates that the record was formulated according to AACR2.

000/19 **Linked record requirement**
Mandatory This code indicates whether a note containing basic identification information can be
generated from a Linking Entry field without accessing the actual related record. Linked
records are not within the scope of this book, therefore, you should always leave this
position blank.

000/20 **Length of the length-of-field portion**
Mandatory In USMARC, this value is always **4**; therefore, many systems will automatically insert
this value for you.

000/21 **Length of the starting-character-position portion**
Mandatory In USMARC, this value is always **5**; therefore, many systems will automatically insert
this value for you.

000/22 **Length of the implementation-defined portion**
Mandatory In USMARC, a directory does not contain an implementation-defined portion; therefore,
this value will always be **0**. Many systems will automatically insert this value for you.

000/24 **Undefined entry map character position**
Mandatory In USMARC, this character position is undefined and will always be **0**.

As you can see from the above, while there are many unique sounding position names, many of them are
always the same and are defined by the rules of USMARC. It is because of the criticalness of them to the
correct storage and interpretation of records that system designers will have them system generated and be
hidden or not changeable by the user.

001

001 CONTROL NUMBER

REPEATABLE: NO
MANDATORY: YES
RELATES TO: 003
AUTHORITY: NO

1st indicator
The 1st indicator is always blank.

2nd indicator
The 2nd indicator is always blank.

This field contains the control number assigned by the organization creating, using, or distributing the record. For interchange purposes, documentation of the structure of the control number and input conventions must be provided to exchange partners by the organization initiating the interchange. The National Union Catalog (NUC) symbol identifying whose system control number is present in field **001** can be found in tag **003 - Control Number Identifier**. An organization receiving a record may move the control number from field **001** to field **035** and place its own system control number in field **001**. (Since the 035 should be machine-created, it is not covered in this book.) This will usually be done automatically by your system software. You should never have to enter information into this tag; it should be system provided.

SUBFIELD CODES

There are no subfield codes for this tag.

EXAMPLES

001   86104385
003   DLC

001   206039
003   TxDaISD

001   flb78889876
003   ICrlF

LOCATION

This information will not appear in the item being cataloged. It is used exclusively by your system for maintenance and "housekeeping" purposes. Many systems hide this number from the user since you will not usually need to do anything with it.

NOTES

Some systems will use this number to allow the entry of items that may have duplicate LCCN, ISBN, or ISSN numbers so that they can be kept separate and not merged together. It can also be used for inventory, system maintenance and operational purposes, as well as forming the basis for a union catalog.

PUNCTUATION

There is no punctuation at the end of this tag.

003 CONTROL NUMBER IDENTIFIER

REPEATABLE: NO
MANDATORY: YES
RELATES TO: 001
AUTHORITY: NO

1st indicator
The 1st indicator is always blank.

2nd indicator
The 2nd indicator is always blank.

This field contains the National Union Catalog (NUC) symbol of the system whose control number is present in field **001**. The NUC is an authoritative-agency data element. The Library of Congress maintains the Symbols of American Libraries and is the authoritative-agency for the United States. To apply for a NUC code for your library, contact the Library of Congress at *rbar@loc.gov*. There currently is no charge for this service.

Whenever the number in field **001** is changed, institutions must make certain that the NUC symbol in field **003** applies to the number found in the **001** field.

SUBFIELD CODES

There are no subfield codes for this tag.

EXAMPLES

001   86104385
003   DLC

001   206039
003   TxDaISD

001   flb78889876
003   ICrlF

LOCATION

This information will not appear in the item being cataloged. It is used exclusively by your system for maintenance and "housekeeping" purposes. Many systems hide this number from the user since you will not usually need to do anything with it.

NOTES

Some systems will use this number to allow the entry of items that may have duplicate LCCN, ISBN, or ISSN numbers so that they can be kept separate and not merged together. It can also be used for inventory, system maintenance and operational purposes, as well as forming the basis for a union catalog.

PUNCTUATION

There is no punctuation at the end of this tag.

005

005 DATE AND TIME OF LATEST TRANSACTION

REPEATABLE: NO
MANDATORY: YES
RELATES TO: 008/00-05
AUTHORITY: NO

INDICATOR VALUES

1st indicator
The 1st indicator is always blank.

2nd indicator
The 2nd indicator is always blank.

SUBFIELD CODES

There are no subfield codes for this tag.

EXAMPLES

    005   19860901141236.0
                [September 1, 1986, 2:12:36 P.M.]
    005   19610311023244.1
                [March 11, 1961, 2:32:44.1 A.M.]

LOCATION

This information is not part of the bibliographic description of the item, so you will not record it from the item in hand when cataloging.

NOTES

This field contains 16 characters that specify the date and time of the latest record transaction (not usage). The date and time serve as a version identifier for the record.

The date is recorded according to *Representation for Calendar Date and Ordinal Date for Information Interchange* (ANSI standard X3.30) The date requires 8 numeric characters in the pattern *yyyymmdd* or 4 for the year, 2 for the month, and 2 for the day.

The time is recorded according to *Representations of Local Time of the Day for Information Interchange* (ANSI standard X3.43) The time requires 8 numeric characters in the pattern *hhmmss.f* or 2 for the hour, 2 for the minute, 2 for the second, and 2 for a decimal fraction of the second, including the decimal point. The 24-hour clock format is utilized.

The date entered on file in the **008** never changes once created. The **005** is used to record when the record was last updated or changed, but not if it is viewed or utilized. This information is usually system generated. It can be useful if you need to verify when the last time a change was made to a bibliographic record in your system.

Both ANSI documents are available from the American National Standards Institute. You should not need these documents, as the information in the **005** is usually system generated.

PUNCTUATION

Apart from the decimal point utilized in the tag to denote the fractional portion of a second, there is no punctuation in this tag.

See pages 178 to 211

See pages 178 to 211

010 LIBRARY OF CONGRESS CONTROL NUMBER (LCCN)

REPEATABLE: NO
MANDATORY: NO
RELATES TO: 260$c
AUTHORITY: NO

1st indicator
The 1st indicator is always blank.

2nd indicator
The 2nd indicator is always blank.

SUBFIELD CODES

a   **LC Control Number (NR)**
z   **Cancelled/invalid LC control number(R)**

EXAMPLES

$a89-45171
$a83-70864
$a80-39
$a88-1329 /AC
$a74-750178 /R
$a4-78932
$a47-8932
$a76-647633$z75-587

LOCATION

The LCCN will usually be located on the verso of the title page of the book. In older books, it may be on the title page, but newer publications will include it with the Library of Congress Cataloging in Publication (CIP data). Some older sound recordings, particularly record albums, may have LCCNs. Most newer items, unless they are part of the Library of Congress's music collection and distribution program, will not have LCCNs on the item, although they will be in bibliographic records distributed by LC.

NOTES

This field contains unique numbers that have been assigned to a bibliographic record by the Library of Congress. The field can have as many as 12 characters, but most book items will only use 8. These numbers are very important! If they are on the item, they should be entered. These numbers are used as system control numbers by some systems, as well as a primary de-duping criterion when a union database is created. The numbers should always be entered in **$a**, unless you know for a fact that the number duplicates another number somewhere, then you should enter it into **$z**. When entering, you may or may not need to enter any leading zeros and or the dash that separates the first two digits from the rest of the number. Depending on the automation system that you are using, your system may automatically provide these. You should check your user's manual to determine what your system will do automatically.

010

These numbers, in essence, function as the Library of Congress's accession and system control numbers. They are their unique automated system ID numbers. This is why you will often see them in the **001** tag System Control number. You should remove the LCCN from the **001** and insert your own control number. If there is another control number there from a different vendor or system, you should move that number down to the **035** tag, along with a notation as to the source of the number and enter your own number in the **001**. It is also possible that your own automation system will enter a unique system identifier into the **001** automatically.

The Library of Congress started assigning LC Numbers in 1898. Since this means that they will have duplicate numbers starting with 1998, they have decided that they will continue the structure of using the first two digits of the year, but not use numbers used prior. Also, when the year 2000 comes, they will adopt a structure of using 00, again, not reusing numbers used earlier.

THE SUBFIELDS IN DETAIL

a **LC Control Number**

It is in this subfield that you will record the LCCN as recorded on the item or from the CIP data.

LCCNs must have at least two digits, one on each side of the hyphen (e.g., 1-1). They can have as many as eight digits; two to the left of the hyphen and six to the right of the hyphen (e.g., 79-123456). The first two digits will usually be within 2 years of the date of publication or copyright of the item that is recorded in the **260$c**. Serial or Pre-MARC items will often have a single digit in the year position. A sign that you have a serial item would be the presence of an International Standard Serial Number (ISSN) which consists of 4 digits, a dash, and then 4 more digits, and words like annual, almanac, yearbook, quarterly, or weekly in the title of the publication. For more information on the ISSN, please consult the **022** tag documentation.

As you can see from the last two examples above, it is very critical that the hyphen be entered correctly, since the numbers 4-78932 and 47-8932 can both be valid numbers, but for different items. Enter the hyphen when searching or entering a number in a record. A computer cannot make "value" judgments. This is your responsibility; to accurately code the information when keying the record.

z **Cancelled/invalid LC Control Number**

This subfield contains a canceled or invalid LC control number. Often, these will be labeled as invalid directly next to the LC number. This is if a publisher has re-used the same LC number from an older work on a newer publication. Please note that this practice on the part of publishers is incorrect; each item should have its own unique LCCN.

As catalogers, we are obligated to enter the number that is on the item, even though we know it is "wrong." The number is correct by virtue of the fact that it is on the item. You should enter the incorrect number, but enter it in a **$z** to indicate that you know that the number is wrong.

Although your patrons will not usually use these numbers, they are very important for matching purposes if you should decide to join a union database at a later date. The LCCN often serves as a unique matching point for de-duping records. Also, some commercial vendors will use this number if you wish to order bibliographic records from them for items that are already in your collection.

A word of warning: Some book jobbers and vendors will use this tag for their own control number. This is incorrect. Their number should be stored and labeled in a **035** tag.

SUFFIXES

Some LCCNs will have a suffix following them. LC uses these as distribution information for card copy. The letters that follow the LCCN are preceded by a "space-slash" (see examples above). Below is a list of the valid letters that can be used and what they mean

A C	Annotated Card, or children's program at LC
A M	Works in Amhtric
A CN	Works in Chinese
A J	Works in Japanese
A K	Works in Korean
F	Works from the audiovisual area of LC
HE	Items written in the Hebrew alphabet
M	Items cataloged in the M schedule of LC Classification scheme
MAP	Atlases
MN	Works classified in ML and MT schedule of LC Classification scheme
MP	Items cataloged in the Motion Picture division of LC
NE	Persian language materials
P P	Prints and photographs
R	Sound recordings

Sometimes the letter AC will precede the LCCN. It should be entered after the LCCN with a "space-slash." All suffixes are capitalized. Do not enter letters before the LCCN. The most common suffix in school libraries is AC, which stands for the Annotated Card program.

SETS

Sometimes you will be entering the records for a set of books and you will notice that each item has the same LCCN on it. This means that the Library of Congress considers the entire group of items to be cataloged under a single record as a set. You should not make separate bibliographic records for each of the items. If you choose to make individual records in an effort to improve access, it would be wise to omit the LCCN from all items, as inclusion could cause matching problems later on if a union database is created. Check with your particular system vendor for guidance on entering the same standard number for multiple items.

Rather than create separate bibliographic records for each item, you may want to create a single set record with as many author and/or title entries as necessary to ensure access to the items. Be certain to assign a different barcode to each physical item and that you have correctly linked that barcode to the correct copy or volume information. How you implement this will depend on your local policies formulated with your reference staff. In some systems, creating set records can cause problems if you have/utilize an AV booking module or function.

PUNCTUATION

There are never any marks of punctuation at the end of the **010** tag.

020 INTERNATIONAL STANDARD BOOK NUMBER (ISBN)

REPEATABLE:	YES
MANDATORY:	NO
RELATES TO:	--
AUTHORITY:	NO

1st Indicator
The 1st indicator is always blank.

2nd indicator
The 2nd indicator is always blank.

SUBFIELD CODES

a   **International Standard Book Number (ISBN) (NR)**
c   **Terms of availability (NR)**
z   **Cancelled/invalid ISBN (R)**

This field contains the International Standard Book Number (ISBN) and all the information related to it. It is repeated for multiple numbers that refer to different printings of a work (e.g., ISBNs for the hard bound and paperback editions), as well as information regarding "sets" of items. Note that some non-book material, like videorecordings (videocassettes and laserdiscs) as well as sound recordings may also have ISBNs.

EXAMPLES

$a0679739483
$a0570-031443
$a089744-962X :$c16.00
$z0835200028 :$c10.00
$a0851573134 (pbk.)
$a0684145421 (Vol. 1) NOTE: *v.* is also acceptable
$a1562827235 (lib. bdg.)

LOCATION

The ISBN will often be recorded as part of the CIP data on newer publications. If there is no CIP data, it will usually be on the verso of the title page or on the dust jacket on the back of the book next to the UPC code. The ISBN listed by the UPC should not be the first place you look for the number; instead, prefer numbers that are given on the verso of the title page. On non-book material, the ISBN will usually appear directly above the UPC barcode. For items that consist of multiple media (like a book and a cassette), you may need to enter multiple ISBNs to accurately describe each piece. Be certain to note which item each individual ISBN is found on. This information would be recorded in parenthesis following the ISBN in **$a**.

You may note that in a card environment, the ISBN was recorded in the notes area, or middle of the card. If you are using your system to print cards, then the system should print the number there. The MARC format has the ISBN at the beginning of the record since it is considered to be a "machine control" number, thus it would fall into the structure of the **0XX** tags.

THE SUBFIELDS IN DETAIL

a **International Standard Book Number (NR)** *(Rule 1.8B)*

This tag contains a valid ISBN for the item. Parenthetical qualifying information, such as the publisher/distributor, binding/format, and volume numbers, is not separately subfield coded.

An ISBN consists of ten digits comprising four groups of numbers separated by hyphens. Sometimes the last digit will be an uppercase *X*, which is used as a validity check by some automation systems. This check uses an algorithm to make certain that the number is formatted according to defined standards. The dashes in the ISBN are determined by another algorithm. You should not enter the hyphens when entering a number into the **020**, as the MARC format specifies that they should automatically be generated as display constants.

You should include any volume, binding, or series information after the ISBN. You should also include the parenthesis and punctuation inside the parenthesis. Never put any punctuation, such as a period, after the number or at the end of the tag. It is important to note set or volume information. Some sets will have an ISBN assigned to the entire collection, as well as individual ISBNs assigned for each volume. You should enter both the set and volume information in as many **020** tags as necessary to contain all the information. This information is useful if the library should need to order only one volume in the event that one volume from the set is lost or stolen.

EXAMPLES

$a0195208090 (Vol. 1)
$a0671704273 (pbk.)

c **Terms of availability (NR)** *(Rule 1.8D, 1.8E)*

This subfield contains the price or a brief statement of availability and any parenthetical qualifying information concerning the item. This price is the price that the item lists for, not what the library actually pays for an item from its jobber or vendor. It should be near the ISBN or stock number.

EXAMPLES

$a0872875113 :$c$37.50
$a1563081423 :$c$37.50 ($45.00 Can.)

Note that the Library of Congress does not apply the optional rule from AACR2 that gives differential pricing information for special audiences, users, or countries. *(LCRI 2.8C)*

z **Cancelled invalid ISBN(R)**

This subfield is used to record an ISBN that is invalid or incorrect. You may choose to record duplicate ISBNs here. Each canceled/invalid ISBN is contained in a separate **$z**. If no valid ISBN exists, only **$z** should be recorded.

Invalid ISBNs are encountered most frequently when a publisher will assign the same number to the entire product line instead of applying to LC for a block of numbers for their items. They can also be labeled as *invalid* by LC in the CIP data. You should check with you system vendor to determine if it searches this subfield when doing ISBN searches.

020

$a0192815075$z0195208137 *(invalid)*

OLDER ITEMS

Sometimes, older items will have nine digits on them. These numbers are SBNs (Standard Book Numbers). If you should come across one of these and the book is in English <u>and</u> published in an English-speaking province or country, place a *0* at the beginning of the number before entering it. If it is not in English or not published in an English speaking country, it is recommended that you do not enter the number unless you have access to the information necessary to recreate the beginning portion of the number. If the item is in English and there are nine digits in the ISBN <u>and</u> the first digit is already a zero, <u>do not</u> put the letter *X* after the ISBN; do not use the ISBN number at all. If there are 4 digits, a dash, and 4 more digits (4589-3349), the number is an ISSN, which goes into the **022** tag, meaning that it is a serial item.

SERIAL ITEMS

Sometimes you will encounter items that have both ISBNs and ISSNs. This arrangement is often used for items that are published annually, such as *yearbooks*, but which some libraries may not want to order every year. The publisher supplies an ISBN so that the library can send that number to their vendor and order only those publications that they wish to receive.

You will need to determine the policy that you wish to follow in your own library. If you purchase an item regularly, it is recommended that you enter the ISSN for the item and not the individual ISBNs for the item, creating an "open-ended" entry. This will permit you to update holding information only for the new copy and not have to create a new bibliographic record each year. You <u>cannot</u> enter a **020** and a **022** in the same record.

NOTES

These numbers are used as system control numbers by some systems, as well as a primary de-duping criterion when a union database is created. Many book jobbers utilize these numbers for accurately processing orders. ISBNs are usually carried in book reviews in leading library publications and catalog, simplifying the ordering of the materials from your jobber.

If you plan to join a union database at some time in the future, these numbers will be very important. Some automation systems will use them to match up the same item.

PUNCTUATION

$c is preceded by a *space:* (space colon)
$c must begin with a dollar sign or other currency mark.
Enclose a qualification to the standard number or terms of availability in parentheses. Do not separately subfield code this information.
There is <u>never</u> any punctuation at the end of the **020**.

022 INTERNATIONAL STANDARD SERIAL NUMBER (ISSN)

REPEATABLE:	YES
MANDATORY:	NO
RELATES TO:	--
AUTHORITY:	NO

1st indicator

The 1st indicator is usually blank.

Note that the NSDP (National Serials Data Program) and ISDS/Canada are permitted to use the values *0* and *1* here in specific instances. You should <u>never</u> enter anything here. If there is a value here and you have downloaded the record from a national library source, do not change the value.

2nd indicator

The 2nd indicator is always blank.

This field contains the International Standard Serial Number (ISSN), a unique identification number assigned to a serial title. Note that serials are <u>not</u> limited to printed items. They can include computer software, videorecordings, and sound recordings.

SUBFIELD CODES

a   **International Standard Serial Number (ISSN) (NR)**
y   **Incorrect ISSN (R)**
z   **Cancelled ISSN (R)**

EXAMPLES

$a0376-4583
$a1056-621X
$a0046-225X$y0046-2254
$a2236-2239

LOCATION

On magazines, the ISSN will usually be recorded in the publisher information. This is the same place that informs you where to send subscription changes, cancellations, claims, etc. If it is not there, your subscription service vendor may be able to provide it, or you may need to refer to a periodical guide, such as *Ulrich's* or *Ebsco's*.

On items that are published every year, this information may be recorded on the verso of the title page or even on the title page itself. It may be in the CIP data, but it almost always will be near the LCCN/ISBN if they are also on the item. If not on the item, your book jobber may be able to provide it on your standing-order list.

022

NOTES

These numbers are assigned by national agencies under the auspicies of the ISSN Network. For a more complete description of the ISSN structure and the procedure for validation of the ISSN by calculating the check digit, you should consult the publication *International Standard Serial Numbering (ISSN) (ANSI Z39.9)*. Individual libraries may <u>enter</u> values into this tag from information supplied on the item, but <u>cannot</u> create ISSNs.

Although possible to have <u>both</u> an ISBN and ISSN for the same item, it is against the rules of *USMARC Bibliographic* to do so. It is <u>not</u> uncommon to find both an ISSN and LCCN in the same record. Theoretically, it is possible to have an LCCN, ISBN, and ISSN in the same record. This is done primarily to simplify ordering for libraries who choose not to purchase an annual every year. It is not incorrect to record an LCCN, ISBN and ISSN all in the same record, but it usually is not wise to do so. By virtue of making a serial record (which would have an ISSN), the library is stating that they chose not to catalog an item with each issue, but rather to create a base record and add on copies and volumes as necessary.

For more information on ISBNs and ISSNs in the same record, refer to the information in the **020** tag.

THE SUBFIELDS IN DETAIL

a   **International Standard Serial Number**   *(Rule 12.8B)*
This subfield contains the valid ISSN for the serial. ISSNs are <u>always</u> four digits, a dash, and then four more digits. It is usually the number on the actual item itself.

y   **Incorrect ISSN**
This subfield is used to record an incorrect ISSN that has been associated with the serial. Each incorrect ISSN is contained in a separate **$y**. Unless you have a way to verify the accuracy of an ISSN, you will probably not be using this subfield frequently.

z   **Cancelled ISSN**
This subfield is used to record a cancelled ISSN that is associated with the serial. Each cancelled ISSN is contained in a separate **$z**. Unless you have a way to verify the accuracy of an ISSN, you will probably not be using this subfield frequently.

PUNCTUATION

There is <u>no</u> punctuation separating the different subfields.
Do not enter any punctuation at the end of the **022** tag.

024   OTHER STANDARD IDENTIFIER

REPEATABLE: YES
MANDATORY: NO
RELATES TO: --
AUTHORITY: NO

1st indicator

1   **Universal Product Code (UPC)**
There are other values that can be used here, but this is the one that most librarians will be entering. If you have the need for other values, then please consult *USMARC Bibliographic* for more detailed information.

2nd indicator

blank   **No information provided**
0   **No difference**
Generally, you will use this value <u>unless</u> you scan the code in with a scanner and see that the number scanned is different than the eye-readable value.
1   **Difference**
Use this value if the number scanned in is <u>different</u> than the eye-readable value on the item.

SUBFIELD CODES

a   **Standard number or code (NR)**
c   **Terms of availability (NR)**
Other subfield codes that can be used here are detailed in *USMARC Bibliographic.*

This field contains a standard number or code published on an item that cannot be accommodated in another field, like the 010, 020, or 022 tags. The type of standard number or code is identified in the first indicator position. The code that is usually entered here is the *UPC* or *Universal Product Code.* This is the same barcode symbol that is scanned on groceries and many other products.

EXAMPLES

024 10   **$a**780836217018
024 10   **$a**780810911871 :**$c**$8.95
024 11   **$a**780679739487 :**$c**$18.00 ($23.00 Can.)

LOCATION

Generally, the UPC code will be found on the back corner of the item. In books, it is usually in the lower right-hand corner near the ISBN. For videorecordings, it is usually on the back of the item along the right edge, either on the top or bottom. For CDs and cassettes it will usually be on the back of the item.

NOTES

It is strongly encouraged that you enter these codes into the record. While many systems do not currently index them, they could prove to be valuable in the future if your software vendor modifies software and scanners so that the UPC could be scanned during searching. This would serve to shorten search times when looking for information in a database, particularly a union database that is used for shared cataloging and holding information. Currently, some systems are able to read the information into the system, but have no way of indexing it. You should check with your particular vendor for plans to use this information.

Prior to January 1995, this tag could <u>only</u> be used for music. As part of Format Integration, it was defined for all materials. The use of it could have implications for future access in your database. The numbers follow a format specified by the Uniform Code Council. It is unnecessary that you understand the structure of the number; rather, it is important that you enter it correctly and accurately.

THE SUBFIELDS IN DETAIL

a   **Standard number or code (NR)**   *(Rule 1.7B19)*
This is where the actual code number is entered. You should use the numbers printed below the barcode symbol on the back of the item.
Do not include those numbers that are in smaller typeface or are directly adjacent to the barcode symbol. It will <u>always</u> be twelve digits in length.

EXAMPLES

$a058008608467
$a008811090623

c   **Terms of availability (NR)**
This subfield contains the price or a brief statement of availability and any parenthetical qualifying information. Do <u>not</u> use the price the library paid for the item; rather, use a price which is pre-printed on the item, if there is any.

EXAMPLES

$a780446513302 *$c$17.95*
$a076714014008 *$c$14.00 ($18.00 Can.)*

PUNCTUATION

$c is preceded by no punctuation.
There is <u>no</u> punctuation at the end of the tag.

028   PUBLISHER NUMBER

REPEATABLE:	YES
MANDATORY:	NO
RELATES TO:	--
AUTHORITY:	NO

1st indicator

0   **Issue number**
Use this value for sound recordings and sheet music.

4   **Videorecording number**
Use this value for publisher numbers for videorecordings.

2nd indicator

0   **No note, no added entry**
This tells your system that it should store the information in the MARC record, but that it should not be displayed in the OPAC or indexed.

1   **Note, added entry required**
The use of this value indicates that you want your system to generate a note and create an entry in your Publisher Number index. You should check with your software vendor to determine if your system supports indexing of this tag.

2   **Note, no added entry**
Use this value if you wish to have a note generated, but not indexed.

3   **No note, added entry required**
Since cataloging rules specify that you need to justify the tracing of an item based on information in other places in the record, you should never use this value.

SUBFIELD CODES

a   **Publisher number (NR)**
b   **Source (NR)**

This field contains formatted publisher's numbers used for sound recordings, printed music, and videorecordings. This number will usually be on the label and/or spine of sound recordings, (CDs, record albums, and cassettes) or on the container for videorecordings, oftentimes along the spine.

EXAMPLES

028 01   **$a**STMA 8007**$b**Tamala Motown
028 01   **$a**ND2-63911**$b**Narada
028 41   **$a**41518**$b**MCA/Universal Home Video
028 42   **$a**40196**$b**Image Entertainment

THE SUBFIELDS IN DETAIL

a   **Publisher number (NR)**   (Rule 1.7B19)
This is where the actual code number is entered. Follow capitalization and spacing exactly as they are on the item.

028

$a1662 CS
$aLD68952-2WS

b   **Source (NR)**

This is the source of the publisher number. Usually, it will be the same as the first **$b** in the **260** tag. Note that the name you enter here will often also be present in the **260** tag.

EXAMPLES

$a**ID8553MM**$b**Image Entertainment**
$a**40183-6**$b**Elektra Entertainment**

PUNCTUATION

$b is preceded by no punctuation.
The tag does not end with a period or any other mark of punctuation.

040   CATALOGING SOURCE

REPEATABLE: NO
MANDATORY: YES
RELATES TO: 003, 008/39
AUTHORITY: NO

1st indicator
The 1st indicator is always blank.

2nd indicator
The 2nd indicator is always blank.

SUBFIELD CODES

a   **Original cataloging agency (NR)**
b   **Language of cataloging (NR)**
c   **Transcribing agency (NR)**
d   **Modifying agency (R)**

This field contains information on the organization that originally cataloged the Item (**$a**), who converted it into Machine Readable form (**$c**), and any agency(ies) that modified the record in any way (**$d**). It may also contain information for the language of cataloging in the record (**$b**). The codes in this field are called National Union Catalog (NUC) codes and are assigned by the Library of Congress that are available free upon request from the Library of Congress. To request an NUC code, contact the Library of Congress at *rbar@loc.gov*. Institutions which plan to participate in a union project should all apply for individual NUC codes. They are also used by some systems for interlibrary loan functions.

EXAMPLES

The most common national codes you will see are:

>   *DLC   Library of Congress*
>   *DNLM   National Library of Medicine*

LOCATION

Since this is not part of the descriptive bibliographic information, you will not find this information on the item being cataloged. Rather, it is supplied by the librarian for record sharing purposes.

NOTES

A library can use the information in this tag to assist in making decisions regarding the quality of information in imported records. Generally, records from DLC and DNLM are presumed to be of higher quality than non-national library records. Also, DLC records are generally preferred over records from the National Library of Canada (NLC) or other national libraries outside the United States, unless your library is in the same country as that particular national library.

You may see some locally assigned codes from libraries in your area if you are editing records from a union database. If you had your shelflist entered by another vendor, their code should appear in the 040. You may wish to ask them what their NUC code is. Be wary of vendors that do not have or enter a unique code in this area. This area is similar to "signing your work." If a vendor does not want to take credit for its work, it may be of questionable quality. With these codes, it is possible for a library to determine the

040

institution/organization that created/modified any particular record. This can assist you in determining the quality of that record based on the information reputation of the vendor and the quality of the information in the record. It will also give you a contact to report errors in the record, which is appreciated by most creators of records, particularly commercial vendors.

If you are entering an original record from a shelflist card that you created or a new item that your library has received, you should enter your code in **$a** and **$c**. If you are updating, adding to, or modifying another institution's copy, you should place your code in **$d**. Note that if you are modifying a record that you entered previously, you should not enter your code in **$d**, as it already appears in **$c**. Some automation systems may automatically supply this information in your MARC editor. Check with your particular vendor to see if this is true for your system.

Be careful to enter the letters in the appropriate case (upper and lower), as these values are case-sensitive.

THE SUBFIELDS IN DETAIL

a **Original cataloging agency (NR)**
This subfield contains the NUC symbol or the name of the organization that created the original record. It means that this institution had the actual item in-hand when they created the cataloging record and applied the rules of AACR2 or another accepted cataloging system in the process of selecting authors, title information, and other bibliographic information.

   $aDLC

b **Language of cataloging (NR)**
This subfield contains a USMARC code for the language of cataloging in the record. The source of the code is *USMARC Code List for Languages* and is maintained by the Library of Congress. It is available for purchase from the Library of Congress's Cataloging Distribution Services (CDS). Unless you are creating catalog records in a foreign language rather than cataloging foreign language items into an English language record, you will not use this subfield. It is presented here so that you may accurately trace the history and development of a record.

   $aCaQQLA
   $bengfre
   $cCaOONL

This information indicates that the record was input by Laval University in French and English and was transcribed by the National Library of Canada.

c **Transcribing agency (NR)**
This subfield contains the NUC symbol or the name of the organization that transcribed the record into machine-readable form. Very often, this value will be the same as **$c**.

   $aDLC
   $cDLC

24

d   **Modifying agency (R)**

This subfield contains the NUC symbol or the name of the organization responsible for modifying a machine-readable record. A modification is defined as any correction to a record, including cataloging, content designation, or keying changes, but excluding the addition of holdings symbols. The NUC symbol for each organization that modifies a record is contained in a separate **$d**. If the same agency transcribing the record also modifies the cataloging record in the process of transcribing it (such as taking the information from a card and entering it into an electronic form), the agency's name or NUC symbol is also recorded in **$d**.

> **$a**DLC
> **$c**DLC
> *$dICrlF*
> *$dTxCatMMA*

PUNCTUATION

There are never any marks of punctuation at the end of the **040** tag.

1XX MAIN ENTRY TAGS

This area will usually contain the name of the person or group chiefly responsible for the intellectual content and creation of an item, be it an individual, corporate, or conference name. It may also contain a uniform title used as the main entry. For a fuller explanation of what constitutes each one of these types of entries, consult that respective entry documentation. If an item does not have a **1XX** tag, it is said to have a "title main entry." Note that you do not make title-main entries; rather, they occur because you do not have any other type of main entry, that is, they occur by default. A record can only have a single **1XX** tag, but it does not <u>have</u> to <u>have</u> a **1XX** tag.

For *books*, the main entry will almost always be found on the title page, usually following the title proper, although in some instances you may have to go to the cover of the book or to internal data to find the main entry for the it.

For *sound recordings*, the main entry is usually on the disc label, or you may need to look at the cover of the item for information if it is a CD or record album. For cassettes, use the face of the cassette itself, or the material lining the case.

For *videorecordings*, you should use the information at the beginning of the recording itself, although you can take it from the label if you so choose.

For *projected graphics*, like motion pictures, filmstrips, slides, etc., you should use the item itself, or a label that is on the item.

For *computer software*, you should take the title information from the title screen first. If you do not have the means to access the software, you can use the disk label. For computer software, you must state where you obtained the title in a **500** tag.

Some older records that you may be editing from other sources may have a value in the <u>2nd indicator</u> position. If they do, ignore it. The 2nd indicator position was used in an earlier version of USMARC. It is unnecessary to go back and change it, although you may do so if you want.

The **1xx** tags described in this book are:

100	**Main entry - Personal name**
110	**Main entry - Corporate name**
111	**Main entry - Meeting name**
130	**Main entry - Uniform title**

The main entry is considered to be the primary access point for an item in a card environment. In card catalogs, the main entry card serves as the unit card on which the other tracings in the collection are listed so that all cards can be pulled if the item is removed from the collection. When the library is formulating call numbers, the Cutter or Author number may be based on the main entry. In an automated system, the concept of main entry is less critical than in a card environment. However, it should still be entered correctly since it could influence how other systems will handle the record. In some systems, for example, the program may try to de-dupe records or match your record with one in a union database. In addition, if a library chooses to print cards or bibliographies from the automated record, the main entry information is very important to assure accurate access to the item.

100 MAIN ENTRY - PERSONAL NAME

REPEATABLE:	NO
MANDATORY:	NO
RELATES TO:	245$c, 700
AUTHORITY:	YES

1st indicator

0	**Forename**	Plato or Jesus Christ
1	**Single surname**	Fitzgerald, David
2	**Multiple surname**	Rousseau-Darnell, Lyse

At one time, the Library of Congress was going to eliminate this value and code all surnames with the value of *1*, but since they are unable to globally change the information in their database, they have decided to retain the separate values of *1* and *2*. How you handle it in your library is a local policy decision.

3	**Family name**	Dunlop family

2nd indicator

The 2nd indicator is always blank.

SUBFIELD CODES

a	**Personal name(NR)**	
q	**Fuller form of name(NR)**	
b	**Numeration associated with name (R)**	
c	**Titles and other words associated with a name (R)**	
d	**Dates associated with name(NR)**	

Note that subfields are not entered in alphabetical order. You should only use those subfields for which you have information, in the order they are listed above.

EXAMPLES

100 1	$aAudubon, John James,$d1785-1851.
100 0	$aAristotle.
100 3	$aKennedy family.
100 0	$aJohn Paul$bII,$cPope,$d1920-
100 1	$aSeuss,$cDr.
100 1	$aKing, Martin Luther,$cJr.,$d1929-1968.
100 2	$aWatson-Bishop, Sylvia.
100 1	$aCummings, E. E.$q(Edward Estlin),$d1894-1962.
100 0	$aLouis$bXIV,$cKing of France,$d1638-1715.
100 1	$aFreeman, Russ.
	(Note: title on disc label is "The Rippingtons featuring Russ Freeman")
100 1	$aBach, Johann Sebastian$d1685-1750.
	Note: disc is a collection of Bach organ works by various performers)

LOCATION

The main entry is usually taken from the chief source of information. For books, this is usually the title page (AACR2 2.0B). For the chief sources of information for other formats, see that individual format below. AACR2 specifies that you should take the personal name that is given prominence on the title page (AACR2 21.6B). This means that if there is only one name, then that name becomes the main entry. If there is more than one name but less than four names, the one that is first should be entered unless one of the other names is given prominence by typeface, wording, or layout. If there are four or more names, none of the names should be entered here.

Usually, all names use normal capitalization.

If the names on the title page include the terms *ed., editor, comp., compiler, translator, or transcriber*, do not enter these names in the **100** tag. You will ultimately enter these in the **245$c** and make added entry(ies) or **7XX** tags for them (AACR2 21.7)

Enter only one name in the **100** tag. If there are two authors, such as John and Mary Smith or Susan and Mortimer Wilson, put the first (or most prominent) name in the **100** tag and make an added entry in the **700** tag for the second one. If there are <u>more</u> than three authors listed on the title page, do not make a **100** tag. Only the first author will be traced in the **7XX** tag.

If an author does illustrations in addition to the text, then you should consider the person primarily as an author, not an illustrator. You would <u>not</u> make an added entry for that person as an illustrator in the **700** tag.

SOUND RECORDINGS

The chief source of information for sound recordings is usually the disc label (AACR2 6.0B1). As a secondary chief source, you can use information on the cover of the item. If the two sources do not agree, prefer the information on the disc label.

If you are cataloging sound recordings by a single artist, then you should enter the name of the artist here (AACR2 21.23B). If the sound recording is for classical music and is predominately by a single composer, then enter that person's name here (AACR2 21.4A1). If the recording is performed by a group, then you will enter that name in the **110** tag. If there is a group with a person's name which is given prominence by either typeface or wording, enter the person's name here and make a tracing for the group's name in the **710** tag (AACR2 21.6B1)

For audio books or books on tape, do not place the author's name here. The item will have a title main entry.

VIDEORECORDINGS

The chief source of information for videorecordings is considered the item itself, such as the title screen (AACR2 7.0B2). If it is not practicable to view the item, then you can use the container and container label. If there is any conflict between the two, prefer the item itself. As a general rule, no single person, including producers, directors, or actors are responsible for the creation of videorecordings. They will usually have a title main entry.

FILMSTRIPS, KITS, MOVIES, COMPUTER SOFTWARE

The chief source of information for these items is considered the item itself, such as the title screen. If it is not practical to view the item, then you can use the container and container label, an accompanying booklet, or a label on the physical carrier of the item. In some circumstances, you may need to go to the container that contains the individual parts of the products.

These generally follow the same rules as given for videorecordings above.

NOTES

Try to be consistent with the form of a person's name through your entire collection. An authority list or system should be consulted and maintained. This is particularly significant for fiction or for researchers, since readers may want to read all of the works by a particular author, or look at everything a particular person has written on a subject.

THE SUBFIELDS IN DETAIL

a **Personal name(NR)**   *(Begin at Rule 22)*
A personal name may be a surname and/or forename; letters, initials, abbreviations, phrases or numbers used in place of a name; or a family name. This subfield is required when the **100** tag is used. (AACR2 22.4B2)

    $aAudubon, John James,$d1795-1851

q **Fuller form of name (NR)**   *(Rule 22.18)*
This subfield contains a more complete form of the name if abbreviations or initials were used in **$a**.

    $aCummings, E. E.$q(Edward Estlin),$d1894-1962.

b **Numeration(R)**   *(Rule 22.17A2)*
This subfield contains a number or a roman numeral. It is used only in a forename heading (first indicator value of **0**). This means that any name in the form Last name, First name cannot have a numeration associated with it. It is usually used with kings, queens, popes, and royalty.

    $aJohn Paul$bII,$cPope,$d1920-

c **Titles and other words associated with a name (R)** *(Begin at rule 22.6)*
This subfield contains titles and other words associated with a name. These include qualifying information such as:

Titles designating rank, office or nobility:
    $aLouis$bXIV,$cKing of France,$d1638-1715

Terms of address:
    $aLucas, Edgar,$cMrs.

Other words or phrases associated with the name:
    $aMoses,$c(Biblical leader)

AACR2 discourages the use of titles except for royalty, nobility, or ranks of office. Thus, you would use terms like king, queen, prince, pope, or marquee, but not terms like Dr., Jr., Sr., or Mr. They allow the use of terms of address or phrases needed to differentiate between two similar names or if the person is commonly known by their title or address, like Dr. Seuss or Martin Luther King, Jr. Multiple adjacent titles or words associated names are contained in a single **$c**. The subfield is repeated only when words associated with a name are separated by subelements contained in other subfields.

d   **Dates associated with a name**   *(Rule 22.17)*
This subfield contains the dates of birth, death, flourishing or any other date used with a name. A qualifier used with the date is also contained in **$d**. Some of these qualifiers and their meanings are:

b.	born	b. 1965
d.	died	d. 1992
ca.	circa or about	ca. 1066
fl.	flourished	fl. 694-675 B.C.
cent.	century	fl. 9th cent. B.C.
?	unknown or questionable	1834?-1890

Dates with a person are most commonly used if there are many people with the same name and some way is needed to differentiate between them.

PUNCTUATION

There is no punctuation before a **$b**.
$c is preceded by a comma.
$d is preceded by a comma.
The information inside of **$q** is placed in parentheses, with the subfield usually being preceded by the period ending the abbreviation in the **$a**.
If the date of death in **$d** is open, meaning that the person is still alive or his death date has not yet been entered into your system, no punctuation follows the hyphen at the end of the subfield.
$e is preceded by a comma.

The **100** tag usually ends in a period. If **$d** is the last subfield, then the **100** tag ends with either a hyphen or a period. If **$q** is the last subfield, then the tag ends with closing parentheses.

110 MAIN ENTRY - CORPORATE NAME

REPEATABLE:	NO
MANDATORY:	NO
RELATES TO:	245$c, 710
AUTHORITY:	YES

1st indicator

1	**Jurisdiction name**	United States
2	**Name in direct order**	Ford Motor Company

1st indicator value 1 will usually be used for governmental entities, such as states, cities, countries, etc. Some entities will have a jurisdictional name, but are not governmental bodies. These should have a 1st indicator value of **2**.

110 1 $aUnited States.$bCongress.$bSenate.
110 2 $aC. S. Hammond & Company.
110 2 $aImages (Musical group)
110 2 $aCars (Musical group)

2nd indicator
The 2nd indicator is always blank.

SUBFIELD CODES

a	**Corporate name or jurisdiction name as entry element (NR)**
b	**Subordinate unit (R)**
t	**Title of a work (NR)**

EXAMPLES

110 2 $aMidwest Express Airlines.
110 1 $aUnited States.$bCongress.$bSenate.
110 2 $aC. S. Hammond & Company.
110 1 $aUnited States.$tConstitution.
110 2 $aUniversity of Illinois at Urbana-Champaign.$bExperimental Music studios.
110 2 $aBoy Scouts of America.
110 2 $aRippingtons (Musical group)
         (Note: disc label says "Rippingtons with Russ Freeman") Compare to
          example in **100** tag.
110 2 $a10,000 maniacs (Musical group)

LOCATION

As with other main entries, corporate names are found on the chief source of information of the item.
(Rule 2.0B)

AACR2 seldom considers corporate bodies main entries (Rule 21.1B2, however, lists six instances when a corporate body can be a main entry). Usually, the only time you will utilize them as main entries is when the company writes an item about itself, such as a corporate history or proceedings, etc., or if you are doing a sound recording that is by a group. Movie production companies are rarely corporate authors, although they may be added entries in a **710** tag.

<u>NOTES</u>

It is very important that you use great care when entering the names of entities here. You should try to be consistent with that company's name through your entire collection. This is where your authority list or system will come in handy. Also, it will help your users to find all the works written by a particular organization. This is particularly significant for patrons doing research on a company or looking for technical manuals, since many of them will be under the company's name. It can also be useful for locating all of a particular organization's annual reports.

THE SUBFIELDS IN DETAIL

a   **Corporate name or jurisdiction name as entry element (NR)**
(Begin at Rule 24.1)

This subfield contains a name of a corporate body or the first entity when subordinate units are present, or a jurisdiction name under which a corporate body is entered. A parenthetical qualifying term, jurisdiction name, or date is generally not separately subfield coded. This subfield is required when the **110** tag is used.

> *$aJohn F. Kennedy Space Center.*
> *$aUnited States.*$bNational Aeronautics and Space Administration.

b   **Subordinate unit (R)**   *(Begin at Rule 24.12)*

This subfield contains a name of a subordinate corporate unit, a name of a city section, or a name of a meeting entered under a corporate or a jurisdiction name. You should enter corporate entities in a subordinate structure if there are several units that could be confused or have the same name.

The subordinate units listed in **$b** can be repeated. This is used if you are showing the hierarchy of an organization, such as an agency of a governmental body that reports to another agency.

> $aUnited States.*$bCongress.$bHouse*
> $aConfederate States of America.*$bArmy.*
> $aUnited States.*$bBureau of Customs.*
> $aIllinois.*$bSupreme Court.*

t   **Title of a work (NR)**   *(Begin at Rule 25)*

This subfield contains a uniform title, a title page title of a work, or a series title used in a name/title field.

> $aUnited States.$bPresident (1861-1865 : Lincoln).*$tEmancipation Proclamation.*

PUNCTUATION

Each **$b** is preceded by a period.
$t is preceded by a period.
The tag ends with a period or a terminal mark of punctuation.

111 MAIN ENTRY - MEETING NAME

REPEATABLE: NO
MANDATORY: NO
RELATES TO: 245$c, 711
AUTHORITY: YES

INDICATOR CODES

1st indicator

0	Inverted name	Used only in rare circumstances.
1	Jurisdiction name	Used only in rare circumstances.
2	Name in direct order	Use this value for most entries.

2nd indicator

The 2nd indicator is always blank.

SUBFIELD CODES

a	Meeting name or jurisdiction name as entry element (NR)
n	Number of part/section/meeting (R)
d	Date of meeting (NR)
c	Location of meeting (NR)

EXAMPLES

111 2 $aLewis and Clark Expedition$d(1804-1806)
111 2 $aOlympic Games$n(23rd :$d1984 :$cLos Angeles, Calif.)
111 2 $aVatican Council$n(1st :$d1869-1870)
111 2 $aUnited Nations Day Conference$d(1975 :$cBoston, Mass.)

LOCATION

As with the other main entry tags, this information should be drawn from the chief source of information.

NOTES

This field contains a meeting or conference name used as a main entry. Main entry under a meeting is assigned to works that contain proceedings, reports, etc. These will most often be the result of the work of a convention or particular conference. The words *proceedings* and *report* of are significance here.

Since the use of meeting names is very limited in the collections of most school and small public libraries, it is rare when you will have a Main Entry Meeting Name. Words that indicate you might have a **111** include *Congress on, Conference on, Expedition, Expo, Olympic games, Colloquia, Exhibitions, Expeditions, Expositions, Fairs, Festivals, Seminars, Shows, Symposia, and Workshops.*

It is very important that you use great care when entering the names of meetings here. You need to be consistent with that meeting's name through your entire collection. This is where your authority list or system will come in handy. Also, the author of a work will help your users find all the works written or presented at a particular meeting or conference. This is particularly significant for researchers, since readers may want to read all of the works of a particular conference or meeting. By using the same form consistently through your entire collection, a researcher will have no difficulty in locating all the publications of a particular meeting or organization.

THE SUBFIELDS IN DETAIL

a　　**Meeting name or jurisdiction name as entry element (NR)**
(Begin at 24; also see 24.3F1 and 24.7)

This subfield contains a name of a meeting or a jurisdiction name under which a meeting is entered. Parenthetical qualifying information is not separately subfield coded. Meeting names are not entered under jurisdiction names in AACR2 formulated 111 fields.

　　　　$a***Pan-American Exposition***$d(1901 :**$c**Buffalo, N.Y.)

n　　**Number of part/section/meeting (R)**　　*(Rule 24.7B2)*
This subfield contains the number of a meeting.

　　　　$a**Vatican Council**$n*(1st :***$d**1869-1870)

d　　**Date of meeting (NR)**　　*(Rule 24.7B3)*
This subfield contains the date a meeting or conference was held. A date added parenthetically to a meeting name to distinguish between identical names is not separately subfield coded.

　　　　$a**Louisiana Cancer Conference**$n(2nd :**$d***1958* :**$c**New Orleans, La.)

c　　**Location of meeting (NR)**　　*(Rule 24.7B4)*
This subfield contains a place name or a name of an institution where a meeting was held. You should follow the same format for entering names here as you would for any other geographic location.

　　　　$a**Conference on Cancer Public Education**$d(1973 :**$c***Dulles Airport)*

PUNCTUATION

$n is preceded by no punctuation.
$d is preceded by no punctuation unless it is preceded by **$n**, then it is preceded by a colon.
$c is preceded by a colon.
$n, $d,** and **$c are enclosed in one set of parenthesis, which are expanded to include all of the subfields.
The tag ends with a terminal mark of punctuation.

130 MAIN ENTRY - UNIFORM TITLE

REPEATABLE: NO
MANDATORY: NO
RELATES TO: 245$a, 740.
AUTHORITY: YES

INDICATOR CODES

1st indicator

0-9   Nonfiling characters
By definition, the Library of Congress states that indefinite articles should be omitted from the title before entry unless the nonfiling characters are an integral part of the name and the searcher would know the title with those articles.

2nd indicator
The 2nd indicator is always blank.

SUBFIELD CODES

a   **Uniform title (NR)**
n   **Number of part/section of a work (R)**
p   **Name of part/section of a work (R)**
l   **Language of a work (NR)**
k   **Form subheading (R)**
s   **Version (NR)**
f   **Date of a work (NR)**

Note that these subfield codes are not in alphabetical order.

EXAMPLES

130 0 $aBible.$lEnglish.$sAuthorized.$kSelections.$f1970.
130 0 $aBible.$pN.T.$pRomans.$lEnglish.$sRevised standard.$f1959.
130 0 $aArabian nights.
130 0 $aMother Goose.
130 0 $aBremer Stadtmusikanten.

LOCATION

If a work is a uniform title, the uniform title will probably not be on the chief source of information in the correct form. You may need to refer to an external authority file to determine what the correct uniform title is.

NOTES

Every **130** must contain a **$a**. If there is a **130** tag, there cannot be a **240** tag in the same record.

A main entry under uniform title is used when a work is entered directly under a title and the work has appeared under varying titles, and a single form of the title is selected to represent all variations. The actual title that appears on the work being cataloged is contained in field **245**. Uniform titles most often used for the Bible and other sacred writings, classical literature, music, and the titles of folklore and fairy tales. It may be necessary to consult other sources to determine the correct main entry for an item.

You should retain a list in your library of the uniform titles used, or you can do this online via your system's authority control system, if so equipped. Since uniform titles are often the most difficult concept to understand, you may wish to ask your supplier of bibliographic records to send you some good examples of records with uniform titles on them, or if you are part of a union project, view them in your system's database or product.

THE SUBFIELDS IN DETAIL

a **Uniform title (NR)**   *(Begin at Rule 25)*

This is where the actual uniform title used as the main entry is entered. Parenthetical information added to make a title distinctive is not separately subfield coded except for treaties.

　　　$aGenesis (Anglo-Saxon poem)

n **Number of part/section of a work (R)**   *(Rule 25.6)*

This subfield contains a number designation for a part/section of a work used in a uniform title field. "Numbering" is defined as an indication of sequencing in any form. **$n** is often followed by **$p**.

　　　$aArabian nights.*$nBooks 1-4.*$pPart 1.

p **Name of part/section of a work**   *(Rule 25.18)*

This subfield contains a name designation of a part/section of a work used in a uniform title field. **$p** will often follow **$n**.

　　　$aBible.*$pO.T.*
　　　$aBible.$pN.T.*$pRevelation.*

l **Language of a work (NR)**   *(Rule 25.18A10)*

This subfield contains the name of the language(s) used in a uniform title.

　　　$aBible.$pO.T.*$lEnglish.*

k **Form subheading (R)**   *(Rule 25.9)*

This subfield contains a form subheading used in a uniform title field. Some typical form subheadings are Manuscript, Selections, and Protocols.

　　　$aMother Goose.*$kSelections.*

s **Version (NR)**   *(Rule 25.18A11)*

This subfield contains version, edition, etc., information used in a uniform title field.

　　　$aBible.$lEnglish.*$sAuthorized.*

f   **Date of a work (NR)**   *(Rule 25.18A13)*

This subfield contains the date of publication used in a uniform title field.

$aBible.$lEnglish.$sRevised Standard.*$f1959.*

It is important to note that not all uniform titles will have every one of these subfields. You should use them as the needs of the title warrant.

PUNCTUATION

$n is preceded by a period.

$p is preceded by a comma if it follows **$n**, otherwise it is preceded by a period.

$l is preceded by a period.

$k is preceded by a period.

$s is preceded by a period.

$f is preceded by a period.

If any subfield has parenthesis, the punctuation goes outside of the parenthesis.

The tag ends with a period or a terminal mark of punctuation.

2XX TAGS

The **2XX** tags contain publication information. This is information such as the title of the item, the edition or version of the item, if any, and places, date, and name of publisher. This information is some of the most important information in the bibliographic record. It is very important that you enter this information correctly, since your users, as well as yourself, will depend on it greatly for a variety of tasks.

Because of this importance, these tags have some very detailed information in them. Don't allow yourself to become swamped or intimidated by the information, if you take the pieces of data in small portions, it will be easy to correctly enter them into the MARC record.

Most of the information in these areas comes from mandated areas, usually the title page. If you get information outside of these mandated areas, you will need to enclose it in square brackets ([ ]) to show that the librarian or cataloger supplied the information.

The tags covered in this section of the book are:

222   **Key title**
240   **Uniform title**
245   **Title statement and statement of responsibility**
246   **Varying form of title**
250   **Edition statement**
255   **Cartographic mathematical data**
256   **Computer file characteristics**
260   **Publication, distribution, etc. (imprint)**

222   KEY TITLE

REPEATABLE: YES
MANDATORY: NO
RELATES TO: 245
AUTHORITY: NO

1st indicator
The 1st indicator is always blank

2nd indicator
0-9   Number of nonfiling characters present
This value specifies the number of character positions associated with an article at the beginning of a title which should be disregarded in the filing process.

SUBFIELD CODES

a   **Key title (NR)**
b   **Qualifying information (NR)**

EXAMPLES

222       $aWorldwide art catalogue bulletin. American library edition
222       $aHigh Fidelity. Musical America Edition$b(1980)
222       $aAlliance plus

NOTES

This field contains a unique title which is assigned to a serial in conjunction with an International Standard Serial Number (ISSN) recorded in field **022**. It is formed from title information transcribed from a piece of the serial and is constructed with qualifiers to make it unique when necessary. In the United States, the National Serials Data Program (NSDP) under the auspices of the International Serials Data System (ISDS) assigns key titles.

When entering records, the key title generally will not be on the item. It will usually be on records provided by the vendor or from your subscription service company. You will usually encounter key titles on records from vendors or you may find them on some catalog cards if you are doing a retrospective conversion project. Very often, they are associated with a specific ISSN that is not recorded here, but in the **022** tag. You should check with your system vendor to determine if they are traced in your system, and if so, under which search keys.

THE SUBFIELDS IN DETAIL

a   **Key title (NR)**   *(Start Rule 12.8C)*
Subfield a contains the actual key title, including any number, name, or edition information.

> *$a101 gardening and outdoor ideas*
> *$aJournal of polymer science. Part B. Polymer letter*

b   **Qualifying information**   *(Rule 12.8E1)*

This subfield contains information that qualifies the title to make it unique. Subfield **b** is always enclosed in parentheses.

> **$a**Economic education bulletin**$b***(Great Barrington)*
> **$a**Russian history**$b***(Pittsburgh)*

Note that subfields **n**, **p**, and **h** are not used here.

PUNCTUATION

$b is preceded by no punctuation, but is always enclosed in parenthesis.

The tag does not end with a mark of final punctuation unless the last word in the field is an abbreviation or closing parentheses.

240   UNIFORM TITLE

REPEATABLE:	NO
MANDATORY:	NO
RELATES TO:	245$a
AUTHORITY:	YES

1st indicator

0   **Uniform Title not printed on cards or displayed on screen.**
1   **Uniform Title printed on cards or displayed on screen.**

2nd indicator

0-9   **Number of nonfiling characters**
          The Library of Congress has stated that, as a rule, initial articles should be dropped from uniform
          titles. Therefore, this value will usually be zero.

SUBFIELD CODES

a   **Uniform title   (NR)**
n   **Number or part/section of a work   (R)**
p   **Name of part/section of a work   (R)**
l   **Language of work   (NR)**
k   **Form subheading   (R)**
s   **Version   (NR)**
f   **Date of work   (NR)**

This field contains the uniform title for a work when the record also has a **100, 110,** or **111** tag. A
uniform title is used when a work has appeared under varying titles, necessitating that a particular title be
chosen to represent the work. The title that appears on the title page (or substitute) of the work being
cataloged is contained in the **245**. This differs from the **130** tag in that the title in a **240** is associated with
a particular author who is recorded in a **1XX** tag. If you have an item that was originally written in
another language, the original language title should be entered in the subfield a with the language statement
that the work in hand represents in subfield **$l**.

This tag will be used most often when you entering sound recordings, folklore, or literature. It cannot be
used when a **130** tag is present.

EXAMPLES

100 1	**a**Menotti, Gian Carlo,**$d**1911-	(Main entry)
240 10	**$a**Amahl and the night visitors.**$l**Spanish	(Uniform title)
245 10	**$a**Amahl y los reyes magos.	(Title on title page)
100 1	**$a**Verne, Jules,**$d**1825-1903.	(Main entry)
240 10	**$a**Vingt mille lieus sous les mers.**$l**English	(Uniform title)
245 10	**$a**20,000 leagues under the sea.	(Title on title page)

100 1	$aTrollope, Anthony,$d1815-1882.	(Main entry)
240 10	$aSelections	(Uniform title)
245 14	$aThe best writings of Anthony Trollope.	(Title on title page)

LOCATION

The actual uniform title will usually not be recorded on the work itself. You may need to verify it in an outside source such as Library of Congress Name Authority File or another authority source. Once you have verified it, you should record the information either in your system's authority module or in your manual authority file.

NOTES

A uniform title is used when a work is entered under a particular author's name, but the actual title of the work may vary from publisher to publisher or from language to language. A uniform title helps pull all these variant forms together, necessitating a particular title be chosen to represent the work. The title that appears on the work being cataloged is contained in field **245**. AACR2 defines a uniform title as "A conventional collective title used to collocate publications of an author, composer, or corporate body containing several works or extracts, etc., from several works." Be careful that the same items are not sometimes entered as a uniform title main entry (**130** tag)

The ability or limitations of a given automation system are often determined by the vendor. Contact your vendor to determine how their particular system handles uniform titles.

THE SUBFIELDS IN DETAIL

a   **Uniform title (NR)**   *(Begin at Rule 25.2)*

This is where the actual uniform title is entered. Parenthetical information added to make a title distinct is not separately subfield coded except for treaties.

100	$aDickens, Charles,$d1812-1870.	(Main entry)
240	*$aMartin Chuzzlewit*	(Uniform title)
245	$aMartin Chuzzlewith's life and adventures.	(Title page title)

n   **Number of part/section of a work (R)**   *(Begin at rule 25.31)*

This subfield contains a number designation for a part/section of a work used in a uniform title field. "Numbering" is defined as an indication of sequencing in any form. For music, the serial opus, or thematic index number, or a date used as a number is contained in this subfield.

100	$aBeethoven, Ludwig van,$d1770-1827.	(Main entry)
240	$aSymphonies.*$nno. 1, op. 21, C Major*	(Uniform title)
245	$aBeethoven's symphony number one	(Title page title)

p   **Name of part/section of a work (R)**   *(Rule 25.32)*

This subfield contains a name designation of a part/section of a work used in a uniform title field.

100	$aVerdi, Giuseppe,$d1813-1901.	(Main entry)
240	$aAida.*$pCeleste Aida*	(Uniform title)
245	$aSelections from Verdi's Aida.	(Title page title)

l   **Language of a work (NR)**   *(Rule 25.5C)*

This subfield contains the name of the language(s) used in a uniform title field. It is the same as the language of the work being cataloged and should agree with the language value in the **008** tag.

100	$aHandel, George Frederic,$d1685-1759.	(Main entry)
240	$aMessiah.*$lSpanish*	(Uniform title)
245	$aHandel's Messiah for Spanish singers.	(Title page title)

k   **Form subheading (R)**   *(Rule 25.6B3 and 25.9)*

This subfield contains a form subheading used in a uniform title field. Some typical form subheadings are Manuscript, Selections, and Protocols.

100	$aBrowning, Elizabeth Barrett,$d1806-1861.	(Main entry)
240	$aPoetry.*$kSelections*	(Uniform title)
245	$aElizabeth Browning's best known poems.	(Title page title)

s   **Version (NR)**   *(Rule 25.12 and 25.18A11)*

This subfield contains version, edition, etc., information used in a uniform title field.

100	$aEmerson, Ralph Waldo,$d1803-1882.	(Main entry)
240	$aPoetry.$kSelectons.*$sLarge print*	(Uniform title)
245	$aSight saving Emerson reader.	(Title page title)

f   **Date of a work (NR)**   *(Rules 25.16 and 25.30E1)*

This subfield contains the date of publication used in a uniform title field.

100	$aMozart, Wolfgang Amadeus,$d1756-1791.	(Main entry)
240	$aConcertos.*$f1938*	(Uniform title)
245	$aComplete concertos of Mozart.	(Title page title)

PUNCTUATION

$f is preceded by a period.
$k is preceded by a period.
$l is preceded by a period.
$n is preceded by a period.
$p is preceded by a comma if it follows a subfield **$n**, otherwise it is preceded by a period.
$s is preceded by a period.
If any subfield has parenthesis, the punctuation goes outside of the parenthesis.
The tag does not end with a period.

245   TITLE STATEMENT

REPEATABLE:	NO
MANDATORY:	YES
RELATES TO:	246$a, 740$a
AUTHORITY:	NO

1st indicator

0	No title added entry	Use if no 1XX tag
1	Title added entry	Use if there is a 1XX tag

2nd indicator

0-9   Nonfiling characters

Count and enter the number of characters for initial articles, like a, an, or the (in any language) plus spaces following them before the first filing word. If there is more than one indirect article, only count the first one. Do not count marks of punctuation at the beginning of the title in nonfiling character counts unless an indirect article precedes them.

SUBFIELD CODES

a	**Title (NR)**
n	**Number of part/section of a work (R)**
h	**Medium (GMD) (NR)**
b	**Remainder of title (NR)**
c	**Remainder of title page transcription/statement of responsibility (NR)**

This field contains the title and statement of responsibility area. The Title Statement field consists of the title proper and may also contain subtitle, other title information, and the statement of responsibility.

EXAMPLES

245 00 $aMap of the Kettle Moraine Bike Trail, Palmyra, Wisconsin.

245 00 $aPrivate eyeballs :$ba golden treasury of bad taste.

245 10 $aLive at Red Rocks$h[sound recording] /$cJohn Tesh.

245 00 $aFlash Gordon$h[videorecording].

245 00 $aStar trek, the next generation$h[interactive multimedia] :$binteractive technical manual.

245 00 $aKuffs$h[videorecording].

245 00 $aMultiplication rock$h[videorecording].

245 00 $aStar trek, the next generation$h[computer file].

245 00 $aRead, man!$h[picture].

24510 $aHe who hunted birds in his father's village :$bthe dimensions of a Haida myth /$cGary Snyder ; preface by Nathaniel Tern ; edited by Donald Allen.

24514 $aThe Green bag :$ba useless but entertaining magazine for lawyers /$cby Caleb Stower and Jack Red.

24510 $aFaust.$nPart two /$cedited by John Chapmann.

245 14 $aThe printer's manual /$cby Caleb Stower ; with a new introduction by John Bidwell. The printer's companion / by Edward Grattan ; with a new introduction by Clinton Sisson.

NOTES

Information is entered exactly as on the chief source of information! If a word seems to be wrong, do not correct it, even if it is "obviously" wrong. Enter errors, abbreviations, numbers, places, names, etc. as shown on the chief source. For information on the chief source of information, consult the **1XX** and accompanying tag information. If you feel that the information needs to be "adjusted" to improve access for your patrons, you should enter the variant form in a **246** tag.

Do not follow standard grammatical rules for capitalization. Capitalize only the first word, proper adjectives, and proper nouns, even if other letters/words are capitalized on the chief source. If there is no **1XX** value and the **245** tag starts with an article, then capitalize the first letter following the article. Do not enter quotation marks if the entire subfield is in quotes. If only part of the subfield is enclosed in quotation marks, then include them.

EXAMPLE

245 14 $a"The dog" that never sleeps /
245 10 $a"Eve" of our destruction
245 05 $aThe "missadventures" of Huckleberry Finn.
                     (The 246 tag will be: *246 30Huckleberry Finn.*)

LOCATION

The information for the **245** is always taken from the chief source of information. If you need to, refer back to the **1XX** information to determine the chief source of information for the various formats. If you obtain information from another place on the item or if the item does not have a title and you have to supply one, you should enclose it in square brackets thus: [information]

THE SUBFIELDS IN DETAIL

a   **Title (NR)**   *(Begin at Rule 1.1 and Rule 4)*
          This subfield contains the title proper and any alternative title. The first letter is capitalized. Again, it is transcribed exactly as on the title page or the chief source of information. If you are uncertain where the title ends and the subtitle begins, the typeface will often give you a clue. The title will be in bolder or more prominent type. The subtitle and statement of responsibility will usually be in smaller type or farther down the page.

> *$aAnimal farm.*
> *$aGulp! Gulp! Gulp!, or ; The pig at the trough.*
> *$aUninstaller.*

n   **Number of part/section of a work (R)**   *(Rule 1.1B9)*
          This subfield contains a number designation for a part/section of a work used in a title. "Numbering" is defined as an indication of sequencing in any form. Note that it does not have to be numerical, but could be alphabetic in nature, e.g., Part A.

> *$aFaust.$nPart one.*
> *$aSpin and Fizz.$nLevel two$h[videorecording].*

h   **Medium (GMD) (NR)**   *(Rule 1.1C1)*

This subfield contains a medium designator used in the title statement. It is always entered in lowercase and enclosed in square brackets {[ ]}   These medium designators are also used in the **246** and **740** tags. Below is a list of the acceptable GMD's and a brief description of each.

Some items do not lend themselves to a particular GMD. This includes items like sound filmstrips, books with an accompanying cassette, items that have a videorecording and models or realia to follow along or examine while playing the tape. You will need to determine which one of the items, if any is predominant. If you feel none of the items is predominant, then use the GMD **kit** (AACR2 1.1C4)

activity card

A card printed with words, numerals, and/or pictures to be used by an individual or a group as a basis for performing a specific activity. Cards used for vocabulary exercises or matching problems often fall into this group.

art original

An original work of art (other than a print or photograph) created by an artist, as opposed to a reproduction of a painting, drawing or piece of sculpture.

art reproduction

A mechanically reproduced copy of a work of art, generally as one of a commercial nature. Art prints mass-produced mechanically often fall into this category.

braille

Material intended for the visually impaired and using embossed characters for reading using raised dots in six-dot cells. A form of this called the Nemeth code is used in mathematics.

chart

An opaque (non-transparent) sheet that exhibits data in graphic or tabular form, like a wall chart or wall graph.

computer file

A data and/or program encoded for manipulation by a computer. Note that some older records may use the term machine-readable data file or MRDF.

diorama

A three-dimensional representation of a scene created by placing objects or figures in front of a two-dimensional painted background. Shoe-box exhibits which students often make are considered to be dioramas.

filmstrip

A length of film containing images that are successive in nature and intended to be projected one at a time. They do not try to create the illusion of movement and can either be silent or accompanied by sound.

flash card

 A card or other opaque material printed with words, numbers, or pictures and designed for rapid display. They are often used to teach math and grammar facts.

game

An item or set of materials designed for play according to prescribed or implicit rules and intended for recreation or instructional use. Note the inclusion of rules that helps to differentiate a game from realia or pictures.

globe

A model of the earth, moon, or other celestial body, depicted on the surface of a sphere.

interactive multimedia

This is a new term that was published as the separate publication *Guidelines for Bibliographic Description of Interactive Multimedia* by ALA in 1994. The information in this book regarding interactive multimedia is formulated according to the specifications stated in Guidelines.

Interactive multimedia is media residing in one or more physical carriers or on computer networks. Interactive multimedia must have user-controlled, nonlinear navigation using computer technology and be a combination of two or more media (audio, graphics, text, animation, video, etc.) that the user manipulates to control the order and/or nature of the presentation.

kit

An item containing two or more categories of materials, none of which is identifiable as the predominant item. They can also be a single-medium package of textual material assembled under a single name or "jackdaw".

manuscript

Writings of any nature made by hand, typescripts, or inscriptions onto natural objects, like clay or stone.

map

A representation, normally to scale and on a flat surface, of a portion or abstract features on or in relation to the surface of the earth or another planetary body. Wall maps usually fall into this category.

microform

A term used to describe any medium, transparent or opaque, bearing images that can be read only via some type of enlargement, usually optical.

microscope slide

A slide designed for holding a minute object that is usually viewed through a microscope.

model

A three-dimensional representation of a real-life object. Can either be fully-functional or static.

motion picture

A length of film bearing a sequence of static images that create the illusion of movement when projected in rapid succession. 16 mm. films used in schools are a common example of these.

music

Printed music or scores used for singing or for musical instruments. Not to be confused with sound recording.

picture

A two-dimensional representation accessible to the naked eye and generally on opaque backing. Use when a more specific GMD is not appropriate. This would be used for things like posters or non-photographic prints.

realia

A manufactured or naturally occurring entity, as opposed to a replica of that item. You would use this if you were cataloging your AV equipment or library furniture.

slide

Transparent film on which there is a two-dimensional image, usually in a plastic or cardboard mount, designed for use in a projector or viewer. They usually do not try to create the illusion of motion.

sound recording

A recording on which sound vibrations have been stored via mechanical or electrical means. This would include cassette tapes, record albums, compact discs and mini-discs.

technical drawing

A cross section or plan made for use in an engineering or other technical context. This would include building plans and blueprints.

toy

A physical object which is used for amusement and enjoyment. Usually does not have a set of rules with it.

transparency

A sheet of transparent material which has an image and designed for use with an overhead projector. May or may not be mounted in a frame and can either be permanent or washable in nature.

videorecording

A recording on which visual images which are usually in motion and accompanied by sound, designed for reproduction on a television set, monitor, or projection screen television. It does not use light shining through it. Note that it is one word and covers items like video tapes, laser discs, DVDs and 8 mm. recordings.

THE GMDs IN SUMMATION

activity card	map
art original	microform
art reproduction	microsope slide
braille	model
chart	motion picture
computer file	music
diorama	picture
filmstrip	realia
flash card	slide
game	sound recording
globe	technical drawing
interactive multimedia	toy
kit	transparency
manuscript	videorecording

For materials for the visually impaired, add (large print) or (tactile), when appropriate, to any of the above terms. Add (braille), when appropriate, to any of the above terms except braille.

> *$h[map (tactile)]*
> *$h[music (braille)]*
> *$h[game (large print)]*

b   **Remainder of title (NR)**   *(Rule 1.1D or 1.1E)*

This subfield contains the remainder of the title information. The data includes parallel titles, and other title (or subtitle) information. If it is extensive (more than 2 lines), do not enter it here but in a **500** tag, preceded by the word *Subtitle:* This is significant since it can affect how your system builds keywords. Since subtitles are usually more descriptive of an item than the actual title, it is often desirable to have keywords built on it. Check with you particular system vendor to determine the keyword indexing rules for your system. If entering parallel title information, precede it with the word *or* and follow the rules of capitalization for **$a** with no **1xx** tag.

> $aWork crew = *$bLew Cris des foret.*
> (Parallel titles are usually in other languages)
> $aFrantic frogs :*$bthe fractured fairy tales for reader's theater.*
> $aTimescapes$h[videorecording] :*$ba video journey thorugh the history of man.*

c   **Remainder of title page transcription/statement of responsibility (NR)**
                                (Begin at Rule 1.1F and Rule 4.1)

This subfield contains the statement of responsibility. It is usually the last subfield in the tag. This subfield will usually contain the name(s) of those involved in the creation of the item. It is in this subfield that you should enter *authors, compilers, editors, illustrators*, and *producers* if they are on the chief source of information. If they are not on the chief source, but elsewhere on the item, you can include them here if you surround the information with square brackets {[ ]}.

> $aAll that jazz /$c*Fats Waller*
> (Single author; title page does not say "by" Fats Waller.)
> $aThinking and reasoning :$bselected readings /$c*edited by P.C. Wason and P.N. Johnson.*
> (Contains a title, subtitle, and two editors.)
> $aPeter Rabbit /$c*Beatrix Potter* ; with new illustrations by Robert Randolf.
> (A title with an author and illustrator.)

If there is a combination of people involved in the creation of the item, you should enter <u>no more</u> than three people who are similar in function. For example, you should not enter more than three authors here, or more than three editors, or more than three compilers/transcribers/translators or illustrators. If there are <u>more</u> than three people involved in any one function, then you should only enter the <u>first</u> or <u>most significant</u> name here, followed by the phrase *[et al.]*. If there are three <u>or fewer</u> entries in this subfield, trace <u>all</u> of them at the end of the record. You may, as a local policy decision, enter the names of all people who would be relevant and significant to your users. Remember that you should not trace anything that you have not included earlier in the record. Translators should only be traced when they have made significant changes to the text as they translated it, or they translated single or collected works of poetry. This will be a judgment call on your part.

$aStories of the Civil War /$cedited by Bruce Catton [et al.].
(The book has more than three editors, only the first of which is listed.)
$aThe children's statistical atlas of the world /$cJohn Stevens and Lester Williams ; maps by Susan Wilson and Kellye Jensen. (All four names would be traced, with the first name going in the **100** tag.)

If there are multiple titles in a book that are bound as one by the publishers, the first title would go in **$a** with the statement of responsibility for that publication recorded in **$c**. After that statement of responsibility, enter a space period space and then proceed to enter the second title, followed by a space slash space and then the second statement of responsibility. You will probably want to enter the second title in a **740** tag and the second author in a **700** tag.

100 1 $aTwain, Mark,$d1835-1910.
245 14 $aThe adventures of Tom Sawyer /$cMark Twain. The adventures of Huckleberry Finn / Mark Twain.
740 02 $aAdventures of Huckleberry Finn.

ORDER

Note that not every **245** will have every one of these tags. If an item does not have information for that subfield, do not use that subfield. The subfields you will use most often are **$a, $h, $b,** and **$c**.

GENRES

Genre phrases such as story, poems, novel, etc. which modify the actual title of the item (**$a**), would be located in **245$b**. This is particularly true when the genre type is preceded by an indirect article.

Often, if the genre type is not preceded by an indirect article and immediately followed by a personal name, it may be a part of **245$c**. This is especially true in instances of mixed responsibility.

EXAMPLES

245 10 $aGreen Monday :
$ba story /
$cby Michael M. Thomas.
("a story" is a genre phrase)
245 10 $aI sing the body electric /
$cstory by Ray Bradbury ; pictures by Kevin Frayer.
("story" is part of the statement of responsibility.)

245

PUNCTUATION

The punctuation for this tag is extremely critical since many systems utilize it to index the information. Remember, when trying to determine the correct punctuation, ask yourself "what information comes next." Once you have determined what comes next, you will be able to correctly enter the punctuation.

$n is preceded by a period.
$h is preceded by no punctuation.
$b is preceded by a "space :"
$c is preceded by a "space /"
Parallel titles are separated by a "space ="
The tag always ends with a question mark, exclamation point, or a period. It cannot end with a bracket, parenthesis, or hyphen. If there is a bracket, parenthesis, or hyphen at the end of the tag, place a period after it.

246 VARYING FORM OF TITLE

REPEATABLE:	YES
MANDATORY:	NO
RELATES TO:	245, 500, 740
AUTHORITY:	NO

1st indicator

0 **Note, no title added entry**

A note is generated, but no title entry is generated in the system. Use this value if you want the relevant information displayed to the user, but not traced in the title index.

1 **Note, title added entry**

Both a note and a title added entry are generated.

Use this for 2nd indicator values **2, 3, 4, 5, 6, 7, 8**.

2 **No note, no title added entry**

No note or title added entry are generated by the system. No occurrence of this information will be accessible to the user.

3 **No note, title added entry**

No note, but a title added entry is generated from the field.

Use this for all other 2nd indicator values.

You should check with your system vendor to determine how your system utilizes these indicator values.

2nd indicator

blank	**No information provided**
0	**Portion of title**
1	**Parallel title**
2	**Distinctive title**
3	**Other title**
4	**Cover title**
5	**Added title page title**
6	**Caption title**
7	**Running title**
8	**Spine title**

246   33
Varint Title

SUBFIELD CODES

a	**Title proper/short title (NR)**
n	**Number or part/section of a work (R)**
h	**Medium (GMD(NR)**
f	**Designation of volume and issue number and/or date of a work (NR)**

EXAMPLES

245 00   **$a**4 corners power review.
246 3   **$a**Four corners power review

245 00   **$a**ALA bulletin
246 2   **$a**American Library Association bulletin

245 04   **$a**The Berkley book of modern writing.

246 30   **$a**Modern writing

245 00   **$a**African semminar series.
246 10   **$a**African seminar series

245 00   **$a**Bangladesh Education Extension Centre bulletin.
246 17   **$a**BEEC bulletin
246 17   **$a**B.E.E.C. bulletin

NOTES

This field contains forms of the title appearing on different parts of the item, or consisting of portions of the title proper or alternative forms of titles, including variant forms of the title. These variant titles are recorded in field **246** only if they differ substantially from the title statement in field **245** and if they contribute to the further identification of the item. Note that many of these titles were previously entered in the **740** tag. Titles from information recorded in the **505** tag that you choose to trace would still be entered in the **740** tag. Note that the subfields are constructed in the same manner as the **245**, with the same punctuation being used.

Because there is no provision for non-filing indicator values in this tag, all non-filing characters, like indirect articles (*a, an, the, le der,* etc.) should be dropped before entering the title <u>unless</u> the user could reasonably be expected to search under them, like *Los Angeles* or *El Paso*.)

You are strongly encouraged to review LCRI 21.30J to observe how the Library of Congress determines when to make variant entries.

THE INDICATORS IN DETAIL

blank   **No information provided**   *(Rule 21.30J1)*

Leave the 2nd indicator position blank if you are creating an entry for a variant form of the title. This would include characters or numbers that are spelled out or spelled out numbers from the **245** which are being entered in their numerical form and for entries for ordinal numbers;

245 10   **$a**30 days in May.
246 3   *$aThirty days in May*

245 14   **$a**The four seasons of love**$h**[sound recording].
246 3   *$a4 seasons of love***$h**[sound recording]

245 00   **$a**Innside Vermont.
246 1   *$aInside Vermont*

245 00   **$a**101 dalmations**$h**[videorecording].
246 3   *$aOne hundred and one dalmations***$h**[videorecording]
246 3   *$aOne hundred one dalmations***$h**[videorecording]

The last example is in accordance with *LCRI 21.30J(8)*

0   **Portion of title**

Use of this value indicates that the title given in the field is a title for which access or an added entry is desired. Use this for entries which are made which are for subfields **b** or **p** from the **245** <u>or</u> when you are making an added entry for a title which has a proper name at the beginning; the title would be entered here without the proper name. It is also used for titles that contain corrections to "obvious" typos from the **245**.

245 14 $aThe how and why wonder book of cars.
246 30   *$aCars*
246 30   *$aWonder book of cars*

245 04 $aThe Sports illustrated guide to ice fishing$h[videorecording].
246 30   *$aIce fishing*$h[videorecording]
246 30   *$aGuide to ice fishing*$h[videorecording]

1   **Parallel title**

Use of this value indicates that the title given in the tag is a parallel title, that is, a title in another language. When one or more parallel titles have been recorded in field **245**, each parallel title is also recorded in a separate **246**. Note that if the item is a <u>translation</u> from another item, the original title would go in a **240** tag.

245 00 $aJapan report =$bNihon.
246 31   *$aNihon*

2   **Distinctive title**

Use of this tag indicates that the title given in the tag is a distinctive title. Distinctive titles are special titles appearing in addition to the regular title on individual issues of an item. They are most commonly found on such items as annual reports, yearbooks, or conference proceedings when an issue is dedicated to a particular topic or theme. Distinctive titles should not be confused with individual titles (e.g., analytics) within a series. The distinctive titles are recorded in the tag if the individual volume is likely to be known by the special title. **Subfield f is always used with indicator value 2.** This value will generally be used with serial items or monographic serials.

245 00 $aAnnual report /$cEconomic Development Administration.
246 12   *$aCreating jobs*$f1980

245 04 $aThe yearbook of American agriculture.
246 12   *$aCrop rotation analysis for the midwest*$f1989

3   **Other title**

Value 3 indicates that the title given in the tag is another title that appears on the piece but which is not specified by one of the other second indicator values. Other titles include, masthead title, half-titles, binder's titles, colophon titles, parallel titles not recorded in field **245**, *cover titles* found in an inverted format at the back of the publication, etc.

245 00 $aComprehensive American subject headings$h[computer file].
246 13   *$aCASH*$h[computer file]
                Title has the word <u>CASH</u> printed on the spine of the publication by the publisher.

4   Cover title

Use of this value indicates that the title given in the tag is a *cover title*. A cover title is the title printed on the original covers of a publication or lettered or stamped on the publisher's binding. This value is used only when the cover is not the chief source of information or if the cover title is different from the title page title. Note that this information used to go in a **740** tag.

> 245 14 $aThe story of a cub riverboat pilot /$cby Samuel Clemens.
> 246 14   *$aLife on the Mississippi*

The story of a cub riverboat pilot is what is printed on the title page of the book. The cover of the book says *Life on the Mississippi*.

5   Added title page title

Use of this tag indicates that the title given in the tag is an *added title page title*. This is usually a title in another language found on a title page preceding or following the title page used as a chief source, or on an inverted title page at the end of the publication.

> 245 00 $aSudan guide.
> 246 15   *$aMurshid al-Sudan$f1982-1983*

6   Caption title

This value indicates that the title given in the tag is a *caption title*, which is the title printed at the head of the first page of text. You should use it only if the title printed at the head of the first page is different than the title from the title page. It will be used primarily for periodical and serial items.

> 245 10 $aNewspaper geog. list$h[microform] /$cCarleton University.
> 246 16   *$aNewspaper index$fJan. 1982-*

7   Running title

This value indicates that the title in the tag is a *running title* that is the title printed on the top or bottom margin of each page of a publication. You should use it only if the title on the bottom or top of each page is different than the *title page title*. It is used most often when cataloging serial titles.

> 245 00 $aDallas Public Schools teacher's newsletter.
> 246 17   *$aDPS teacher's newsletter*

8   Spine title

This value indicates that the title given in the tag is a *spine title* found on the spine of the publication. This title must be a publisher's title, not the title placed on the spine if the library sends an item out to the bindery.

> 245 10 $aChartbook of federal program on aging /$cIrma Schechter.
> 246 18   *$aChartbook on aging*

THE SUBFIELDS IN DETAIL

a   Title proper/short title (NR)

This subfield contains the title proper and any alternative title. The first letter is capitalized.

n   **Number of part/section of a work (R)**
This subfield contains a *number* designation for a part/section of a work used in a title. "Numbering" is defined as an indication of sequencing in any form. Note that it does not <u>have</u> to be numerical in nature, but could be alphabetic in nature, e.g., *Part A*.

$aFaust.*$nPart one.*

h   **Medium (GMD)(NR)**
Enter the General Material Designator for AV items here. The values are identical to those used in the **245** and brackets surround it. For a detailed explanation of these, refer to the **245$h** information.

> activity card
> art original
> art reproduction
> braille
> chart
> computer file
> diorama
> filmstrip
> flash card
> game
> globe
> interactive multimedia
> kit
> manuscript
> map
> microform
> microscope slide
> model
> motion picture
> music
> picture
> realia
> slide
> sound recording
> technical drawing
> toy
> transparency
> videorecording

f   **Designation of volume/issue number and/or date of a work (NR)**
This subfield contains dates or volume/issue numbers that relate the variant title to the record. It should not be used when the second indicator position value is 0 or 1.

246

EXAMPLE

245 04	**$a**The how and why wonder book of cars & trains.
246 30	*$aCars & trains*
	but not
246 30	**$a**Cars and trains.

PUNCTUATION

$n is preceded by a period.

$h is preceded by no punctuation.

$f is preceded by no punctuation **unless** the item preceding $ f is an abbreviation, initial/letter, or data that ends with a mark of punctuation, then it is preceded by a coma.

The tag does <u>not</u> end with a mark of final punctuation unless the last word in the field is an abbreviation, initial/letter, or data that ends with a mark of punctuation.

MAKE A 246 WHEN:

• There is a **500** tag with the notation *Cover title, Spine title,* or *At head of title:* Put the variant title, if it is different from the **245**, in a **246**.

• If there is an "obvious" typo in the **245**. *Note that this is a <u>local</u> policy decision.*

• If there is a non-letter character (&, +, =, $, etc.) in the first <u>five</u> filing words of the **245$a** with the character in spelled-out form.

• If there is an abbreviation in the first five filing words of the **245** that could <u>reasonably</u>be expected to be searched in its spelled out form.

• Numerical values in the first five words of the **245**. It is LC policy to enter these in spelled-out form. Note that numbers ending in "1" such as 101 require <u>two</u> **246** tags.

• Ordinal numbers that are the first filing word in the title. This means that if you have the number *1st, 2nd, 3rd,* etc., you would make a **246** for the spelled out form. If the title has the spelled out form, such as *First, second, third,* etc., then you should make a **246** for the numerical value.

• Arabic ordinal numbers that are in the first five filing positions. Make a **246** for the spelled-out value.

• Words in the first five filing positions that are spelled out that could be searched under an abbreviation, such as "United States". You should make a **246** for "U.S." but not "US".

• There is a parallel title, such as when the title is in Spanish and the English translation of the title is in subfield **b**.

• Titles that start the same as the series name. Make a **246** entry for the title, omitting the series name.

• Notations in the **500** tag that state *Added t.p.* The title information in the **500** should be traced <u>if</u> it differs significantly from the **245** <u>and</u> someone could *reasonably* search under that title.

• Items which are preceded by a prepositional phrase should have a **246** entry created for the subject of the phrase.

• Titles that have the author, editor, translator, or compilers (**100, 110, 700,** or **710**) at the beginning of the **245$a**. The **246** would be entered <u>without</u> the name (s)

• For abbreviations which are the same as the **245** but lack marks of punctuation (e.g. **245** has *U.S.* there would be a **246** for *US* <u>and</u> there would be a **246** for *United States.*)

DO NOT MAKE A 246:

• Titles that have been previously published as another title. You may need to make a **240** for that title also.

• If there is a note in a **500** tag which says *Series Title.*

• For non-letter characters <u>after</u> the first five words in the title.

• For subtitles. *You may wish to trace the subtitle in a 246 if the item is better known by that subtitle.*

• For spelled out years (e.g. title of book is *1776;* do not make a **246** containing *Seventeen Seventy-six.*)

• Fractional values in the **245** are not spelled out in a **246**.

• Titles of respect or professions, such as *Mr., Ms., Miss., Dr.*

• Acronyms that are commonly used as words, such as *AIDS, Radar,* and *NASA.*

• For standard contracted terms, such as *Let's, It's, Here's* etc.

• Spelled out ordinal numbers, e.g. *First, Second, Fifth,* etc. which are <u>not</u> the first filing word in the title.

• Arabic ordinal numerals other than the <u>first</u> one in the title.

• Titles that are either sequels or preceded the item on the card.

• Variant forms of the title which are already a variant of the **245$a** value.

250 EDITION STATEMENT

REPEATABLE:	NO
MANDATORY:	NO
RELATES TO:	245$b
AUTHORITY:	NO

1st indicator

The 1st indicator is always blank.

2nd indicator

The 2nd indicator is always blank.

SUBFIELD CODES

a   Edition statement(NR)
b   Remainder of edition statement(NR)

EXAMPLES

250	$a1st ed.
250	$aDiamond jubilee anniversary ed.
250	$aVersion 6.0.
250	$aLetterbox ed.
250	$aDOS version.
250	$aEuropean ed.
250	$a4th ed. /$brevised by J.G. Le Mesurie and E. Mc Intosh.
250	$aCanadian ed. /$bwith revisions, an introduction, and a chapter on writing by Mary Turner.
250	$a[4th ed., rev.].

The first word of the edition statement (if it begins with a letter), is capitalized.

LOCATION

As a rule, the edition statement will either be on the chief source of information or very near to it (like on the backside of the title page or directly below the title on many AV items.) If you take the edition statement from another source, such as the index, table of contents, the dust jacket, or the cover of the item, you should enclose it in square brackets as shown in the last example above.

Numbers that are written out (e.g., *seventh, first*) can be converted to Arabic numerals (*7th, 1st*) at your discretion. Whether you chose to convert or not is not important, what <u>is</u> important is that you do it <u>consistently</u> throughout your collection. It is acceptable, but not mandatory, to abbreviate the following words whenever they occur in the tag, whether they are spelled out or not on the item. Again, it is more important to be consistent rather than if you choose to abbreviate or not:

	WORDS	NUMBERS
ed.	or edition	1st
rev.	for revised	2nd
enl.	for enlarged	3rd
rev. & enl.	for revised and enlarged	10th

Note that the word *version* when used for computer software is <u>not</u> abbreviated.

NOTES

The edition statement is very important to you and your patrons. It helps your patrons determine if there are several books with the same title and the same publisher, which is the most current. It aids you when you are ordering replacement items, if you want to order the same edition. It is also invaluable during collection development, evaluation, and weeding activities to determine if there is a newer edition of an item out or if the item you have should be replaced. Some specialized edition statements, such as *Golden Anniversary ed.* or *Midwest ed.* can have special significance to your users. You should also be aware of special editions that may target an item to a particular user, such as *Teacher's ed.* or *Student ed.*

COMPUTER SOFTWARE

When cataloging computer software, you should use this tag to enter the version of the software being cataloged, <u>not</u> the version of the operating system software (e.g., *DOS* or *System*) needed to run the actual application. The word *version* <u>must</u> be spelled out; it cannot be abbreviated.

(Start at rule 9.B)

EXAMPLES

250 **$a**Version 1.2.
250 **$a**Version 7.7i.

If the application needs a particular version of DOS or other operating system, the version information for DOS would be recorded in the **538** tag, <u>not</u> in this tag.

VIDEORECORDINGS

When cataloging videorecordings, you can use this tag to record if the recording is non-standard or unusual. Note that this deals only with the <u>presentation</u> of the material, <u>not</u> the physical storage of the information.

(Start at rule 7.2B)

EXAMPLES

250 **$a**Letterbox ed.
250 **$a**Widescreen ed.

The method of recording and storage, like *VHS, CLV or DVD* are recorded in a **538** tag.

THE SUBFIELDS IN DETAIL

a   **Edition statement (NR)**   *(Start at Rule 3.2)*

This subfield contains an edition statement that usually consists of numeric and alphabetic characters and accompanying words and/or abbreviations. If an edition statement appears in more than one language, only the first edition statement is recorded.

> *$a1st ed.*
> *(Recorded only if statement on title page or verso)*

b   **Remainder of edition statement (NR)**   *(Rule 3.2C)*

This subfield contains the remainder of the edition statement and usually consists of a statement of personal or corporate responsibility, and may include a parallel edition statement(s). In punctuation and layout, it is very similar to the **245$c** tag. Be careful <u>not</u> to enter the name of the editor or compiler of the main work in this subfield. This subfield is rarely used.

100	$aWenshall, Constance.
245	$aGuide to reference books /$cConstance Wenshall ; 4th edition revised and enlarged by Sally Fields
250	$a4th rev. & enl. ed. /$bSally Fields.

(This edition is still considered the work of Wenshall, the original author, but an additional person helped with the 4th ed.)

PUNCTUATION

$b is preceded by a "*space /*"

The tag always ends with a period, even after a bracket or parenthesis, but there should not be two periods together. (e.g., two periods after "*4th ed..*")

260   PUBLICATION, DISTRIBUTION, ETC. (IMPRINT)

REPEATABLE: NO
MANDATORY: YES
RELATES TO: 010
AUTHORITY: NO

1st indicator

The 1st indicator is always blank

2nd indicator

The 2nd indicator is always blank

> Note: If you are editing older records from another source, they may have a value in one or both of the indicator positions. These values were invalidated in 1990. If you come across a record with a value in either indicator position, it is unnecessary to remove it, although you may do so if you wish.

SUBFIELD CODES

a   **Place of publication, distribution, etc. (R)**
b   **Name of publisher, distributor, etc. (R)**
c   **Date of publication, distribution, etc. (R)**

LOCATION

This information can usually be found on the chief source of information. This should be the source for your information. If you get the information from other sources, you will need to enclose it in square brackets.

EXAMPLES

260	$aChicago :$bElsevier,$c1988.
260	$aSpringfield, Mo. :$bSimpson's Press,$c1986.
260	$aBerlin ;$aNew York :$bSpringer Verlag,$c1977.
260	$bFollett,$c[19--]
260	$bUMI Books,$c1967, c1965.
260	$aParis :$bGauthier-Villars ;$aChicago :$bUniversity of Chicago Press, $c1986.

BUT NOT:

260     $aChicago :$bUniversity of Chicago Press ;$aParis :$bGauthier-Villars,$c1986.

NOTES

This field contains information relating to the publication, printing, distribution, issue, release, or production of a work. It is very important to correctly enter this information, as it is often necessary to reorder materials. It is also used when evaluating items for deselection or weeding, or if the library is part of an accreditation evaluation. Users will also use this information to determine if an item is timely enough before actually retrieving it.

260

Some of the detailed address information used to be entered in a **265** tag. The **265** has been removed from the *USMARC Bibliographic*. If you wish to enter detailed address or publication information, it should now be entered in the appropriate subfields in this tag.

THE SUBFIELDS IN DETAIL

a   **Place of publication, distribution, etc. (R)** *(Start at Rule 1.4 and 3.4)*

This subfield contains the place of publication and any additions to the name of a place, bracketed correction to erroneous information, or bracketed clarification of a fictitious place. This subfield is **not** required.

An abbreviation for the state is used with the city only if there are two cities by that name that could be confused, or if it is not a reasonably well known city. "Reasonably well known" is usually considered to mean that a librarian in another part of the country would have no difficulty in locating the state in which the city is. You have the option to abbreviate states, but it is <u>not</u> mandatory to do so. If you choose to abbreviate states, use the form as specified in AACR2 for state abbreviations. These abbreviations are <u>not</u> the Postal Service abbreviations; rather, they are the "old" ways of abbreviating states. (*Wisconsin* is abbreviated as *Wis.* and *California* is abbreviated as *Calif.*) Locations in foreign countries should be followed by the country name, unless they are considered to be reasonably well known. If multiple locations are given, they should each go into a separate *$a*. Record locations in the order they appear on the chief source of information. Continue entering locations until you enter one that is located in the United States; do not enter any locations after the one in the United States. If none of the locations is in the United States, enter only the first location.

> *$aNew York.*
> (Title page said *New York ; London*)
> *$aLondon ;$aNew York.*
> (Title page said *London ; New York ; Chicago*)
> *$aMilwaukee, Wis. (4650 N. Port Washington Rd., Milwaukee, WI, 52312-1063.*

When you have multiple publishers of an item, see the section below entitled *Multiple publishers.*

The abbreviation [*S.l.*] should be used in the subfield if the place, publisher, and date are not known. It <u>is</u> acceptable to enter the state or country only, without the name of a city if that is the only location information that is given on the item.

b   **Name of publisher, distributor, etc. (R)**   *(Rule 1.4D ; 3.4D)*
This subfield contains the name of the publisher or distributor.

Common terms, such as "company," "publishers," or "inc." should not be entered unless they are necessary to differentiate between two publishers whose names are similar. The term "*press*" does not have to be included <u>unless</u> the item is published by a college or university press; then it <u>must</u> be included. The term *Press* should also be entered if it is a fundamental part of the publisher's name (e.g., *Children's Press* or *University of Utah Press*).

> *$aNew York :$bH.W. Wilson.*
> (*Not* Wilson *or* H.W. Wilson & Company)
> *$aEnglewood, Colo. :$bLibraries Unlimited.*
> (*Not* Libraries Unlimited, Inc.)

See the section below entitled *Multiple publishers* if you have more than one publisher listed on the item.

The abbreviation [*s.n.*] should be used if the name of the publisher is not known.

c   **Date of publication, distribution, etc. (R)**   *(Rule 1.4F; 3.4F)*
This subfield contains the date of publication. Record the date on the chief source of information if given or check the package and/or container for other dating. If the date of publication is not known, you can use the year as given in the first two digits of the LCCN. Put a question mark after it and enclose it in brackets *[1993?]*. If there is no year of any type given on the item, enter *[19--], [18--]* depending on which century or decade you feel the item was published.

The librarian is supposed to show only the latest copyright data. Some publications will have multiple adjacent publication dates such as a date of publication and copyright date. They should both be entered in a single subfield but <u>DO NOT</u> enter printing dates as publishing dates. They are not entered in the record unless a <u>significant</u> change has been made between printings. Then a new record should be made.

If the date is shown with the copyright sign, type a lower case c before the date. If no "c" is shown, do not enter one.

Some sound recordings will use the production mark, which is similar to the copyright mark, except that it is the letter *p* inside of a circle, not a *c*. It is used primarily with sound recordings and should be handled the same way that a copyright mark is. If the copyright symbol precedes the production mark, then use *c*, not *p*.

$aNew York :$bGRP Records,$cp1993.
$aMilwaukee, Wis. :$bNarada Productions,$cc1993.
$aNew York :$bChrysalis Records,$cp1980, 1987.
$aOak Ridge, Tenn. $bU.S. Dept. of Energy,$cApril 15, 1977.

Exercise caution when doing videorecordings. The standard VHS videotape was not available prior to 1975, so if you see a date before that on a videotape, you should be suspicious. Generally, these are items which had been released on 16 or 35 mm. film and were transcribed to videotape. If the pre-1975 date is the only date on the item, you should enclose the date in brackets.

MULTIPLE PUBLISHERS

Sometimes you will have an item with multiple publishers in multiple locations. In these circumstances, you will need to enter locations and names of publishers (with each different publisher being attached to its respective location) until you come to one in the United States; any subsequent ones can be ignored. If there is only <u>one</u> publisher listed, then enter locations until you come to one in the United States.

If you have two cities in the United States with two different publishers, enter <u>both</u> cities/publishers only if one of them has a different function (e.g., distributor, printer, etc.). If they both function as publishers (e.g., *jointly published by...*), enter only the first entry. If there are two publishers separated by a slash (/), then they <u>both</u> must be entered in a separate **$b**. (AACR2 1.4D5d) This does <u>not</u> apply if the publisher's name has a slash in it as a result of a merger (e.g., *MGM/UA*).

260

(Rule 1.4G1)

In rare circumstances, particularly on older items, the place of publication, publisher, and date are <u>all</u> unknown. In these circumstances, brackets would surround the entire tag.

> 260   **$a**[S.l. :**$b**s.n.,**$c**19--?]

There is no punctuation at the end of the tag (after the bracket), but the usual internal punctuation remains the same.

If you have an item where the place and publisher are not known, but the date is, then the brackets would enclose **$a** and **$b**, but not **$c**.

> 260   **$a**[S.l. :**$b**s.n.],**$c**1973.

Note that the comma preceding **$c** goes <u>outside</u> the brackets.

If the place of publication and the date(s) are known, but the publisher is not, then **$b** is enclosed in brackets.

> 260   **$a**Chicago :**$b**[s.n.],**$c**1973.

When entering unknown information, one set of brackets should be used to enclose all of the unknown information. This means that the brackets may have to be expanded to enclose one, two, or three subfields.

It may seem that this tag is particularly difficult. In reality, for most of the items you will be cataloging, it is not as difficult as it may seem. The examples and scenarios given here are designed to expose you to as many possibilities as possible, so if you are faced with a situation outside the norm, you will be able to accurately catalog it.

PUNCTUATION

Multiple **$a** are preceded by a *space;*
$b is preceded by a *space*:
Multiple **$b** are preceded by a *space*:
$c is preceded by a comma with no *space*.
The tag ends with a terminal mark of punctuation.

3XX TAGS

The **3XX** tags contain information relating to the physical description or frequency of an item. Many librarians consider the physical description of an item insignificant, since it is not searchable. While this may be correct, they overlook the fact that the information on the screen can help the user and the librarian determine if an item is in a particular format (a videorecording as opposed to a motion picture) or if it is worth retrieving before actually going to the shelf and get it. It allows the librarian to tailor the materials to the skill and educational level of the user. Already, some systems are becoming available which will re-create a representation of the shelf where the item is, complete with title, call number, and relative size of the items. This is only possible if the **3XX** tags have been accurately completed.

Because of this importance, these tags have some very detailed information in them. Don't allow yourself to become intimidated by the information. What you enter here will prove to be very useful to you and your patrons when searching for items in your collection.

The **3XX** tags covered in this book are:

300   Physical description
306   Playing time

There are multiple **300** tag entries in this book. This is designed to accommodate the different types of materials that you may have in your library. To combine all the forms into one entry would be confusing and difficult to use. Each section is laid out with the names of the GMDs in the following pages.

300 PHYSICAL DESCRIPTION
[books]

REPEATABLE:	YES
MANDATORY:	YES
RELATES TO:	--
AUTHORITY:	NO

1st indicator
The 1st indicator is always blank.

2nd indicator
The 2nd indicator is always blank.

SUBFIELD CODES

a   **Extent (R)**
b   **Other physical details (NR)**
c   **Dimensions (R)**
e   **Accompanying material (NR)**

This field contains the physical description of the item that consists of the extent of the item and its dimensions and may also include other physical details of the item and information concerning accompanying material. This information is important since it will allow the user to "preview" the item before they retrieve it from the stacks.

EXAMPLES

300	$a151 p. :$bill (some col.) ;$c21 cm.
300	$a12 v. :$bill., maps, ports. (some col.)
300	$a[ ] p. :$bill.
300	$a3 v. (600 p.)
300	$a25 p. :$bill. (chiefly col.) ;$c12 x 28 cm.
300	$a v. ;$c29 cm.
300	$a4 v. :$b col. ill., maps (some col.), ports ;$c21 cm.
	(note that the v in all of the above examples is lower case.)

LOCATION

There is no single place to find this information. You will need to inspect the book to determine it. This includes looking at the introductory material, final page number, illustrations, and physical size. You will also need to leaf through the book to determine the quantity and type of illustrations that it contains.

NOTES

This tag is probably one of the most overlooked during cataloging. Most librarians feel that it serves no useful purpose since it is not usually searchable, including keyword searches. Nothing could be further from the truth. As pointed out earlier, this tag helps the user, as well as the librarian evaluate a book before time is devoted going to the stacks to retrieve the item. For example, for a patron doing research on dinosaurs, and needing a picture of a specific dinosaur, it would be a waste of the patron's time to give them a book that has no illustrations in it. By the same token, the user who is more advanced would not be interested in a book that is chiefly illustrated and has few pages in it. That book would be more appropriate for a juvenile reader.

Some vendors are currently developing software that will allow the user to actually view a representation of the shelves where a selected book is located. This is the ultimate attainment of browsing: browsing the shelves without actually having to go there. While this software is still in the development stages, it serves to highlight the many wonderful things that can be accomplished if you create detailed, thorough MARC records.

THE SUBFIELDS IN DETAIL

a   **Extent (R)**   *(Rule 1.5B, 3.5B)*

This subfield contains the extent of the item, which usually consists of the number of pages, volumes, etc. of each type of unit. For multipart items, it includes volumes (and pagination when pages are numbered consecutively). **$a is required**.

Enter the pages shown in the book. This includes introductory material at the beginning that is often enumerated by lower case Roman numerals (i, ii, iv, xxi, etc.) The final number of pages will be the last numbered page in the book. If the last numbered page is not the last page in the book, you should still use the number unless doing so gives a completely false impression of the size of the book. A good guide is that if the actual number of pages is greater or less than five percent of the numbered pages, you should use the actual pages, enclosing the value in square brackets. It is not acceptable to leave this subfield blank or to enter *unp.* in it.

> *$a139 p.*
> *$ax, 343 p.*
> *$avi, 269, x p.*

If there are no page numbers, you should do one of three things, in order of desirability:

1.   Physically count the number of pages. You should then enter this number in the subfield enclosed in square brackets.
        $a[32] p.

2.   Make a reasonable estimate as to the number of pages. You should enter this value in subfield a preceded with the notation **ca.** for circa.
        $aca. 32 p.

3.   Enter no page numbers, but instead use the notation **1 v.** in the subfield.
        $a1 v.

If the work is in more than one volume, you only need to enter the number of volumes, followed by a space and the letter **v.** If you choose to also record the total pagination for a multi-volume work, enter the information in the subfield after enclosing the page numbers in parenthesis.
        $a3 v.
        $a3 v. (798 p.)

If the item is a multivolume work that is still being published or a serial item, *enter 3 spaces* and then a *v.*

If you have one of the two unique types of material below, you should enter the qualifiers after the pagination information. They should be entered exactly as given below.
        (loose-leaf)
        (large print)

300

b   **Other physical details (NR)**   *(Rule 1.5C, 3.5C)*

This subfield contains information that further specifies other physical characteristics of an item, such as identification of illustrative matter, coloration, portraits, etc. If you have an illustrator in the **245$c** or **7XX** tags, you must indicate some type of illustrations in this subfield.

Below is a list of the acceptable abbreviations that can be entered in this subfield, along with their meanings. Use of the abbreviated form, if available, is highly recommended.

coats of arms	(no abbreviation)
col.	colored
facsim.	facsimile (singular)
facsims.	facsimilies (plural)
forms	(no abbreviation)
geneal.	genealogical (tables, trees)
ill.	illustrations
map	(no abbreviation)
maps	(no abbreviation)
music	(no abbreviation)
plans	(no abbreviation)
port.	portrait (singular)
ports.	portraits (plural)
samples	(no abbreviation)

DO NOT enter terms like charts, graphs, photographs, diagrams, or drawings. These are considered *ill.* and should be entered as such. You may find many older records that carry these notations. They were created according to rules formulated by AARC1.

If there is more than one type of the above items, enter *ill.* first, followed by the appropriate terms in alphabetical order.

> **$a**324 p. :*$b*ill., *music, ports.*

If parts of the items are in color, then note them as such. Some items, such as maps, may be in color, but portraits may not be. Indicate coloration for each item separately. If the book is primarily illustrations with very little text, then make the notation *chiefly ill.* If the illustrations in that book are mostly in color, then enter chiefly *col. ill.*

> **$a**[32] p. :*$b*col. ill.
> **$a**245 p. :*$b*ill., col. maps.

The information you enter here should agree with other information in the record. Title statements like *The illustrated book of birds* indicates that you will need to enter *ill.* in this subfield. If the title was *The illustrated color book birds*, then you should state *ill. (chiefly col.)* This means that, while most of the pictures in the book are in color, not all of them are, and that the book is primarily text, not illustrative in nature.

c   **Dimensions (R)**   *(Rule 1.5D, 3.5D)*

This subfield contains the dimensions of an item in centimeters. This information is particularly important to help distinguish oversize or "folio" books.

Dimensions are given in centimeters (cm.), unless the item is *less* than 10 cm. in height, then it is given in millimeters (mm.) If you measured the item using inches, convert the inches to centimeters by multiplying the number of inches by 2.54 and then rounding up. Give the *height only* unless:

The item is wider than it is high;

      **$a**24 p. :*$c 24 x 35 cm.*

             or

The item is more than twice as high as it is wide

      **$a**171 p. :*$c25 x 11 cm.*

In these circumstances, give both dimensions, height first with the *by* sign (x) between them.

The most effective way to measure an item is to take a ruler with centimeters on it and cut it off so that the end starts at "0". Remember, you are measuring the complete size of the book, including the binding, so do not open the book and measure only the height and/or width of the pages.

e   **Accompanying material (NR)**   *(Rule 1.5E1)*

This subfield contains a description of accompanying material. It may include any associated physical description statements enclosed in parentheses. It is used primarily when doing AV material, although some game and activity books may use this information.

      $a**387 p. :**$bill ;**$c**27 cm. +*$e3 maps*

      $a**271 p. :**$bcol. ill. ;**$c**21 cm. +*$e1 computer disc.*

PUNCTUATION

$b is preceded by a space colon (space :)

$c is preceded by a space semi-colon (space ;)

$e is preceded by a space plus (space +)

Note that the plus sign goes in the subfield directly preceding it, not in **$e** itself.

The tag ends with a terminal mark of punctuation or a period.

300 PHYSICAL DESCRIPTION
[computer file] [interactive multimedia]

REPEATABLE:	YES
MANDATORY:	YES
RELATES TO:	256, 500, 538
AUTHORITY:	NO

1st indicator
The 1st indicator is always blank.

2nd indicator
The 2nd indicator is always blank.

SUBFIELD CODES

a   **Extent (R)**
b   **Other physical details (NR)**
c   **Dimensions (R)**
e   **Accompanying material (NR)**

This field contains the physical description of the item that consists of the extent of the item and its dimensions and may also include other physical details of the item and information concerning accompanying material. This information is important since it will allow the user to "preview" the item before they retrieve it from the stacks.

EXAMPLES

300   **$a**1 computer disk ;**$c**5 1/4 in.
300   **$a**1 computer disk :**$b**col. ;**$c**3 1/2 in. +**$e**1 user's guide.
300   **$a**1 computer optical disc :**$b**sd., col. ;**$c**4 3/4 in.
300   **$a**1 videodisc, 3 computer disks (3 1/2 in.), 1 connector cable, 1 guide, 2 folded wall maps, 1 poster.

LOCATION

There is no single place to find this information. You will need to inspect the software and possibly even run it. This includes looking at the physical format and the accompanying material (if any.) You will need to use your discretion regarding the level of detail you want to go into here.

NOTES

This tag is probably one of the most overlooked during cataloging. Most librarians feel that it serves no useful purpose since it is not usually searchable, including keyword searches. Nothing could be further from the truth. As pointed out earlier, this tag helps the user, as well as the librarian evaluate the material before they request or retrieve it. It is also significant since it allows the user to determine if they are able to actually use this particular type of software on their computer. Also, in some circumstances, a patron (especially a teacher in a school library) may specifically want a particular piece of software to demonstrate an idea or to create a presentation.

<u>THE SUBFIELDS IN DETAIL</u>

a **Extent (R)**   *(Rule 1.5B, 9.5B)*

This subfield contains the SMD, or Specific Material Designation of the item. The phrase will usually start with the word computer followed by the physical form of the item (e.g. computer disk, computer optical disc, computer tape reel. **$a** is required.

If the medium is magnetic in nature ("floppy" disks), then use the spelling disk. If the medium is optical in nature (like compact discs or videodiscs), then use spelling disc.

> *$a3 computer disks*
> *$a1 computer optical disc*
> *$a2 computer tape reels*
> *$a1 computer optical disc (4 3/4 in.), 2 computer disks (5 1/4 in.), teacher's guide (24 p. : ill. ; 29 cm.)*

b **Other physical details (NR)**   *(Rule 1.5C, 9.5C)*

This subfield contains information that further specifies other physical characteristics of the computer file. This would include if it is encoded to produce sound or if it is designed to display in two or more colors.

> **$a**1 computer disk :*$b*sd.
> **$a**1 computer optical disc :*$b*sd., col.

c **Dimensions (R)**   *(Rule 1.5D, 9.5D)*

This subfield contains the dimensions of an item in inches. When measuring disks, measure the diameter of the disk in inches, rounding up to the next 1/4 in. Do not give any size or dimensions for computer reels.

If there are more than one physical carrier and they differ in size, give the smallest or smaller and the largest or larger size, separated by a hyphen, but no space.

> **$a**1 computer disk : **$b**sd., col. ;*$c3 1/2 in.*
> **$a**1 computer optical disc :**$b**sd., col. ;*$c4 3/4 in.*
> **$a**2 computer reels.
> **$a**2 computer disks :**$b**sd., col. ;*$c3 1/2-5 1/4 in.*

Do not use the "fraction" keys on your keyboard, if it has any. You should "make" the fractions using the numbers and slashes.

If you want to specify how many of each type of disk there are in a package, you should specify that in a **500** tag (see below)

e **Accompanying material (NR)**   *(Rule 1.5E, 9.5E)*

This subfield contains a description of accompanying material. It may include any associated physical description statements enclosed in parentheses. It is used primarily when describing any accompanying material with the software, particularly study guides, teacher's manuals, or documentation.

> **$a**1 computer disk ;**$c**5 1/4 in. + *$e1 booklet (45 p. : col. ill. ; 28 cm.)*
> **$a**1 computer optical disc :**$b**sd., col. ;**$c**4 3/4 in. +*$e1 user's manual (255 p.: col. ill. ; 18 cm.)*

300

Note that the information for **$e** which is inside the parenthesis is created and punctuated identically to the way it is in the **300** tag for books.

RELATED TAGS

If you are working on this tag, there are some other tags into which you may need to enter information. The tags most often used when working with computer software are the **256, 500** and **538** tags.

256 TAG

This field is used to record characteristics pertaining to a computer file. It may contain information about the type of file (e.g., Computer program) as well as the number of records or files. If you cannot ascertain how many files or records there are, then enter *Computer program* in this area.

    256   **$a**Computer data (2 files).
    256   **$a**Computer programs (2 files : 4300, 1250 bytes).

For more information on this tag, consult the **256** tag in this book.

500 TAG

When doing software, you must give the source of the title proper (Rule 9.7B3) This can either be from the title screen, from the disk label, or from supporting documentation.

    500   **$a**Title from title screen.
    500   **$a**Title from disk label.
    500   **$a**Title supplied by cataloger.

538 TAG

This tag is used to make a note on the system requirements of the file if the information is readily available (Rule 9.7B1b)

    538   **$a**System requirements: Apple family 48K RAM; DOS 3.3 or higher.
    538   **$a**System requirements: IBM PC or compatible; 8MB RAM; DOS 5.0 or higher; CD-ROM drive; color monitor recommended.

For more detailed information about this tag, consult the **538** tag in this book.

PUNCTUATION

$b is preceded by a space colon (space :)
$c is preceded by a space semi-colon (space ;)
$e is preceded by a space plus (space +)

Note that the *plus sign* goes in the subfield directly <u>preceding</u> it, not in **$e** itself.
The tag ends with a terminal mark of punctuation or a period.

300 PHYSICAL DESCRIPTION
[activity card] [art original] [chart] [filmstrip] [flashcard] [picture] [slide]
[technical drawing] [transparency]

REPEATABLE: YES
MANDATORY: YES
RELATES TO: 500,546
AUTHORITY: NO

1st indicator
The 1st indicator is always blank.

2nd indicator
The 2nd indicator is always blank.

SUBFIELD CODES

a   **Extent (R)**
b   **Other physical details (NR)**
c   **Dimensions (R)**
e   **Accompanying material (NR)**

This field contains the physical description of the item that consists of the extent of the item and its dimensions and may also include other physical details of the item and information concerning accompanying material. This information is important since it will allow the user to "preview" the item before they retrieve it from the stacks.

EXAMPLES

300     $a5 activity cards :$bcol. ;$c16 x 24 cm.
300     $a25 flash cards :$bcol. ;$c11 x 25 cm.
300     $a1 flip chart (15 sheets) :$bcol. ;$C35 x 26 cm.
300     $a1 postcard :$bcol. ;$c15 x 11 cm.
300     $a1 transparency (5 overlays) ;$c25 x 12 cm.

LOCATION

There is no single place to find this information. You will need to inspect the item in hand. This includes looking at the physical format, the accompanying material (if any), and possibly actually playing the item. You will need to use your discretion regarding the level of detail you want to go into here.

NOTES

This tag is probably one of the most overlooked during cataloging. Most librarians feel that it serves no useful purpose since it is not usually searchable, including keyword searches. Nothing could be further from the truth. As pointed out earlier, this tag helps the user, as well as the librarian evaluate the material before they request or retrieve it. In some circumstances, a patron may specifically want a graphic item instead of a book. This will allow them to determine if the material fits their particular needs.

300

THE SUBFIELDS IN DETAIL

a **Extent (R)**   *(Rule 1.5B, 8.5B)*
This subfield contains the SMD, or Specific Material Designation of the item.

Below is a list of acceptable SMD terms: *(Rule 8.5B1)*

activity card
art original
art reproduction
chart
filmstrip
flash card
flip chart
photograph
picture
postcard
poster
radiograph
slide
stereograph
study print
technical drawing
transparency
wall chart

EXAMPLES

$a1 activity card
$a35 photographs

b **Other physical details(NR)**   *(Rule 1.5C, 8.5C)*
This subfield contains information that further specifies other physical characteristics the item.

$a1 art original :*$boil on canvas.*
$a1 art reproduction :*$bcolotype.*
$a1 picture :*$bb&w ;$c13* x 7 cm.
$a2 wall charts :*$bcol. ;$c98* x 25 cm. folded to 30 x 12 cm.
$a1 technical drawing :*$bblueprint ;*$c 100 x 50 cm.

c **Dimensions (R)**   *(Rule 1.5D, 8.5D)*
This subfield contains the dimensions of an item measured height by width in centimeters, or the next whole centimeter up.

> $a1 wall chart (25 sheets) :$bcol., double sided ;*$c105 x 35 cm.*
> $a125 photographs :$bcol. *;$c15 x 9 cm.*
> $a4 posters :$bcol. and b&w ;*$c250 x 35 cm. folded to 35 x 15 cm.*
> $a25 slides :$bcol. ;*$c7 x 7 cm.*
> (Note: Do not give the size of slides if they are 5 x 5 cm.)

e **Accompanying material (NR)**   *(Rule 1.5E, 8.5E)*
This subfield contains a description of accompanying material.   It may include any associated physical description statements enclosed in parentheses. It is used

primarily when describing any accompanying material with the item. It is particularly important if you have something which is mixed-media and you have selected something else as the predominant item. You will need to describe the other item(s) here.

> **$a**1 filmstrip (35 fr.) :**$b**sd., col. ;**$c**35 mm. +*$e2 sound discs (60 min.: analog, 33 1/3 rpm, mono. ; 12 in.*
> **$a**1 study print ;**$b**b&w ;**$c**29 x 12 cm. +*$e1 biographical fact sheet (29 cm.)*

Note that the information for **$e** which is inside the parenthesis is created and punctuated identically to the way it is in the **300** for those particular items.

RELATED TAGS

If you are working on this tag, there are some other tags that you may need to enter information into. The tags most often used when working with graphic items are the **500** and **546**.

500 TAG

You should give the source of the title proper if it is a container or if it is other than the chief source of information.   *(Rule 8.7B3)*

> 500   **$a**Title from cover of box.

You should make notes relating to the edition being described or to the history of the item, particularly if it is based on another work.   *(Rule 8.7B7)*

> 500   **$a**Based on a book by Gay Patrick.

Make notes on important physical details that are not included in the physical description area, particularly if these are necessary to aid the user in determining if this item is usable as is or if they will need supplementary equipment to use the item.

> 500   **$a**Can only be used with viewer supplied in lesson one.

546 TAG

Indicate language(s) of the spoken or written content of the graphic item unless this is apparent from the rest of the description.   *(Rule 8.7B2)*

> 546   **$a**Captions in Spanish.

PUNCTUATION

$b is preceded by a space colon (space :)
$c is preceded by a space semi-colon (space ;)
$e is preceded by a space plus (space +)

Note that the ***plus** sign* goes in the subfield directly preceding it, not in **$e** itself.
The tag ends with a terminal mark of punctuation or a period.

300 PHYSICAL DESCRIPTION
[maps] [globes]

REPEATABLE:	YES
MANDATORY:	YES
RELATES TO:	255, 500
AUTHORITY:	NO

1st indicator
The 1st indicator is always blank.

2nd indicator
The 2nd indicator is always blank.

SUBFIELD CODES

a   **Extent (R)**
b   **Other physical details (NR)**
c   **Dimensions (R)**
e   **Accompanying material (NR)**

This field contains the physical description of the item that consists of the extent of the item and its dimensions and may also include other physical details of the item and information concerning accompanying material. This information is important since it will allow the user to "preview" the item before they retrieve it.

EXAMPLES

300       $a1 map :$bcol. ;$c29 x 35 cm.
300       $a1 globe :$bcol., plastic, on plastic stand ;$c20 cm. in diam.
300       $a1 relief model :$bcol., plastic ;$c47 x 35 x 10 cm.

LOCATION

There is no single place to find this information. You will need to inspect the item in hand. This includes looking at the physical format and any accompanying material. You will need to use your discretion regarding the level of detail you want to go into here.

NOTES

This tag is probably one of the most overlooked during cataloging. Most librarians feel that it serves no useful purpose since it is not usually searchable, including keyword searches. Nothing could be further from the truth. As pointed out earlier, this tag helps the user, as well as the librarian evaluate the material before they request or retrieve it. Also, in some circumstances, a patron may specifically want a map or globe instead of a book. This will allow them to determine if the material fits their particular needs.

THE SUBFIELDS IN DETAIL

a   **Extent (R)**   *(Rule 1.5B, 3.5B)*

This subfield contains the SMD, or Specific Material Designation of the item. Below is a list of acceptable SMD terms: *(Rule 3.5B1)*

diagram
globe
map
map section
profile
relief model
remote-sensing image
view

If the item would be in more than one class (a map on a poster or an atlas on a CD-ROM disc), consult the rules in this chapter in conjunction with those of the chapter appropriate to the item. LC prefers to catalog the content of the item, not its physical form.

                                        (Rule 3.0A1)

EXAMPLES

$a1 globe
$a35 identical maps

b   **Other physical details (NR)**   *(Rule 1.5C, 3.5C)*

This subfield contains information that further specifies other physical characteristics the item.

       $a1 map :*$bcol.*
       $a1 atlas (vii, 237 p.) :*$b250 col. maps*
       $a1 globe :*$bcol., wood on brass stand*

c   **Dimensions (R)**   *(Rule 1.5D, 3.5D)*

This subfield contains the dimensions of an item measured in centimeters, giving it in the format height by width, always rounding up to the next largest centimeter. For an *atlas*, measure exactly as you would a book. For *globes*, give the diameter, stating that it is the diameter.

       $a1 wall map :$bcol. ;*$c55 x 225 cm.*
       $a1atlas (101 p.) :$bcol. ;*$c35 cm.*
       $a1 globe :$bwood, on plastic stand ;*$c25 cm. in diameter.*

e   **Accompanying material (NR)**   *(Rule 1.5E, 3.5E)*

This subfield contains a description of accompanying material. It may include any associated physical description statements enclosed in parentheses. It is used primarily when describing any accompanying material with the item. It is particularly important if you need to include a description of any material that may be needed to more fully utilize the item being cataloged.

$a1 globe :$bcol. ;$c23 cm. in diam. +$ewith teachers guide (64 p. : ill. ; 29 cm.)

Note that the information for **$e** which is inside the parenthesis is created and punctuated identically to the way it is in the **300** for those particular items.

RELATED TAGS

If you are working on this tag, there are some other tags that you may need to enter information into. The tags most often used when working with maps are the **255** and **500**.

255 TAG

This field contains mathematical data associated with map material, including a statement of scale, statement of projection and/or a statement of coordinates. It usually includes information regarding the scale to which the map or globe was created, if any. It lists the scale and the projection used, if available. For more information regarding this tag, you may wish to consult the **255** tag information earlier in this book.   *(Rule 3.3B1)*

255    $aScale 1:59,000,000 at equator only.
255    $aScale not given.
255    $aScale [ca. 1:13,835,000] ;$bMercator.

500 TAG

Give notes on the nature or scope of the cartographic item unless it is obvious from the rest of the description, or if there is an unusual or unique aspect of the item.   *(Rule 3.7B1)*

500    $aGraphically depicts the Great circle route
500    $aSuggested bike routes indicated by light green lines. Dangerous routes indicated by solid red lines.

You should give the source of the title proper if it is a container or if it is other than the chief source of information.   *(Rule 3.7B3)*

500    $aTitle from globe box.

PUNCTUATION

$b is preceded by a space colon (space :)
$c is preceded by a space semi-colon (space ;)
$e is preceded by a space plus (space +)

Note that the *plus* sign goes in the subfield directly preceding it, not in **$e** itself.
The tag ends with a terminal mark of punctuation or a period.

300 PHYSICAL DESCRIPTION
[diorama] [game] [kit] [microscope slide] [realia] [toy]

REPEATABLE:	YES
MANDATORY:	YES
RELATES TO:	500
AUTHORITY:	NO

1st indicator
The 1st indicator is always blank.

2nd indicator
The 2nd indicator is always blank.

SUBFIELD CODES

a   **Extent (R)**
b   **Other physical details (NR)**
c   **Dimensions (R)**
e   **Accompanying material (NR)**

This field contains the physical description of the item that consists of the extent of the item and its dimensions and may also include other physical details of the item and information concerning accompanying material. This information is important since it will allow the user to "preview" the item before they retrieve it.

EXAMPLES

300   **$a**2 dioramas.
300   **$a**35 microscope slides.

LOCATION

There is no single place to find this information. You will need to inspect the item in hand. This includes looking at the physical format and the accompanying material (if any). You will need to use your discretion regarding the level of detail you want to go into here.

NOTES

This tag is probably one of the most overlooked during cataloging. Most librarians feel that it serves no useful purpose since it is not usually searchable, including keyword searches. Nothing could be further from the truth. As pointed out earlier, this tag helps the user, as well as the librarian evaluate the material before they request or retrieve it. It is also significant since it allows the user to determine if they are able to actually use this format of material on their equipment. Also, in some circumstances, a patron may be searching for a physical specimen rather than a book. This will allow them to determine if the material fits their particular needs.

THE SUBFIELDS IN DETAIL

a   **Extent (R)**   *(Rule 1.5B, 10.5B)*

This subfield contains the SMD, or Specific Material Designation of the item. Below is a list of acceptable SMD terms: *(Rule 10.5B1)*

If none of these are appropriate, give the specific name of the item or the names of the parts of the item as concisely as possible.   *(Rule 10.5B1)*

art original
art reproduction
diorama
game
microscope slide
mock-up
model

EXAMPLES

$a1 game
$a1 model
$a2 jigsaw puzzles (50 pieces)
$a1 skeleton

b   **Other physical details (NR)**   *(Rule 1.5C, 10.5C)*
This subfield contains information that further specifies other physical characteristics the item.

     **$a**2 jigsaw puzzles (55 pieces) :*$bwood*
     **$a**1 quilt :*$bcotton and wool, multicolored*
     **$a**2 paperweights :*$bquartz and obsidian.*
     **$a**1 stuffed toy :*$bnylon fur and polystyrene, brown and white*
     **$a**1 microscope slide :*$bglass, stained*

c   **Dimensions (R)**   *(Rule 1.5D, 10.5D)*
This subfield contains the dimensions of an item measured height by width in centimeters, or the next whole centimeter up. If you give multiple dimensions, you should give them in the order height x width x depth, unless you are doing microscope slides, then you should give them in the order of height x width.

If the object is in a container, give the name of the container and its dimensions either after the dimensions of the object or as the only dimensions.

     **$a**1 statue :*$bmarble, white ; $c250 cm. high.*
     **$a**25 microscope slideS :*$bstained ;$c3 x 8 cm.*
     **$a**4 jigsaw puzzles :*$bcardboard, multicolored ;$cin box 29 x 15 x 4 cm.*

e   **Accompanying material (NR)**   *(Rule 1.5E, 10.5E)*

This subfield contains a description of accompanying material. It may include any associated physical description statements enclosed in parentheses. It is used primarily when describing any accompanying material with the item. It is particularly important if you have something that is used for instructional purposes and has an accompanying teacher's guide.

> $a1 hand puppet :$bred and blue ;$c29 cm. high +$e1 story book (25 p. : ill. ; 29 cm.)
>
> $aTalking model :$bcloth and metal, brown ;$c35 cm. high +$e2 sound cassette tapes (analog, mono.) + 1 activity guide (25 p. : ill. ; 28 cm.)

Note that the information for **$e** which is inside the parenthesis is created and punctuated identically to the way it is in the **300** for those particular items.

RELATED TAGS

If you are working on this tag, there are some other tags that you may need to enter information into. The tag most often used when working with graphic items is the **500**.

500 TAG

Give the nature of the item unless it is obvious from the rest of the description.

(Rule 10.7B1)

    500      $aRepresentation of Clifford the big red dog.

You should give the source of the title proper if it is a container or if it is other than the chief source of information.   *(Rule 10.7B3)*

    500      $aTitle supplied by cataloger.
    500      $aTitle taken from study guide.

Make notes on important physical details that are not included in the physical description, particularly if they affect the use of the item.

(Rule 10.7B100)

    500      $aPattern: Boston friendship duck.
    500      $aRequires external electrical source.

PUNCTUATION

$b is preceded by a space colon (space :)
$c is preceded by a space semi-colon (space ;)
$e is preceded by a space plus (space +)

Note that the *plus sign* goes in the subfield directly preceding it, not in **$e** itself.
The tag ends with a terminal mark of punctuation or a period.

300 PHYSICAL DESCRIPTION
[sound recording]

REPEATABLE:	YES
MANDATORY:	YES
RELATES TO:	500, 505,538
AUTHORITY:	NO

1st indicator
The 1st indicator is always blank.

2nd indicator
The 2nd indicator is always blank.

SUBFIELD CODES

a   **Extent (R)**
b   **Other physical details (NR)**
c   **Dimensions (R)**
e   **Accompanying material (NR)**

This field contains the physical description of the item that consists of the extent of the item and its dimensions and may also include other physical details of the item and information concerning accompanying material. This information is important since it will allow the user to "preview" the item before they retrieve it.

EXAMPLES

300	$a1 sound disc (20 min., 35 sec.) :$banalog, stereo, 33 1/3 rpm.
300	$a1 sound disc (35 min.) :$banalog, 33 1/3 rpm, mono. ;$c 12 in.
300	$a1 sound disc (45 min., 24 sec.) :$bdigital, stereo. ;$c 4 3/4 in. +$e1 booklet (32 p. : col. ill., 25 cm.)
300	$a1 sound cassette (1 hr., 30 min.) :$banalog, mono.
300	$a2 sound cassettes (3 hrs.) :$banalog, stereo.
300	$a1 sound cassette (55 min., 37 sec.) :$bdigital, stereo.

LOCATION

There is no single place to find this information. You will need to inspect the sound recording to determine it. This includes looking at the physical format, the accompanying material (if any), and possibly actually playing the item. You will need to use your discretion regarding the level of detail you want to go into here.

NOTES

This tag is probably one of the most overlooked during cataloging. Most librarians feel that it serves no useful purpose since it is not usually searchable, including keyword searches. Nothing could be further from the truth. As pointed out earlier, this tag helps the user, as well as the librarian evaluate the material before they request or retrieve it. It is also significant since it allows the user to determine if they are able to actually play this format of material on their equipment. Also, in some circumstances, a patron may specifically <u>want</u> a sound recording instead of a book. This will allow them to determine if the material fits their particular needs.

For read-along packages (a book and a cassette or a book and a record), the librarian will need to determine which item (the sound recording or the book) is most significant and follow the cataloging rules for that particular item, making certain to create a **006** tag for the other item(s) in the set. Because of the way many libraries organize their material, book/cassette and book/record materials are usually classified as *sound recordings*. Be certain to apply your policy consistently in your cataloging.

THE SUBFIELDS IN DETAIL

a **Extent (R)**   *(Rule 1.5B, 6.5B)*
This subfield contains the SMD, or Specific Material Designation of the item. The phrase will usually start with the word Soun*d* followed by the physical form of the item (e.g. cartridge, cassette, or disc as necessary.) **$a** is required.

You can also give the running time of the item if you know it. Some CD's will have this information printed on the label, or you may choose to actually load the disc into a player to determine the playing time. You may also add up times on the label or ignore the information completely. Note that the word *disc* is used for <u>both</u> record albums and CDs.

> *$a1 sound disc (50 min.)*
> *$a1 sound cassette (ca. 90 min.)*
> *$a3 sound cassettes (45 min. each.)*

You should precede the time with the letters *ca.* if you are not certain of the running time.

b **Other physical details (NR)**   *(Rule 1.5C, 6.5C)*
This subfield contains information that further specifies other physical characteristics of the sound recording. This would include the type of recording, playing speed, and the number of sound channels.

> *$a1 sound disc (45 min.) :$banalog, 33 1/3 rpm, mono.*
> *$a1 sound disc (71 min., 41 sec.) : $bdigital, stereo.*
> *$a1 sound cassette (45 min.) :$banalog, stereo.*

Note that if you are doing either a standard cassette or a compact disc, you do <u>not</u> include the playing speed if it is the standard speed of 1 7/8 ips. for cassettes or 1.4 meters per second for CDs. Generally, this will be most of your material <u>unless</u> you are working with very specialized materials, which most libraries do not.

c **Dimensions (R)**   *(Rule 1.5D, 6.5D)*
This subfield contains the dimensions of an item in inches. Unlike books, you should <u>not</u> convert this information to centimeters.

> *$a1 sound disc (20 min.) :$banalog, 33 1/3 rpm, stereo. ;$c12 in.*
> *$a1 sound disc (56 min., 45 sec.) :$bdigital, stereo. ;$c4 3/4 in.*
> *$a2 sound cassettes (ca. 90 min.) $banalog, stereo.*

Note that if you are cataloging standard cassettes (3 7/8 x 2 1/2in. with a tape 1/8 in. wide), you do <u>not</u> enter the size in **$c.**

300

e   **Accompanying material (NR)**   *(Rule 1.5E, 6.5E)*

This subfield contains a description of accompanying material. It may include any associated physical description statements enclosed in parentheses. It is used primarily when describing any accompanying material with the recording, be it a booklet, a libretto, or the book for a read-along package.

> $a1 sound disc (50 min.) :$banalog, 33 1/3 rpm, stereo. ;$c12 in. + *$e1 booklet (11 p. : col. ill. ; 24 cm.)*
>
> $a1 sound cassette (ca. 30 min.) :$banalog, mono. + *$e1 book ([32] p. : col. ill. ; 29 cm.)*
>
> $a1 sound disc (41 min., 23 sec.) :$bdigital, stereo. ;$c4 3/4 in. +*$e1 booklet ([4] p. : ill. (some col.) ; 12 cm.)*

The information for **$e** which is inside the parenthesis is created and punctuated <u>identically</u> to the way it is in the **300** tag for books.

RELATED TAGS

If you are working on this tag, there are some other tags which you may need to enter information into. The tags most often used when working with sound recordings are the **500**, **505**, and **538** tags.

500 TAG

When doing sound cassettes, you should not assume any type of noise reduction. If *Dolby* noise reduction is indicated on the item by the "double D" symbol, you should enter that information in the **500** tag in the format *Dolby encoded*.   *(Rule 6.7B10)*

> 500 $aDolby encoded.
> 500 $aSurround sound.

If a sound recording is originally captured in a different form than the final recording, note that here. That is, if a CD were originally recorded analog, you would say *analog recording*. If you have a cassette or record album that was originally captured digitally, you would state *digital recording* here. You should base this information if it is listed on the item or indicated by the SPARS code, which is a three letter code, often on the disc itself or on the back of the case. It is in the format of three capital letters, with the last letter <u>always</u> being *D*. Alternatively, the accompanying information may tell you how it was originally captured or recorded.

> 500 $aAnalog recording.
>   (For a digital product made from an analog original)
> 500 $aDigital recording.
>   (For an analog recording made from a digital source)

If the item is in the same format that it was originally recorded (e.g., a CD which had the original recording made digitally <u>or</u> an analog recording made from an analog master), then you would make <u>no</u> notation here.

505 TAG

This tag is used to list the titles of the individual works contained on a sound recording. Add to each title statements of responsibility not included in the title and statement of responsibility and the duration of the piece. *(Rule 1.5B4, 6.7B18)* Make certain that you use the proper indicator. Note the order of the information (title, time, then statement of responsibility) and that the spacing and punctuation are similar to what is in the **245** tag.

     505 0   **$a**Quatrain II (16:35) -- Water ways (1:57) -- Waves (10:49)

     505 2   **$a**Let's stay together (4:47) / The Rippingtons featuring Russ Freeman -- Night of the roses (5:05) / Deborah Henson-Conant -- Through the test of time (4:12) / Patti Austin -- Outback oasis (5:27) / Don Grusin -- The kiss (3:59) / Lee Ritenour -- Cast your fate to the wind (3:13) / David Benoit.

If the individual titles in the **505** have their own timings, it is <u>not</u> necessary to add those times for inclusion in the 300, although you <u>may</u> do so if you wish. *(LCRI 6.5B2* and *LCRI 6.7B10]* If there is a total time given on the recording, either on the disc label or on the cover of the item, you should enter that value in the **300$a.**

For more information on the indicators and formatting of the **505** tag, including information on separately subfield coding the author and title, consult the specific information for that tag.

538 TAG

If you are doing compact discs (CDs), you must indicate that here by the statement *Compact disc.*
                                              (Rule 6.7B10)

     538   **$a**Compact disc.

If you are doing mini-discs, you must indicate that here by the statement *Mini-disc.*
                                              (Rule 6.7B10)

For more information regarding the **538** tag, you should consult the information for that tag directly.

PUNCTUATION

$b is preceded by a *space colon* (space :)
$c is preceded by a *space semi-colon* (space ;)
$e is preceded by a *space plus* (space +)
Note that the *plus sign* goes in the subfield directly <u>preceding</u> it, not in **$e** itself.
The tag ends with a terminal mark of punctuation or a period.

300 PHYSICAL DESCRIPTION
[videorecording] [motion picture]

REPEATABLE: YES
MANDATORY: YES
RELATES TO: 500, 538,546
AUTHORITY: NO

1st indicator
The 1st indicator is always blank.

2nd indicator
The 2nd indicator is always blank.

SUBFIELD CODES

a   **Extent (R)**
b   **Other physical details (NR)**
c   **Dimensions (R)**
e   **Accompanying material (NR)**

This field contains the physical description of the item that consists of the extent of the item and its dimensions and may also include other physical details of the item and information concerning accompanying material. This information is important since it will allow the user to "preview" the item before they retrieve it.

EXAMPLES

300     $a1 videocassette (90 min.) :$bsd., col. ;$c1/2 in.

300     $a1 videodisc (2 hrs., 25 min.) :$bsd., b&w ;$c12 in. +$e1 study guide (34 p. : ill. ; 23 cm.)

300     $a1 videodisc (2 hrs., 5 min.) :$bsd., col. ;$c4 3/4in.
            $a14 film reels (157 min.) :$bsd., col. ;$c35 mm.

300     $a2 film reels (2 hours, 25 min.) :$bsd., b&w. ;$c16 mm. +$e1 study guide (37 p. : col. ill. ; 23 cm.)

LOCATION

There is no single place to find this information. You will need to inspect the videocassette, motion picture, or disc to determine it. This includes looking at the physical format, the accompanying material (if any), and possibly actually playing the item. You will need to use your discretion regarding the level of detail you want to go into here.

NOTES

This tag is probably one of the most overlooked during cataloging. Most librarians feel that it serves no useful purpose since it is not usually searchable, including keyword searches. Nothing could be further from the truth. As pointed out earlier, this tag helps the user, as well as the librarian evaluate the material before they request or retrieve it. It is also significant since it allows the user to determine if they are able to actually play this format of material on their equipment. Also, in some circumstances, a patron (especially a teacher in a school library) may specifically <u>want</u> a videocassette or motion picture instead of a book. This will allow them to determine if the material fits their particular needs.

Much of the descriptive statements used for laserdiscs will be used for DVDs as they share the same basic concept: A signal is played back by interpreting the reflections of a laser beam as it bounces off of a reflective surface.

THE SUBFIELDS IN DETAIL

a   **Extent (R)**   *(Rule 1.5B, 7.5B)*

This subfield contains the SMD, or Specific Material Designation of the item.   The phrase will usually start with the word film or video... followed by the physical form of the item (e.g. *film reel, film cartridge, videocassette,* or *videodisc* as necessary. **$a** is **required.**

You can also give the running time of the item if you know it.   Most recordings will have this information printed on the label or packaging. If you choose to enter the time, then you should do it <u>in the form given on the item</u>.   Note that *videocassette* and *videodisc* are <u>one</u> word.

> *$a3 film reels.*
> *$a1 videocassette (119 min.)*
> *$a2 videodiscs (121 min.)*
> *$a1 film cartridge (4 min.)*
> *$a1 videodisc (98 min.)*

You should precede the time with the letters *ca.* if you are not certain of the running time.

If you are doing videodiscs with still images (many collections of artwork use this format), you have <u>the option</u> of giving the number of frames on the disc *(Rule 7.5B1)*

> *$a1 videodisc (45,876 fr.)*

b   **Other physical details (NR)**   *(Rule 1.5C, 7.5C)*

This subfield contains information that further specifies other physical characteristics of the videorecording. This would include the sound characteristics, and any information on colorization.

> $a1 film reel (30 min.) :*$bsd., col.*
>   (This is for an item that has sound and is in color)
> $a1 videocassette (24 min.) : *$bsd., col. with b&w sequences*
>   (This is for an item which has sound, <u>primarily</u> in color with a <u>few</u>
>   black and white sequences.
> $a1 videodisc (45 min.) :*$bsl., b&w*
>   (This is for an item that is silent and in black and white.)

c   **Dimensions (R)**   *(Rule 1.5D, 7.5D)*

This subfield contains the dimensions of an item in centimeters for films and inches for videorecordings. If you need to convert the inches to centimeters, multiply the number of inches by <u>2.54</u> and then round the number up to the nearest centimeter.

> $a1 film reel (12 min.) :$bsd., b&w ; *$c16 mm.*
> $a1 film reel (21 min.) : $bsd., col. ; *$c standard 8 mm.*
> $a1 videocassette (ca. 90 min.) : $bsd., col. ; *$c1/2 in.*
> $a1 videocassette (4 min.) : $bsd., col. ; *$c3/4 in.*

300

$a1 videodisc (65 min.) : $bsd., col. ; *$c12 in.*

$a1 videodisc (98 min.) :$bsd., col. ;*$c4 3/4 in.*

This last example is for a *DVD* disc.

Note that the size of tape in standard VHS or Beta cassettes is 1/2 in. Tape for U-Matic cassettes, which were popular in libraries for some time, is 3/4 in. You should <u>not</u> indicate if it is VHS or U-Matic in this tag. It is more correctly recorded in the **538** tag.

e   **Accompanying material (NR)**   *(Rule 1.5E, 7.5E)*

This subfield contains a description of accompanying material. It may include any associated physical description statements enclosed in parentheses. It is used primarily when describing any accompanying material with the recording, particularly study guides or teacher's materials.

$a1 film reel (21 min.) :$bsd., col. ;$c16 mm. + *$e1 booklet (12 p. : col. ill. ; 28 cm.)*

$a1 videocassette (ca. 30 min.) :$bsd., col. + *$e1 study guide ([64] p. : col. ill. ; 29 cm.)*

The information for **$e** which is inside the parenthesis is created and punctuated <u>identically</u> to the way it is in the **300** tag for books.

RELATED TAGS

If you are working on this tag, there are some other tags that you may need to enter information into. The three most often used when working with films and videorecordings are the **500, 538** and **546** tags.

500 TAG

When doing visual items, you should note if the item has any unique sound characteristics, like Dolby, stereo., or surround sound encoded.   *(Rule 7.7B10)*

500   $aDolby stereo, mono. compatible.
500   $aDolby surround sound.
500   $aTHX encoded.

538 TAG

This tag is used to give the system used for a videorecording.   *(Rule 7.7B10f)*

538   $aVHS Hi-fi.
538   $aLaser optical CLV.
538   $aLaser optical DVD.
538   $aU-Matic.
538   $aBeta II.

For more information regarding the **538** tag, you should consult the information for that tag directly.

Indicate language(s) of the spoken or written content of the graphic item unless this is apparent from the rest of the description.   *(Rule 8.7B2)*

546 TAG

546	*$aCaptions in Spanish.*
546	*$aDialoge in English and French, with English, French, and Spanish subtitles.*
546	*$aClosed-captioned.*

PUNCTUATION

$b is preceded by a *space colon* (space :)

$c is preceded by a *space semi-colon* (space ;)

$e is preceded by a *space plus* (space +)

Note that the *plus sign* goes in the subfield directly <u>preceding</u> it, not in **$e** itself.

The tag ends with a terminal mark of punctuation or a period.

306 PLAYING TIME

REPEATABLE: NO
MANDATORY: NO
RELATES TO: 300,500,505
AUTHORITY: NO

1st indicator
The 1st indicator is always blank

2nd indicator
The 2nd indicator is always blank

SUBFIELD CODES

a   **Playing time (R)**

EXAMPLES

$a011189
$a000623
$a020600

NOTES

This field contains a formatted numerical representation of the playing time of the item. Note that this information is also recorded in natural language in tags **300** and **500/505**.

This tag will be used when you are entering musical and non-musical sound recordings, as well as printed music and videorecordings. This information is <u>not</u> specified in AACR2. Rather, it is part of *USMARC Bibliographic.*

THE SUBFIELDS IN DETAIL

a   **Playing time (R)**
This subfield contains the playing time of an item. It is six characters in length and formatted *hhmmss* which means 2 character positions for the hour, 2 for the minute, and 2 for the second. If the recording is less than 1 hour, the hour is recorded as two zeros; if less than a minute, the minute is also recorded as two zeroes. This subfield is repeatable to allow the recording of the playing time of two or more pieces.

For printed or manuscript music, the stated running time of performance can be recorded here.

$a002016
　　　　[Playing time is 20 min., 16 sec.]

$a014500
　　　　[Playing time is 1 hour and 45 min.]

$a011025
　　　　[Playing time is 70 min., 25 sec.]

$a003100$a001839
　　　　[Playing times are 31 min. and 18 min, 39 sec. respectively]

PUNCTUATION

$a is preceded by no punctuation.

The tag does not end with a period or any other mark of punctuation.

The **4XX** tags contain information relating to any series aspect of the item. It is important to differentiate between <u>series</u> and <u>serial</u>. A series is an item, usually with its own unique title, that comes from the same publisher and is part of a larger set or collection. A <u>series</u> may or may not have a fixed number of volumes or topics, and they usually appear at irregular intervals. They can be by the same author, but usually they are by different authors and have different titles. The series statement usually is on the title page or on the dust cover of the book, or you may discover that the item is part of a series based on a catalog listing or a listing of titles contained within the book. Many videorecordings will state that they are part of a series on the box; whereas book/cassette combinations will often have the information printed inside of the book or on the packaging material. A <u>serial</u> is an item that appears on a regular interval, usually more often than yearly, each of which has the same title. They will usually come from the same publisher and are usually a collection of different titles, articles, or sections. Magazines, quarterly journals, and newspapers are good examples of serials.

It is important to record the series title of an item since this will allow the user to find all the items in the series that the library owns. The series statement can help you order other titles in a particular series that are requested frequently by your patrons. The Library of Congress serial information is available on their website or from other commercial sources. Some bibliographic utilities, as well as state databases, have an authority component. As a last resort, if you are part of a union catalog, either local or state, you can look to see how other libraries have handled the same or similar items. What is most important is to be consistent.

The **4XX** tags covered in this book are:

440	**Series statement/Added Entry -- Title**
490	**Series statement**

440 SERIES STATEMENT/ADDED ENTRY - TITLE

REPEATABLE: YES
MANDATORY: NO
RELATES TO: --
AUTHORITY: YES

1st indicator

The 1st indicator is always blank.

2nd indicator

0-9 **Number of non-filing characters**

These are entered in the same manner and capitalization as the non-filing values in the **245** tag. Generally, non-filing characters are dropped from the entry, so this value will usually be *0*.

SUBFIELD CODES

a **Title (NR)**
n **Number of part/section of a work (R)**
p **Name of part/section of a work (R)**
v **Volume number/sequential designation (NR)**

EXAMPLES

440 0 $aGems of American life
440 0 $aFolger Shakespeare Library slide set ;$vno. 2
440 4 $aThe dayparts series ;$vv. 2
440 0 $aDay in the life of series

LOCATION

Very often, this information will be located on the *title page*, often above the title, or you may find a narrative phrase stating that it is part of a series. For AV items, this information will often be on the *container* of the item. A very good indication of a series statement are phrases such as *part of the ... series* or *other books in this series are ...* , on the inside of the book or the dustjacket, or the phrase *if you enjoyed this videotape, you will want to watch the others in the series,* or you may find a listing of items in the series on the back cover or dust jacket of the book or on the container of AV items. If you do make a series entry, you should make a note of this in your authority file so that you can consistently use the same name of the series in your catalog.

For videorecordings, the series statement will often be on the box containing the videocassette, usually with the word *series* in the phrase, like *The kids in the hall series.* Sound recording or readalong book/cassette packages may say something like *The I can read it myself* series. You should interpret the series information liberally on audio-visual items, but be certain to keep a record of the form you have used in your authority file.

This field contains a series title. There will not be an additional **7XX** field for the series title. Series information is often overlooked by most librarians and is often considered unimportant. The best utilization of the series information is to find all the items in your collection that are part of the same series. Since a single producer usually does the items in a particular series, they tend to be similar in writing style, layout, and readability. This can help your users find information in a format they enjoy or find useful.

Series authority records, which are created or approved by the Library of Congress, are available on their website, or they can be purchased on microfiche. Some bibliographic utilities, like OCLC, have authority files. If you are getting bibliographic records from your jobbers, find out what source they are using as authority control for their records. You may wish to make a note of the series entries they are using so that your local original cataloging conforms to them, thereby promoting consistency in your database.

THE SUBFIELDS IN DETAIL

a   **Title (NR)**   *(Rule 1.6B, 3.6B)*
This subfield contains the title portion of the series.

Capitalization rules are the same as for the **245$a**.

> *$aLibrary science text book*
> *$aA Libraries Unlimited data book*
> *$aThe toast of the town series*

Be careful when entering this information, as some items will "run" the series and title information together (see below). This can be particularly noticeable on the spine and covers of books, and it may also happen on the packaging material of audiovisual items. You should consult your authority file to determine how you have done this, or similar, items in the past. If you have not done this particular series in the past, be aware of supporting information (see <u>LOCATION</u> above) to help determine the series statement proper.

> 245 $aThe how and why wonder book of cars.
> 440   *$aHow and why wonder book series*

<u>Please note that these are NOT serial titles.</u> A serial title is something that always has the same title on it and comes out on a regular basis, such as magazines or yearbooks. Series come out in no set pattern (usually) and each publication will have its own unique title.

n   **Number of part/section of a work (R)**   *(Rule 1.6G, 3.6G)*
This subfield contains a *number* used in a series title or listing. "Numbering" is defined as an indication of sequencing in any form. In music titles, the serial opus, or thematic index number is contained in subfield **$n**. Note that it does not <u>have</u> to be numerical in nature.

> *$aBeatrix Potter jigsaw puzzles.$nNo. 1*

p   **Name of part/section of a work (R)**   *(Rule 1.6H, 3.6H)*
This subfield contains a *name* of a part/section of a series title, usually called a subseries. Usually, you will <u>not</u> trace this information in a **246** or **740** tag. Some automation

system will automatically trace this information as part of the series or title index. Check with your system vendor for the capabilities of your particular software.

> $aHow to read series.$nPart 1,$pBlue level

> $aGreat music of the world.$nSection B,$pBach

v   **Volume number/sequential designation (NR)**
This subfield contains the volume number or other sequential designation used in a series statement. It will always contain some type of numerical data.

> $aEnvironmental science research ;$vv. 6
> $aReference shelf ;$vv. 26, no. 5

You should be aware of the fact that if the **440** is similar or identical to the start of the **245**, you may wish to consider entering the subject or noun of the title into a **246** tag.

245 04 $aThe How and why book of airplanes.
440 0 $aHow and why library

In this circumstance, you should make a **246** for *Airplanes.*

PUNCTUATION

$v is preceded by a *space; (*space semi-colon)
$n is preceded by a period.
$p is preceded by a period unless it is preceded by **$n**, then it is preceded by a comma.
Do not type the parenthesis that surrounds the series information, but include the brackets if they are inside of the parenthesis. The parentheses are part of the MARC format and should be system supplied.
There is **NO** punctuation at the end of the tag unless it ends with an abbreviation.

490 SERIES STATEMENT

REPEATABLE: YES
MANDATORY: NO
RELATES TO: 800, 810, 811, 830
AUTHORITY: YES

1st indicator

0   **Series not traced**   (This is the value you will usually use.)
1   **Series traced differently**

2nd indicator
The 2nd indicator is always blank.

SUBFIELD CODES

a   **Series statement (R)**
v   **Volume number/sequential designation (R)**

This field contains a series statement for which no series added entry is to be made or for which the series added entry is in a form different from that which appears in the series statement. These series are usually publishers' series that really indicate a segment of publishing or a certain format rather than a true series. The Library of Congress has determined that some series should <u>not</u> be traced, or that they should be traced under a particular author's or creator's name. You may see some of these on records that you receive from your book jobbers or on records that you download from a union database. By a strict interpretation of cataloging rules, an automation system should not trace this tag, but many will to simplify searching and improve access for the searcher. Check with your vendor to ascertain how your system handles this tag.

EXAMPLES

490 0   **$a**Berkley/Splash book
490 0   **$a**Laurel-Leaf books   *(All the paperbacks of a publisher)*
490 0   **$a**Bantam pathfinder edition
490 0   **$a**Pelican books   *(Their paperbacks only)*
[There would be <u>no</u> 800-830 tag in the record for any of the above entries.]

490 1   **$a**Uniform crime reports
490 1   **$a**West Virginia University bulletin   *(Indicates a news format)*
[All of these tags would have a subsequent **8XX** tag in the record.]

LOCATION

If you purchase records from a vendor, you may see this tag used, or you may come across it when transcribing CIP data from the front of a book. It will usually be at the bottom of the entry, in the added entries area, preceded by a Roman numeral and a person's, often the author's name.

490

The tag helps to bring together all the series items that are uniquely linked to a particular person in a single searchable place in the record. Depending on how your particular system handles the series statements, they may or may not be traced in your search screens.

Note that there are **NO** non-filing indicator values for this tag. If there is a word that you would not normally file on (such as an article), remove the article.

Many of the **490** tags will be preceded by the words *His, Hers,* or *Its*. You should remove these before entering the information. If it is present in a record from a jobber, you should remove it. If your system has an *Authority control* module, this would be a good way to change all the occurrences of a particular series statement in a short period of time.

> 490   1   *$aHis enchantment of America*
>   would be entered as:
> 490   1   *$aEnchantment of America*

Be aware that there will probably be an **800** tag for this entry. It would read:

> 800   1   *$aCarpenter, Allan,$d1917- $tEnchantment of America.*

THE SUBFIELDS IN DETAIL

a   **Series statement (R)**   *(No applicable rule in AACR2)*
         This subfield contains the title of the series. It may also contain a statement of responsibility, other title information, dates, or volume numbers preceding or appearing as part of the title. Do not enter any nonfiling character values as you would for the **440** tag; there is no indicator value provision to make them non-filing.

         Capitalization rules are the same as for the **245$a**.

v   **Volume number/sequential designation (R)**
         This subfield contains the volume number or other sequential designation used in a series statement. It will always contain some type of numerical data. If a volume number is a Roman numeral, the abbreviation changes from *v.* to *vol*

PUNCTUATION

$v is preceded by a *space*; (space semi-colon)
Do not type the parenthesis that surrounds the series information, but include the brackets if they are inside of the parenthesis. The parenthesis are system supplied by the MARC format.
There is **NO** punctuation at the end of the tag unless it ends with an abbreviation.

100

5XX NOTES -- GENERAL INFORMATION

The note tags are something of a "catch-all" for information that does not fit anywhere else. Some of the note tags can only contain specific types of information and have special rules of punctuation; others can have information entered "free-form." **5XX** tags are used extensively when cataloging non-print materials.

Many libraries depend heavily on the **5XX** tags since they are used to hold information important during keyword searching which cannot be elsewhere entered the record. It is in the **5XX** tags that you can take full advantage of the power of keyword searching. Do not be hesitant to create **5XX** tags. Pay particular attention to the **500, 505,** and **520** note areas. While they do take time and effort to create, the dividends they pay during keyword search strategies are immeasurable.

A record does not have to contain a note tag, but sometimes they are <u>mandatory</u>, depending on other information that you have entered in the record or pieces of information that are obligatory under AACR2. Also, some of these tags are not <u>specifically</u> required or indicated by AARC2, but the librarian may find them useful in the future.

The **5XX** tags covered by this book are:

500	**General Note**
504	**Bibliography Note**
505	**Formatted Contents Note**
508	**Creation/Production Credits note**
511	**Participant or performer note**
516	**Type of file or data note**
520	**Summary, Etc. Note**
521	**Target Audience Note**
530	**Additional Physical Form Available Note**
536	**Funding Information Note**
538	**System Details Note**
546	**Language Note**
586	**Awards Note**
590	**Local Note**

When evaluating records for purchase from an outside source, see if the vendor has made liberal use of the **5XX** tags. The more they have, the more time they have devoted to creating a good, thorough, useful record. The more detailed record you can purchase, the more time you will save later enhancing marginal records, and the better your users will be able to find information that they are searching for.

500

500   GENERAL NOTE

REPEATABLE: YES
MANDATORY: NO
RELATES TO: --
AUTHORITY: NO

1st indicator
The 1st indicator is always blank.

2nd indicator
The 2nd indicator is always blank.

This field contains a note that provides general information for which a specialized note field (e.g., a specific defined **5XX** field) has not been defined.

SUBFIELD CODES

a   General note (R)

EXAMPLES

500	$aTranslated from French.
500	$aCover title: Comprehensive American social heuristics.
500	$aSpine title: CASH
500	$aIncludes index and glossary.
500	$aProgram notes by Michael Murray on album.
500	$aBased on the author's book with the same name.
500	$aSequel to: Gone with the wind.
500	$aRevision and updating of the movie: Desk set.
500	$aDolby Surround sound.
500	$aDisc recorded in AC-3 format.

LOCATION

Since the information here is drawn from many areas of the item, such as the title page, physical examination of the index, bibliography, or information on the dust jacket is necessary. For audio-visual items, you will need to look at any external packaging material, accompanying documentation, indirect evidence from actually utilizing the item, and notes on the container itself. There is no one single place to look for information. You should enter any information that you feel will be useful to your patrons. If you want to include such information like *mostly photographs* or *leather binding*, feel free to do so. AACR2 and the MARC formats give librarians a large degree of latitude for this area. As a <u>general</u> rule, if you cannot ascertain where a particular piece of information not specified for elsewhere goes, the **500** tag is usually a safe assumption for it.

NOTES

This tag is designed to serve as a "catch all" for information that does not quite fit anywhere else. It is designed to help users more fully evaluate the item to determine if it is appropriate for their needs. The information you enter in this tag is very important, since many automated systems will look at this tag when it does keyword searching.

This field will contain such information as cover and spine titles, translation statements, index statements, bibliographic history, etc. Information such as cover and spine titles (if different from the title page title) need to be entered here so you can justify tracing them in the **246** tags. You should also be liberal with information recorded here which is subsequently recorded in the **246** tag, like *title on tape box ...* or *title on label is ...*

The information on the *spine title* is particularly important if it differs from the title page title that is used for cataloging. The spine title is what the user will see as they walk along the stacks looking for the item as they try to link the title with the call number.

Cover title information is useful, especially if it differs from the title page title. Many users will go by the title on the cover or box of the item when it is first removed from the shelf in determining if it is, in fact, the item they want. Other title information can be entered here if you have made some type of modification of the title page to make sense of the information there. You may also want to make entries for unique forms of the name. Many movies and television programs have become known by slang terms. *Gone with the wind* is often referred to as *GWTW*. If it is a reasonable access point, enter it and trace it in a **246** tag.

The information on *sequel to* and *followed by* can be useful to a user who is following a storyline through a set of books or movies. The notation *Revision and updating of...* can aid the researcher who seeks to compare the current version of the work with an earlier one.

If there is a statement on the item like *Previously published as...* , then enter that title information into a **240** if you have a **100** or **110** tag and enter it in the **500** tag. If you do not have a **100** or **110** tag, enter it into a **730** tag instead of a **240** tag.

If the title in the **500** is in a different language than the title in the **245** tag, enter the appropriate language in **$l** of the **240/730** tag following the title. The value in **$l** should agree with the language which the book-in-hand is written in and with the **language** code in the **008** tag.

If you have a long subtitle (**245$b**), then you should record that subtitle here preceded by the notation *Subtitle:* This can be useful since the subtitle of an item often contains words or phrases that are more descriptive of the title. These words can be beneficial in a keyword search, especially if your particular system does not utilize the **245$b** when doing keyword searches.

Do not enter summaries or individual chapter notes here since there are other dedicated tags for that information. In general, if you are not certain where to put descriptive information about an item, the **500** tag is probably where it belongs. This includes "dashed on" information usually found in the note area of cards, which often relate to a previous or related item. Also do not enter information regarding the physical characteristics of the item. There are dedicated note tags for that information.

Information such as "previously published as" and other bibliographic history information used to be contained in the **503** tag. The **503** has been discontinued in the *USMARC* Format, therefore, you should no longer utilize it.

THE SUBFIELDS IN DETAIL

a   **General note (R)**   *(Begin at Rule 1.7 ; 2.7)*
             This subfield contains the entire text of the note. For more specific information regarding the use of the **500** tag for non-print materials, you should consult that particular form in the information on the **300** tag.

                    $aOriginal soundtrack for the motion picture of the same name.
                    $aOn cover of book, word degrees *is replaced by minus sign.*

> *$aTranslation of: Le enfant terrible.*
>
> *$aSpine title: Better grades.*
>
> *$aSeries title from cover of book.*
>
> *$aShows southernmost extent of the midnight sun.*
>
> *$aAnalog recording.*
>
> *$aWith audible and inaudible film advance signals.*
>
> *$aTitle from disk label.*
>
> *$aTitle supplied by cataloger.*

SPECIFIC MEDIA

Following are some special rules you should be aware of when doing non-book materials.

COMPUTER DISKS

When cataloging computer software, count the total quantity of disks in the package, including backup disks, data disks, and student disks. Record this value in the **300$a**. If there are multiple disk sizes <u>in the actual package</u>, it will be necessary to record the sizes of the disks, as well as the quantity of each.

Make a note in the **500** tag as to how many backup disks there are. The other disks <u>do not</u> need to be accounted for. If you chose to do so, they must be listed in the **505** tag.

EXAMPLES

300	**$a**6 computer disks.
500	*$aIncludes 3 backup disks.*

300	**$a**10 computer disks.
500	*$aIncludes 2 backup disks.*
505	**$a**AppleWriter diskette -- Music data diskette -- Spelling data diskette -- Backup disks.

300	**$a**5 computer disks ;$c3 1/2-5 1/4 in.
500	*$a2 3 1/2 in. disks, 3 5 1/4 in. disks.*

KITS

When cataloging *Kits*, it is recommended that you list the component parts of the kit. You should start the **500** with the narrative phrase *Kit contains:* There should be a *space + space* between each separate item in the kit. Descriptions of particular components of the kit should be enclosed in parenthesis and formatted as you would a **300** tag.

EXAMPLES

500	**$a**Kit contains: 1 puppet + 1 sound recording + 4 teacher's guides.
500	**$a**Kit contains: 1 game +1 puzzle + 1 sound disc (analog, 33 1/3 rpm. ; 12 in.) + 4 teacher's guides.

SLIDES

Notations regarding the carriers for slides, be they carousel trays or glass frames must be indicated in the **500** tag.   *(AACR2 8.7B10)*

EXAMPLES

500	**$a**Slides in carousel tray.
500	**$a**Slides in glass frames.

SOUND RECORDINGS

When doing sound cassettes, do not assume any type of noise reduction. If *Dolby* noise reduction is indicated on the item by the "double D" symbol, you should enter that information here in the format *Dolby encoded.*

If a sound recording is originally captured in a different form than the final recording, note that here. That is, if a CD is originally recorded analog, you would say *analog recording.* If you have a cassette or record album that was originally captured digitally, you would state *Digital recording* here. ONLY enter this information if it is listed on the item or indicated by the SPARS code.

EXAMPLES

500 $aAnalog recording.
500 $aDolby encoded.

VIDEORECORDINGS

If the videorecording is Dolby or surround encoded, you must note that also. This will usually apply only to newer recordings.

EXAMPLES

500 $aDolby Surround-sound encoded.
500 $aAC-3 encoded.
500 $aTHX mastered.
500 $aSide one widescreen version, side two standard version.

PUNCTUATION

The tag ends with a period unless a terminal mark of punctuation is present.

504 BIBLIOGRAPHY, ETC. NOTE

REPEATABLE: YES
MANDATORY: NO
RELATES TO: 500
AUTHORITY: NO

1st indicator
The 1st indicator is always blank.

2nd indicator
The 2nd indicator is always blank.

This field contains a note indicating the presence of a bibliography(ies), discography(ies), filmography(ies), and/or other bibliographic references in an item. It may also indicate the presence of a bibliography, etc. in accompanying material that is described in the record.

SUBFIELD CODES

a   **Bibliography, Etc. note (NR)**   *(Rule 2.7B18)*

If the item has both a bibliography and an index, they can be combined in the **504** field <u>if</u> there is no specific page information for the bibliography.

EXAMPLES

Bibliography: p. 345-347 Includes index.
These two statments should not be combined into one 504 field. You will need to make a 504 tag for the bibliography <u>and</u> a 500 tag for the index. Alternately, make a 504 tag such as incldues bibliographial /references (p.345-347) and index.

Bibliography   Index
These two items <u>can</u> be combined into one 504 tag. It would read as:

504      $aIncludes bibliography and index.
(This form is used to indicate that there is no pagination information for the bibliography and/or the index.)

504      $aBibliography: p. 238-239.
504      $aDiscography: p. 105-111.
504      $aFilmography: p. 344-360.
504      $aSelected bibliography: p. 351-358.
504      $aIncludes discography and videography.
504      $aIncludes bibliographical references (p. 234-237) and index.
504      $aContains bibliographical information.
(Use this form if the bibliographies are at the end of chapters or are just in footnotes.)

LOCATION

Information on the presence of a bibliography will usually be found in the back of the book or at the end of each chapter; sound recordings may have this information as part of the accompanying material on the booklet in the case. If the item does, you should make a **504** the same as the last example above. Some sound recordings may contain a listing of other works (either sound recordings or videos) by the artist or group on the accompanying material. You should include this information as listed in the third to last example above.

Remember that bibliographic information is not limited to bound printed matter. Some videorecordings have listings on the end of suggested sources. Filmstrips may contain a frame of suggested reading, and computer software may reference other interesting or relevant software.

DEFINITIONS

Bibliography A listing of bibliographic items, books or journals that were utilized in the preparation of the current book in hand. It may suggest sources for further reading.

Discography A list of sound recordings. These will usually appear in books about famous singers or performers, or in books that have a musical topic. Some sound recordings will list other works by the same artist or on the same label in the container. This would also be considered a discography.

Filmography A list of movies, videotapes, laserdiscs, etc. These will often be found in biographies of actors and actresses, books about movie as a genre, or about histories of the movie industry.

Videography A list of videos, including videotapes and discs. These will often be found in biographies of actors and actresses, books about movie as a genre, or about histories of the movie industry. You may also find them in the accompanying material for musical artists referring to music videos that they have done.

Note that there is no specified order for *bibliography, discography, filmography,* or *videography* information. You should consider them to be equal to each other, and to apply the same rules when considering if index information can be merged with it.

NOTES

This information is very important to a researcher, especially someone who has just started research on a topic that they know little about. An item with a bibliography will aid the user in finding other books, sound recordings, or videos on the topic, or for the experienced researcher, make it possible for the facts and citations to be verified for accuracy.

For the reference staff, the presence of discographies and filmographies can be very useful when helping users with questions about the cinema or music industry, or when doing biographical research on famous people.

Check with your system vendor about keyword searching capabilities on this tag.

<u>THE SUBFIELDS IN DETAIL</u>

a   **Bibliography, Etc. note (NR)**
This subfield contains the entire text of the note.

> *$aBibliography: p. 504.*
> *$aIncludes bibliographical references.*
> *$aDiscography: p. 334.*
> *$aIncludes bibliography, discography, and index.*
> *$aIncludes videography.*

<u>PUNCTUATION</u>

This tag ends with a period unless there is another terminal mark of punctuation.

505   FORMATTED CONTENTS NOTE

REPEATABLE:	YES
MANDATORY:	NO
RELATES TO:	740$a
AUTHORITY:	NO

1st indicator

0	**Complete contents**		(Use if you enter entire contents area)
	250	**Incomplete contents**	
	251	**Partial contents**	(Use if you only enter part of the contents area)

2nd indicator

blank Basic

0   Enhanced   (Use if you used subfields **g**, **t**, and **r**)

This field contains a formatted contents note. A contents note usually contains the titles of separate works, or parts of an item, and may also include statements of responsibility associated with the works or parts. It can also include individual tracks or sections of sound recordings, chapter titles on videodiscs, titles of component parts of computer software, individual titles of videotapes when cataloged as a set, and the names of parts of kits. Volume numbers and other sequential designations are also included in a contents note, but chapter numbers are generally omitted. Sometimes, other data may be included (e.g., the number of pages or pieces in each part or running and playing times.)

SUBFIELD CODES

a	**Formatted contents note (NR)**	*(Rule 1.7B18 ; 2.7B18 ; 6.7B18; 7.7B18 ; 8.7B18 ; 9.7B18)*
g	**Miscellaneous information (NR)**	
t	**Title (R)**	
r	**Statement of responsibility (R)**	

EXAMPLES

505 0 $aFuture lake use plan -- Recommended shoreline improvements -- Existing beachfront use -- Suggested zoning changes.

505 00 $tChildren of darkness /$rStephen B. Oates --$tHayfoot, strawfoot! /$rBruce Catton -- $tFear of the city /$rAlfred Kazin --$tBig Bill Taft /$rStephen Hess --$tWhen I landed, the war was over /$rHughes Rudd.

505 20 $tNowhere fast --$tSorcerer --$tTonight is what it means to be young.

505 0 $aBelt sanders -- Table saws -- Lathes.

505 00 $tArrival of the Queen of Sheba from "Solomon"$g(2:53) /$rGeorge Frideric Handel --$t Harmonious blacksmith from Harpsichord suite #5$g(4:49) /$rGeorge Frideric Handel --$tCanon$g(5:21) /$rJohann Pachelbel --$tPrelude and fugue in D major$g(3:38) /$rJohann Sebastian Bach --$tAir on the G string$g(5:20) /$rJohann Sebastian Bach --$tTrumpet voluntary$g(1:59) /$rJeremiah Clarke --$tNew Irish tune$g(3:37) /$rHenry Purcell --$tGigue$g(2:29) /$rArcangelo Corelli --$tSonata in A major$g(2:29) /$rDomenico Scarlatti --$tAdagio for strings and organ$g(6:47) /$rTomaso Albinoni.

505

505 0	**$a**v. 1. The Earth -- v. 4. The sky.	
505 0	**$a**v. 1. Star Trek -- v. 2. Star Trek; The next generation -- v. 3. Space 1999 -- v. 4. Battlestar: Galactica.	

LOCATION

This information will usually be found on the *table of contents* page at the front of the book, although in the case of multi-volume works or sets, the individual title of each item could be entered here. For sound recordings, you should check the label or the back of the container; for videodiscs, the back cover will contain the information. For component parts of other items cataloged under a collective title, you will need to examine each item.

NOTES

Information from the table of contents should be entered here. This would include the names of individual stories, poems, and plays for anthologies. You should also enter the author of each one of these works if different. In an academic environment, this will be useful to your students when they are looking for works that an instructor discussed in class. In a school library, you may wish to work with the different instructors to ascertain which items are the most important and relevant to the curriculum. In a public library, you may wish to focus on works in anthologies by authors that your patrons have asked for or checked out frequently in the past.

For *sound recordings*, this tag is particularly useful for items that are a compilation of different pieces by various artists. When doing *videorecordings*, it is useful to list the chapter stops on videodiscs and DVDs, particularly if there are multiple units or sessions on a disc.

For *books*, titles are entered from the table of contents, with each title separated by a *"space -- space"*. Timings for sound recordings and videorecordings are entered following the title, but before the slash. Standard cataloging capitalization rules apply.

If there are authors for each item, such as in a short story or poetry anthology, construct statements of responsibility like you would a **245$a** and **245$c**, with a *"space / space"* between the title and the author, with each title/author combination separated by a *"space -- space"*. It is important that you follow this prescribed punctuation, since in the future many systems will be able to provide author and/or title access searches on the relevant information in this tag. This will be possible <u>only</u> if you give the system the correct "signposts" to follow. Until then, this information is still important since many systems will use this information when doing keyword searches.

You may wish to create individual **740** tags for each title/author combination that you enter here, or for only a few of them to provide direct title/author access from your patron search screen. While most systems will provide keyword access to this tag, you may wish to simplify searching for your patrons by providing direct title/author access to the information here. Check with your system vendor for any limitations as to the number of entries you can make.

Prior to *Format Integration*, the only way a system could determine where the titles and authors began and ended was through the punctuation. Through the use of subfields **t** and **r**, it is now possible for a system to build these into the respective author and title indexes. You will need to make the decision whether to separately subfield code these pieces of information. You should contact your automation vendor to determine if they plan on using these subfields in the future, or if they will have an automated conversion program to take care of them.

Do not use 1st indicator values **1** or **2** unless you are working under significant system limitations or the set has not completed publishing.

a   **Formatted contents note (NR)**   *(Rule 1.7B18)*

This subfield contains the formatted contents note, whether complete, incomplete, or partial. The text of the contents note may include titles, statements of responsibility, volume numbers and sequential designations. For records formulated according to AACR2 rules, these elements are usually separated by ISBD punctuation.

Do not enter the word *Contents* at the beginning of the tag as it should be supplied by the software as part of the *USMARC Bibliographic* protocols.

> *$aBean basics -- Drinks -- Breakfast fare -- Entrees -- Side dishes -- Sauces -- Frozen deserts.*

NOT

> *$aContents: Bean basics -- Drinks -- Breakfast fare -- Entrees -- Side dishes -- Sauces -- Frozen deserts.*

CORRECT FORM

> *$aForever your girl (4:58) / Paula Abdul -- Don't rush me (3:47) / Taylor Dayne -- Buffalo stance (5:42) / Neneh Cherry -- Mercedes boy (5:10) / Pebbles -- I wanna have some fun (4:08) / Samantha Fox -- The way you love me (4:56) / Karyn White -- Typical male (4:14) / Tina Turner -- Head to toe (5:01) / Lisa Lisa and Cult Jam -- Come go with me (4:15) / Exposé -- Strut (3:59) / Sheena Easton.*

> *$aOpening & flight to Jupiter -- The Jupiter encounters -- The Saturn encounters -- The long voyage to Uranus -- The Uranus encounter -- The Neptune encounter.*

t   **Title (R)**

This subfield contains a title used in the coding-enhanced contents note. Note that your **second indicator** value <u>must</u> be **0**.

> *$tBreakfast fare --$tEntrees -- $tSide dishes --$tSauces --$tFrozen deserts.*

> *$tOpening & flight to Jupiter --$tThe Jupiter encounters --$tThe Saturn encounters --$t The long voyage to Uranus --$tThe Uranus encounter --$tThe Neptune encounter.*

g   **Miscellaneous information (R)**

This subfield contains any information other than the statement of responsibility or title, used in a coding-enhanced note. If you use this subfield, then your **second indicator** value <u>must</u> be **0**.

> *$tOpening$g(6:18) --$tFloe$g(5:32) --$tIsland$g(7:39) --$tRubric$g(6:04) -- $tFacades$g(7:19) --$tClosing$g(5:56)*

505

r   **Statement of responsibility (R)**

This subfield contains the statement of responsibility of the article or part in the coding-enhanced contents note. If you use this subfield, then your **second indicator** value <u>must</u> be **0**.

$tLinus & Lucy$g(3:35) /$rDavid Benoit --$tSpain$g(5:52) /$rChick Corea --$tWaltz for Suzy$g(4:05) /$rDudley Moore --$tTequila mockingbird$g(4:42) /$rRamsey Lewis --$tFlapstick blues$g(2:15) /$rMcCoy Tyner --$tOn golden pond$g(3:35) /$rDave Grusin --$tCarmel$g(5:36) /$rJoe Sample --$tI'll remember April$g(6:10) /$rBilly Taylor --$tBop-be$g(6:58) /$rKeith Jarrett --$tSteepian Faith$g(6:01) /$rKenny Kirkland.

PUNCTUATION

Subfield **$t** is preceded by a *space--* (space dash dash)

Subfield **$g** is preceded by no punctuation

Subfield **$r** is preceded by a *space /* (space slash)

The tag ends with a period unless another terminal mark of punctuation is present.

508 CREATION/PRODUCTION CREDITS NOTE

REPEATABLE: NO
MANDATORY: NO
RELATES TO: 245$c, 511,700$a, 710$a, 711$a
AUTHORITY: NO

1st indicator
The 1st indicator is always blank.

2nd indicator
The 2nd indicator is always blank.

SUBFIELD CODES

a **Creation/Production credits note (NR)** *(Rule 7.7B6 ; 6.7B6)*

EXAMPLES

508 **$a**Producer, Joseph N. Ermolieff ; director, Lesley Selander ; screenplay, Theodore St. John ; music director, Michael Michelet.

508 **$a**Music, Michael Fishbein ; camera, George Mo.

LOCATION

Generally, you will be able to get this information from either the box accompanying a *videotape* or *videodisc*, or from the credits at the beginning or end of the production. For *sound recordings*, you will need to look at either the dust jacket for record albums, at the enclosed flyleaf for cassettes, and at any accompanying booklets for CDs.

NOTES

This field contains a note that states the credits for persons or organizations, other than members of the cast, who have participated in the artistic or technical production of the work. Narrators may be recorded here or in tag **511**. Generally, voice-over narrators are recorded in tag **508**, on-screen narrators are recorded in tag **511**.

Sometimes it will be necessary to duplicate information from the **245** in this tag. Many systems build keywords based on this tag, which can be useful for finding all the works which a particular person or organization participated in. You should check with your system vendor to determine if keywords can be built on this tag. Many times, you may find it desirable to trace the names here in **700** or **710** tags, depending on your library's policies. If you choose to trace the names, then you should do it for <u>all</u> items; consistency in your cataloging is very important.

Producers and engineers on sound recordings can be entered here if they make a significant artistic or interpretive contribution to the work *(6.1F1)*. What a "significant" contribution is, is a decision the cataloger will have to make. If you enter a name or names here, you also have the option of tracing them in **700** or **710** tags as appropriate.

508

EXAMPLES

508	**$a**Film editor, Martyn Down ; narrator, Margaret Throsby ; consultant, Robert F. Miller.
508	**$a**Educational consultant, Roseanne Gillis.
508	**$a**Music by John Williams ; screenplay by Michael Crichton and David Koepp ; directed by Steven Spielberg.
508	**$a**Engineered by Doug Rider, Jeff Lorber ; mastered by Steve Hall ; executive producer, Bruce Lundvall.

PUNCTUATION

This tag ends with a period unless another mark of punctuation is present.

511 PARTICIPANT OR PERFORMER NOTE

REPEATABLE:	YES
MANDATORY:	NO
RELATES TO:	245$c,508, 7XX
AUTHORITY:	NO

1st indicator	Display constant controller
0	**No display constant generated**
1	**Cast**

2nd indicator
The 2nd indicator is always blank.

SUBFIELD CODES

a   **Participant or Performer note(NR)**   _(Rule 6.7B6 ; 7.7B6)_

EXAMPLES

511 0 $aMarshall Moss, violin ; Neil Roberts, harpsichord.
511 1 $aSharon Stone, Michael Douglas.
511 0 $aPresenter: Billy Crystal.
511 0 $aNarrator: Sally Struthers.

LOCATION

Generally, you will be able to get this information from either the box accompanying a _videotape_ or _videodisc_, or from the credits at the beginning or end of the production. For _sound recordings_, you will need to look at either the dust jacket for record albums, at the enclosed liner notes for cassettes, and at any accompanying booklets for CDs.

For _videorecordings_, the production information that is often duplicated in advertisements for the production is an excellent source.

NOTES

This field contains a note giving information about the participants, players, narrators, presenters, or performers. The note is usually displayed and/or printed with an introductory term that is generated as a display constant based on the first indicator value. You should <u>not</u> enter the phrases listed under _Display constant controller_ as they should be system-supplied. You will need to verify this information with your vendor. On-screen narrators are recorded in 511. Generally, voice-over narrators are recorded in 508.

Put narrators for **motion pictures** and **videorecordings** in this tag. For **sound recordings,** it is acceptable to enter the names of the performers on a recording in this tag. Sometimes it will be necessary to duplicate information from the **245** in this tag. Many systems build keywords based on this tag, which can be useful for finding all the works which a particular person or organization participated in. You should check with your system vendor to determine if keywords can be built on this tag. Many times, you may find it desirable to trace the names here in **700** or **710** tags, depending on your library's policies. If you choose to trace the names, then you should do it for <u>all</u> items; consistency in your cataloging is very important.

511

Enter information in the **245$c** or in this tag but not in both. For more detailed instructions, refer to that tag.

EXAMPLES

511 0		**$a**Hosted by Hugh Downs.
511 1		**$a**Jackie Glanville.
511 1		**$a**Colin Blakely, Jane Lapotaire.
511 0		**$a**Anchor, Dan Rather.
511 0		**$a**Narrator: Burl Ives.
511 0		**$a**Russ Freeman, Tony Morales, Kim Stone, Jeff Kashiwa, Steve Reid, Mark Portman.
511 0		**$a**Bob James, keyboards ; Lee Rittenour, guitars ; Nathan East, bass ; Harvey Mason, drums.
511 1		**$a**Steve Martin, Victoria Tennant, Richard E. Grant, Marilu Henner.
511 1		**$a**Arnold Schwarzenegger, Maria Conchita Alonso, Yaphet Koto, Richard Dawson.

PUNCTUATION

The tag ends with a period unless another mark of punctuation is present.

516 TYPE OF FILE OR DATA NOTE

REPEATABLE: YES
MANDATORY: NO
RELATES TO: 008/26
AUTHORITY: NO

1st indicator

b **blank**
8 **No display information generated**

2nd indicator

b **blank**

SUBFIELD CODES

a **Type of file or data note (NR)**

This field contains information that characterizes the file. It is related to the value given in the **008** (Type of computer file). In addition to a general descriptor (e.g., text, computer programs, numeric), more specific information, such as the form or genre of textual material (e.g., biography, dictionaries, indexes) may be recorded in this field.

If the software includes both the program and data for the program, then you <u>must</u> use the phrase:

Computer data and program.

EXAMPLES

516    $aComputer programs
516    $aNumeric (Summary statistics)
516    $aText (Law reports and digests)

LOCATION

Generally, you will find this information based on direct physical examination of the software or from the accompanying documentation. Again, consulting any user documentation or guides will prove to be helpful.

THE SUBFIELDS IN DETAIL

a **Type of computer file or data note (NR)**

This subfield contains the entire text of the note. Do not enter the phrase *Type of file* as this may be system generated.

$aText (Law reports and digests)
$aBibliogrphic data file

PUNCTUATION

The tag does not end with a mark of punctuation unless the tag ends with an abbreviation, initial/letter, or other data that ends with a mark of punctuation.

520

520 SUMMARY, ETC. NOTE

REPEATABLE:	YES
MANDATORY:	NO
RELATES TO:	--
AUTHORITY:	NO

1st indicator

blank **No information provided**
0   **Subject**
1   **Review**
8   **No display constant generated**

2nd indicator
The 2nd indicator is always blank.

This field contains an unformatted note that describes the scope and general contents of the described materials. This could be a summary, abstract, annotation, review or only a phrase describing the material. How much detail you go into here depends on the audience for a particular item. You can use this tag to record review material.

SUBFIELD CODES

a   **Summary, etc. note (NR)**   *(Rule 1.7B17 ; 2.7B17)*

EXAMPLES

520   **$a**Describes associations made between different animal species for temporary gain or convenience as well as more permanent alliances formed for mutual survival.

520   **$a**Miguel has always wanted to go on the drive up to the mountains, and now, maybe his chance has come, but at what price to his brother?

520   **$a**Records the events, people, and places that made news in 1973 and updates the information from the encyclopedia's first year.

520   **$a**Kate and Ben follow their rabbit into a haunted house and discover the source of the house's ghostly sound.

520   **$a**A number of possible methods of measuring the relaxation of flexural stress in thin carbon/carbon composites are described and critically reviewed. An acoustic method is considered to be the most advantageous and is selected for use and further development.

520 1   **$a**"Pictures the highlights of the play Julius Caesar using photographs of an actual production"--School Library Journal.

520   **$a**"A textbook for 6th form students"--Publisher's Weekly.

LOCATION

Many librarians will take this information from the dustjacket or publisher's blurb for books or from the packing material or box in the case of AV items. If you are among these, be certain to evaluate this information, as it often does not accurately describe the contents of the item.

One of the best locations for summary information is the introduction. This is where the author, editor, or creator of an item will usually explain what they are trying to do or attempts to set the tempo and atmosphere for the item. Skim books for topics discussed, chapter titles, etc. and other relevant words. For AV items, you may wish to examine any accompanying study guides or documentation, actually view or listen to the opening segments of a production, or to use a review source or catalog. You may wish to include descriptive words that cannot be entered in the subject tags, as they will be accessible through a keyword search.

If entering reviews, you should not exclusively use reviews printed on the item as they may be biased toward the book. As a matter of legal protection, you should try to present at least two opposing reviews from reputable sources. If there are not opposing viewpoints to a particular work, be certain that you are able to support the purchase of the item and have other items in your collection to balance the points of view presented in the work.

NOTES

Try not to duplicate the words in the **505** Contents area since that area is usually keyword indexed, rather, you should select unique and new words for keyword indexing. Assign terms in a narrative phrase that will be useful to your users when they do keyword searches.

As you can see from the examples above, summaries can pique the curiosity of the reader, encourage the browser to look at the item, or contain key, relevant, poignant phrases that an experienced researcher will be looking for.

Ultimately, a good summary depends on you knowing your clientele, as well as spending some time with the item. While this may seem time-consuming, the benefits in improved accessibility and reduced time in wasted retrievals is a good investment for you and your patrons.

If the summary is taken from the introduction of the book, or if it is taken from a review source, such as *Library Journal* or *Publisher's Weekly*, be certain to use a **first indicator** value of **1** and enclose the summary in quotations, followed by two dashes, and the source of the quotation.

THE FIRST INDICATOR IN DETAIL

blank No information provided
By leaving the first indicator blank many systems will automatically provide the notation *Summary* at the beginning of the note. You should check with your vendor to determine if it does or not.

520        $aAn illustrated collection of nursery rhymes set to music.

520        $aLetters, primarily to Angelica Schuyler Chruch, wife of John Barker Church and daughter of Philip John Schuyler.

520        $aDemonstrates the interval method of aerobic exercise, plyometric routines, and non-ballistic stretching. Incorporates floor work and step work in the demonstrations.

520

0   Subject

This value is used to generate the display constant *Subject*. You would use this if you are creating a description or *subject* of an artwork or other graphic material.

520 0 $aTwo head-and-shoulder portraits in separate ornamental oval frames, one frame held by eagle.

1   Review

This value is used to generate the display constant *Review*.   It would be possible to actually record the review for a particular item here. Usually, they will be taken from an outside reviewing source and will need to be credited by the librarian.

520 1 $a"Combines the most frequently asked questions regarding AIDS with the most prominent US physician, former Surgeon General C. Everett Koop, resulting in an informative 38-minute production"--Video rating guide for libraries, Winter, 1990.

8   No display constant generated

The use of this value results in no display constant being generated. Many libraries use this as their default value.

THE SUBFIELDS IN DETAIL

a   Summary, etc. note (NR)

This subfield contains the text of the note. Do not enter the phrase *Summary* as it should be provided by the software according to *USMARC Bibliographic* protocols.

> *$aUsing the concepts of interval training and plyometrics, many of the common causes of illness and more serious body harm can be avoided.*

> *$aA comprehensive guide to cooking with coffee, including main courses, appetizers, and as refreshment.*

PUNCTUATION

The field ends with a period unless another terminal mark of punctuation is present.

2. TARGET AUDIENCE NOTE

REPEATABLE:	YES
MANDATORY:	NO
RELATES TO:	008/22,500, 520
AUTHORITY:	NO

1st indicator

blank	**No information provided**
0	**Reading grade level**
1	**Interest age level**
2	**Interest grade level**
3	**Special audience characteristics**
4	**Motivation interest level**
8	**No display constant generated**

2nd indicator

The 2nd indicator is always blank.

SUBFIELD CODES

a	**Target audience note (R)**
b	**Source (NR)**

This field contains a note about the target audience of the described materials. It is primarily used when the contents of an item are considered appropriate for a specific audience or intellectual level (e.g., elementary school students). Information about juvenile target audiences and/or intellectual level should also be recorded in coded form in the **008** tag. This tag is also used to record the *Motion Picture Association of America (MPAA)* rating for videorecordings. This tag can also be used to record the rating of computer software and games for children. The *Parent's Music Resource Center (PMRC)* advisory for sound recordings could also be recorded here.

NOTES

Exercise care when entering this information. Unless you have specialized training in the assignment of the information, it may be wise to only use information that would be in vendor supplied records or from an outside review source. It is also possible to use the information supplied on or with the item by the publisher if your experience shows it to be valid and accurate. Do not hesitate to consult with the relevant professional staff in your school or community for assistance on these values.

THE INDICATORS IN DETAIL

blank   **No information provided**
No information is provided. This value is used if the note contains information on the *Audience*.

> *$aThose who have completed the basic requirements of the primary degree and wish to commence study for an advanced degree.*

0   **Reading grade level**

The grade level at which the item is meant to be read. This value can be used to generate the display constant *Reading grade level:*

$a3.1.
(The reading level is that for the first month of the third grade)

1   **Interest age level**

This indicates that the numbered information in **$a** pertains to the age level at which the item will most likely be of interest. The value is used to generate the display constant *Interest age level:*

$a004-006.
(The item is of interest to those ages 4 through 6.

2   **Interest grade level**

This value indicates that the numbered information in **$a** pertains to the grade level at which the item will most likely be of interest. The value is used to generate the display constant *Interest grade level:*

$a9 & up.
(The item is of interest to those in the ninth grade and up.)

3   **Special audience characteristics**

This value indicates that the information in **$a** pertains to special characteristics of the audience to which the item will most likely be of interest. The value is used to generate the display constant *Special format characteristics:*

$aVision impaired$afine motor skills impaired$aaudio learner.
(The item is of interest to vision and fine motor skills impaired audio learners.)

4   **Motivation/interest level**

This value indicates that the information in **$a** identifies the motivation and/or interest level of the audience for which the item is best suited. The value is used to generate the display constant *Motivation/interest level:*

$aHighly motivated$ahigh interest.
(The item is appropriate for highly motivated, highly interested audiences)

8   **No display constant generated**

Use this value if you do not want your system to place any display constants before the body of the note. This would be useful if you are writing broad, general, target audience notes that are best described narratively, rather than by grade or age levels. It is also used for recording the MPAA rating for movies or PMRC advisory for sound recordings, as well as ratings values for video games.

> *$aFor advanced and self-paced learners.*
> *$aMPAA rating: PG.*

<u>THE SUBFIELDS IN DETAIL</u>

a   **Target audience note (R)**   (Rule 1.7B14 ; 2.7B14 ; 7.7B14)
This subfield contains the text of the note. It is repeatable if necessary.

521   *$aProgram designed for geographers, planners, geologists, meteorologists and others who have a professional interest in analyzing spatial data.*

521 1   *$a009-012.*
           (*Note*: The interest level is that for ages 9-12)

521 2   *$a7 & up.*
           (*Note*: The interest level is that for grades 7 and up.)

521 0   *$a5.*
           (*Note*: The reading level is that for the fifth grade.)

521 8   *$aFor remedial reading programs.*

521   *$aPrimary/intermediate.*

521 2   *$aK-3.*

521 8   *$aMPAA rating: G.*
           (*Note:* This is the form used for the rating on motion pictures assigned by the MPAA)

b   **Source (NR)**
This subfield is used to record the name or abbreviation of the agency or entity assigning the information.

521 2 $aK-3.*$bFollett Library Book Co.*
521 3 $aVisually impaired*$bLENOCA.*
521 8 $aPG-13.*$bMotion Picture Association of America.*

LOCATION

There is no specified location for this information. Many publishers will put it on the front or back cover, particularly for children's books, or it may be recorded on the title page verso. You may also find a narrative phrase that is appropriate, a citation in an outside, secondary source, or you may enter a value based on your knowledge and experience.

PUNCTUATION

$a is preceded by no punctuation.
$b is preceded by a period if the value before it is numerical, otherwise it is preceded by **no** punctuation.
The tag ends with a period unless another terminal mark of punctuation is present.

530 ADDITIONAL PHYSICAL FORM AVAILABLE NOTE

REPEATABLE: YES
MANDATORY: NO
RELATES TO: 300,500
AUTHORITY: NO

1st indicator
The 1st indicator is always blank.

2nd indicator
The 2nd indicator is always blank.

SUBFIELD CODES

a   Additional physical form available note (NR)

This field contains information concerning a different physical format in which the described item is available. The additional form may be published and/or made available for use at a repository in the additional form.

EXAMPLES

530	$aIssued as Beta 1/2 in. or VHS 1/2 in. or U-Matic 3/4 in.
530	$aAlso available on cassette.
530	$aIssued also for Macintosh.
530	$aMaps also available on CD-ROM.
530	$aGame pieces also available with different team jersey colors.
530	$aAlso available on microfiche.

LOCATION

Generally, you will need to get this information from a catalog from the publisher, from a review source, or from examining the accompanying documentation. You should not use information for similar records in a shared database as proof that a variant form is also available. It is also acceptable to obtain this information from direct physical examination (observing multiple formats at a retail outlet, etc.)

NOTES

Field **530** is used only for notes describing different physical formats. Notes conveying information about other editions (e.g., earlier versions, shorter versions, different language versions) are recorded in fields **250** or **500** as appropriate.

When doing a filmstrip/sound recording combination where the sound recording is available in another format *(cassette vs. sound disc)*, a notation should be made in the **530**-- *Kit available with sound cassette.* You should use this phrase <u>only</u> if your library actually has that alternative form.

<u>THE SUBFIELDS IN DETAIL</u>

a   **Additional physical form available note (NR)**   *(Rule 1.7B16 ; 3.7B16 ; 6.7B16 ; 7.7B16 ; 8.7B16 ; 9.7B16)*

This subfield contains a description of the additional physical form(s) and any text not belonging in the other subfields.

530   *$aIssued also as cassette (VHS or Sony U-Matic)*

530   *$aIssued also as cassette and as cartridge.*

530   *$aAlso available with sequenced sound recording.*

530   *$aData also issued in print and microform.*

530   *$aAlso available with wooden playing pieces.*

530   *$aIssued also as 16 mm. motion picture.*

530   *$aIssued also as 16 mm. filmstrip in cartridge and as slide set and as videorecording*

<u>PUNCTUATION</u>

The tag ends with a period unless another terminal mark of punctuation is present.

536

536 FUNDING INFORMATION NOTE

REPEATABLE: YES
MANDATORY: NO
RELATES TO: --
AUTHORITY: NO

1st indicator
The 1st indicator is always blank.

2nd indicator
The 2nd indicator is always blank.

SUBFIELD CODES

a   **Text of note (NR)**   *(No AACR2 rule)*

EXAMPLES

536    $aSponsored by the World Health Organization
536    $aMade possible by a grant from the J.L. Hesburg foundation.

LOCATION

This information may or may not be recorded on the item. It is particularly found on specially commissioned or produced audio-visual works, videotapes, or concerts.

NOTES

It is important to remember that this tag is used to record the <u>agency</u> or agencies that made possible the <u>production</u> of the item, <u>not</u> its purchase or funding source for acquisition.

THE SUBFIELDS IN DETAIL

a   **Text of note**
This subfield contains information concerning the sponsors or funding agencies.

536   *$aSponsored by the U.S. Energy Research and Development Administration.*
536   *$aMade possible through a grant from the Byron R. Lewis Memorial trust.*
536   *$aFunding for the original compositions on the recording originally provided by the Friends of the Symphony and the Symphony Ladies' Auxiliary.*

PUNCTUATION

The tag does not end with a mark of punctuation unless the field ends with an abbreviation, initial/letter, or other data that ends with a mark of punctuation.

538 SYSTEM DETAILS NOTE

REPEATABLE:	YES
MANDATORY:	NO
RELATES TO:	516
AUTHORITY:	NO

1st indicator

The 1st indicator is always blank.

2nd indicator

The 2nd indicator is always blank.

SUBFIELD CODES

a   **System details note (NR)**

EXAMPLES

538       $aSystem requirements: IBM PC AT or XT or compatible; 8MB RAM; 540 MB hard drive; CD-ROM player and drive.

538       $aSystem requirements: Personal or multimedia computer with a 486 or higher processor; 8MB RAM (Windows95), 16MB RAM (Windows NT) (more memory may be required to run additional applications simultaneously); 60-167MB hard disk space required depending on configuration; CD-ROM drive; VGA or higher resolution video adapter (Super VGA 256-color recommended); Microsoft mouse, Microsoft IntelliMouse or compatible pointing device.

538       $aSystem requirements: Apple II or higher; 48K; DOS 3.3; Applesoft BASIC.

538       $aVHS.

538       $aLaser optical CAV.

538       $aCompact disc.

538       $aLaser optical DVD.

LOCATION

For *computer software*, this information will usually be on the outside of the packaging box, prefaced by the words *System requirements*. This information is usually provided on the outside so that the purchaser can determine if they are able to run the software on their computer before purchasing it.

For *videorecordings*, this information will usually be on the packaging container, or it may be on the item itself. You should look for words like *VHS* or *Laserdisc*.

NOTES

For *computer software*, this field contains technical information about the file. This includes the presence or absence of certain kinds of codes or the physical characteristics of the file such as recording densities, parity, or blocking factors. For software, data such as software programming language, computer requirements (e.g., computer manufacturer and model, operating system, or memory requirements), and

538

peripheral requirements (e.g., number of tape drives, number of disk or drum units, number of terminals, or other peripheral devices, support software, or related equipment) can be recorded.

If the software is designed to run on two platforms, e.g. Windows95 and Macintosh, then you will need <u>two</u> **538** tags, with each on beginning with a statement which platform the requirements are for:

538   *$aSystem requirements for Windows95:*

538   *$aSystem requirements for Macintosh:*

For *videorecordings*, including videotapes and videodiscs, information about the trade name or recording system(s) (e.g. VHS, Beta, etc.), number of lines of resolution, and modulation frequency should be included if given on the item.

For *sound recordings*, you should record the specific format here. Formerly, this information was recorded in the **500** tag.

THE SUBFIELDS IN DETAIL

a   **System details note (NR)**   *(Rule 7.7B10 ; 9.7B1 ; 9.7B10)*

When entering the information for computer software, begin the note with the phrase *System requirements:*. Give the following characteristics in the order in which they are listed below. Precede each characteristic, other than the first, by a semi-colon space.

(Rule 9.7B1b)

the make and model of the computer(s) on which the file is designed to run
the amount of memory required
the name of the operating system
the software requirements (including the programming language)
the kind and characteristics of any required or recommended peripherals

538   *$aU-Matic.*

538   *$aOne side CAV, one side CLV.*

538   *$aSystem requirements: Apple //e; 128K; 2 disk drives; 1 color monitor.*

538   *$aSystem requirements: IBM compatible PC; 640K; 40 megabyte hard drive.*

538   *$aSystem requirements: IBM or compatible PC, 386/33 MHz or better; 8MB RAM; Windows 3.1; VGA card with 256 colors and 640 x 480 resolution; color monitor; Double-speed CD-ROM drive; MPC compliant sound card and mouse or other compatible pointing device.*

538   *$aLaser optical CAV.*

538   *$aVHS Hi-fi*

538   *$aMiniDisc.*

PUNCTUATION

The tag ends with a period unless another terminal mark of punctuation is present.

546   LANGUAGE NOTE

REPEATABLE: YES
MANDATORY: NO
RELATES TO: 008/35-37, 041
AUTHORITY: NO

1st indicator
The 1st indicator is always blank.

2nd indicator
The 2nd indicator is always blank.

SUBFIELD CODES

a   **Language note (NR)**   *(Rule 7.7B2 ; 6.7B2)*

EXAMPLES

546   $aIn Hebrew and Greek.
546   $aText in Latin; critical apparatus in English and German.
546   $aEnglish, French, or German.
546   $aClosed-captioned
546   $aWith sign language interpreter.

LOCATION

You will need to physically inspect the item to determine the language(s) used in the publication.

NOTES

This field contains a textual note giving the language(s) of the described materials. The field is also used to describe the alphabets, script, or other symbol system appearing in the information. This information is presented in coded form in the **008/35-37 (Language)** tag and the **041** tag. The **041** tag is outside the scope of this book.

If the item is closed captioned as indicated by the closed-captioning symbol on it (primarily for *videorecordings*), then you will have to have a subject heading entry stating *Video recordings for the hearing impaired.*

THE SUBFIELDS IN DETAIL

a   **Language note (NR)**
The subfield contains the text of the language note.

546   *$aIn Hungarian; summaries in cyrillic and Japanes*
546   *$aEnglish, French, or German.*
546   *$aIn Spanish*

PUNCTUATION

The tag ends with a period unless another terminal mark of punctuation is present.

586 AWARDS NOTE

REPEATABLE: YES
MANDATORY: NO
RELATES TO: --
AUTHORITY: NO

1st indicator

b   Display constant *Awards:* generated   (Depends on local system parameters)
8   No display constant generated   (Depends on local system parameters)

2nd indicator
The 2nd indicator is always blank.

SUBFIELD CODES

a   **Awards note (NR)**   *(Rule 1.7A3)*

EXAMPLES

586     $aAcadamy Award for Best Picture, 1987
586 8 $a"Emmy Award for Best Classical Program in the Performing Arts, 1980/81"
586     $aNewbery Medal, 1983
586     $aNational Book Award, 1991
586     $aPulitzer Prize for Nonfiction, 1987

LOCATION

This information will usually be recorded somewhere on the publication, either on the title page or on the front or back dustjacket. For *videorecordings*, it will usually be on the packaging container. For *sound recordings*, it will usually be on the jacket or on the accompanying material.

You can also verify if an item received an award by checking a review source or reference book. You may wish to keep a list of the awards that your library considers important enough to tag. Do not begin this tag with the word *Awards*; this should be system generated if you are leaving the **first indicator** blank. To supress any display constants, use the **first indicator** value of **8**.

NOTES

This information can be useful when helping to order materials for your library, as you may wish to collect all the titles that have won a particular award. Parents and librarians can also use this information in the compilation of selection lists to help select items that a third party considers being noteworthy. For the librarian, this field can be useful to aid the defense of the library's collection development policy if a particular item is challenged as being unsuitable for the collection.

There must be a date given for each entry. If there is no date for a particular award, enter the information in a **500** tag.

a   **Awards note (NR)**
This is where the actual text of the award is recorded.

> *$aNewbery Medal, 1993*
> *$aBlue Ribbon Award, State Library Association, 1987*
> *$aGrammy Award, Best New Singer, 1994*
> *$aAcademy Award, Best Sound, 1993*

PUNCTUATION

The tag does <u>not</u> end with a mark of punctuation, unless the field ends with an abbreviation, initial/letter, or other data that ends with a mark of punctuation.

590   LOCAL NOTE

REPEATABLE: YES
MANDATORY: NO
RELATES TO: --
AUTHORITY: NO

1st indicator:
The 1st indicator is always blank.

2nd indicator:
The 2nd indicator is always blank.

SUBFIELD CODES

a   **Local note (NR)**   *(Rule 1.7B20 ; 2.7B20)*

EXAMPLE

590    $aLibrary's copy is number 220 out of a numbered series of 500.
590    $aSigned by the author.
590    $aGift of the Ford Foundation.
590    $aLibrary has volumes 1-4.
590    $aLibrary lacking 1974 yearbook.
590    $aPurchased with Chapter IV funds.

LOCATION

Since this information is not part of normal cataloging rules, there is no specific location for it. The library should enter information here in accordance with locally formulated guidelines.

If you are exchanging information with other libraries or contributing records to a union database, you may not want to have the information in this tag recorded in the product since it pertains only to specific situations in your particular library. You should check with the vendor compiling your union information if this tag can be stripped out prior to addition to the database.

Do not add copy/volume information here. Also, do not add acquisition, vendor, or unique identifiers here. They are more correctly entered in the local copy information area of the MARC record, usually the **852** tag.

NOTES

This tag is used for information that is institution specific and would not apply to any other institution or library.

a   **Local note (NR)**
This subfield contains the contents of the local note. It is entered in accordance with the policies of your automation system, local library, or consortium.

> *$aDonated to the library by the author.*
> *$aPurchased with funds donated by Friends of the Library.*
> *$aLibrary lacking volume 5.*
> *$aCannot be checked out to users under the age of 18.*

PUNCTUATION

This tag ends with a period unless another terminal mark of punctuation is present.

6XX SUBJECT ACCESS FIELDS -- GENERAL INFORMATION

The subject tags are possibly the most important tags in the MARC record. This is where you record the subjects of the work, whether topic, a person's name for biographical works, or place names for geographic works. These are called topic headings. It is also used to record form headings, like *Encyclopedias and dictionaries* and *video recordings for the hearing impaired.*

In the past, cataloging rules stated that if you needed more than two subject headings to adequately describe a topic, you should use a broader heading. Many librarians wanted to create more subject headings for their patrons, but were constrained by the time involved in typing and filing cards, as well as the physical limitations of the cards themselves. With automated systems, those limitations are gone, so you should feel free to enter all the subject headings that your patrons will find useful. Note that a record does not have to contain **6XX** tags, but even with the power of keyword searching, they are still invaluable for access. Most searches in a library are done on subjects, and most keyword hits come from the subject tags, so they are still very important.

The **6XX** tags described in this book are:

600	**Subject Added Entry** --	**Personal name**
610	**Subject Added Entry** --	**Corporate name**
611	**Subject Added Entry** --	**Meeting name**
630	**Subject Added Entry** --	**Uniform title**
650	**Subject Added Entry** --	**Topical term**
651	**Subject Added Entry** --	**Geographic name**

When you purchase records from an outside source, you should evaluate them for the number of subject headings that they contain. Many vendors do not include subject headings with their records since they are primarily designed for circulation, not online access. You may wish to discuss this with your jobber in an effort to aid them in improving their cataloging.

6XX

6XX SUBJECT ACCESS TAGS -- OVERVIEW

REPEATABLE: YES
MANDATORY: NO
RELATES TO: --
AUTHORITY: YES

The **6XX** tags contain subject access entries and terms. These tags are similar in format to their counterparts in the **1XX** area (e.g., **600** is for personal names, **610** is for corporate names, etc.) Note that there are no corresponding **1XX** values for the **650** and **651** tags, as topics and places cannot be the main entry of an item or create items, like books and sound recordings.

The values for the first indicator are the same as those for its counterpart in the **1XX** area. Refer to the documentation for that specific tag if you need more detailed information on the application of the first indicator value. The second indicator values are:

2nd indicator

0	**Library of Congress Subject Headings (LCSH)**	
1	**LC Subject Headings for children's literature (LCAC)**	
2	**Medical Subject Headings (MeSH)**	
7	**Source specified in subfield 2**	(Depending on source of records, may use **8** below)
8	**Sears Subject headings**	(Depending on source of records, may use **7** above)

EXAMPLES

600 10	$aNixon, Richard M.$q(Richard Milhouse),$d1913- $xDrama.
610 20	$aAmerican Airlines$xOfficials and employees
600 10	$aKennedy, John F.$q(John Fitzgerald),$d1917-1963$xSpeeches$zNew York.
650 0	$aAutomobiles$zUnited States$xHistory.
650 0	$aVideo recordings for the hearing impaired.
650 0	$aEncyclopedias, Juvenile.
651 8	$aUnited States$xHistory$y1861-1865, Civil War$xPersonnal narratives.$2Sears
651 0	$aCanada$xSocial life and customs$vIndexes.

THE INDICATORS IN DETAIL

0   **Library of Congress Subject Headings (LCSH)**
If you use LCSH for your collection, this would be the value you would use. LCSH, print version is available for purchase from the Library of Congress. Its drawbacks are that it is large (the print version currently is four volumes), costly, and often requires supplemental publications to be used most effectively. Many districts will use this scheme, even in their elementary schools if they have a district-wide centralized processing structure. The print LCSH is kept current by the *Weekly List of Subject Headings* and *Cataloging Service Bulletin (CSB)*. The Library of Congress provides access to their authority files via their web site. It is also available from the bibliographic utilities and on CD-ROM from secondary vendors.

1   **LC Subject Headings for children's literature (LCAC)**
This value is to denote those headings that are part of the Library of Congress's annotated card (AC) program. As a <u>general</u> rule, they duplicate LCSH, although there have been

some modifications made to make them more appropriate for the use of younger library users. Those that are different are printed at the front of the LCSH schedules, and they are also available in print from Libraries Unlimited. If the records are coming from the Library of Congress or another source, records that have **6XX** tags in them with a second indicator value of 1 often will also have a **500, 505,** and/or **520** tags. They can be combined in the same record with LCSH entries, provided each is identified by its relevant indicator value.

2   **Medical Subject Headings (MeSH)**

This heading should only be used if you are using subject headings formulated by the National Library of Medicine (NLM). While most school and small public libraries will not be using them, you may see them on some records that are cataloged by NLM for the Library of Congress. If using CIP data, these headings will usually be in parenthesis.

7   **Source specified in subfield 2**

This is the indicator used by some vendors if they make entries based on *Sears List of Subject Headings*. If they use this value, they <u>must</u> have a **$2** with the word **Sears** in it. This is the form that you should use for all new original cataloging, or when updating records. Note that Sears entries will not appear in records from the Library of Congress.

8   **Sears Subject headings**

This is another value which can be used for *Sears* headings. Jobbers and vendors use this value most often. Many school and smaller public libraries use Sears subject headings. These subject headings are derived from the *Sears List of Subject Headings* by H.W. Wilson & Company and can be obtained from your book supplier. Note that this form should no longer be used for <u>original</u> cataloging.

Note that when you are purchasing records from a vendor (book jobber or retrospective conversion agency), you should specify which subject scheme they should use for your library. Some will allow you to mix multiple forms, while others limit you to only one. While it may seem desirable to mix headings, this can cause difficulties when attempting to maintain consistency in headings via authority control practices.

<u>SUBFIELD CODES</u>

In addition to the subfield codes introduced in the **1XX** tags, there are three that are unique to the **6XX** tags. They can be used in any of the **6XX** tags, <u>do not have to be in alphabetical order</u>, and can be repeated as needed, depending on the subject scheme you are using.

v   **Form subdivision (R)**

This subdivision contains an entry that is a **form** subdivision. These are usually items that describe the physical or intellectual form of the subfield before it. As of this writing, the Library of Congress has only recently started to distribute records using this subfield. Until more records are distributed, or if you are working with older records, you may see many of these terms in **$x**. It <u>MUST</u> be the last subdivision in a subject string if it is used.

x   **General subdivision (R)**

This subfield contains an entry that is used to modify the entry preceding it. These can be assigned as necessary by the cataloger. They are what are generally known as "free-floating subdivisions" in LCSH and "standard subdivisions" for Sears.

The Library of Congress sells a separate publication containing just these and the subject areas that they can be used in. Detailed information on LC's application of these can also be found in the publications <u>Subject Cataloging Manual</u>, or the <u>H</u> series of books, which serve as guidelines to LC's application of LCSH.

Sears records the list of standard subdivisions at the beginning of the book under the heading *Standard subdivisions.*

EXAMPLES

Computer programs
History
Songs and music

Note that each scheme will assign unique subdivisions for selected terms. At other times, they may specifically disallow a particular subdivision, especially if it is not logical, like the phrase *Diseases$xBiography.*

y **Chronological subdivision (R)**
This subfield contains a subject subdivision that represents a period of time. The period of time can be specific dates, such as *1971-1980,* it can be the name of a period, such as *Geometric period,* or it can be a combination of both, like *Civil War, 1861-1865.* Chronological subdivisions usually are not free-floating, rather, they are directly linked to the country that they apply to. You will need to consult the schedules for the subject scheme you are using to determine which periods, if any, are valid for the entry you have created. Hint: If there is a **$x** with the entry "History," there will probably be a **$y** that contains specific dates and/or a time period.

EXAMPLES

$aUnited States$xHistory$y1775-1783.
$aVocal music$zSpain$y18th century.

z **Geographic subdivision (R)**
This subfield contains a geographic subject subdivision. This will usually be the name of a place, such as a city, region, or country. In the past, it was typically the last subfield in the tag, but after further study and consultation with many libraries, LC has revised their policy and has been moving it to directly <u>after</u> the <u>first</u> subfield. Again, you should consult LCSH for specific entries. If you are using it in a **651** tag, you may need to create another **651** tag with the entries in **$a** and **$z** reversed.

EXAMPLES

$aMotion picture industry$zUnited States
$aAutomobiles$zUnited States$xHistory.
$aWorld War, 1939-1945$xCampaigns$zEgypt.
$aSpain$xBorders$zFrance.
$aFrance$xBorders$zSpain.

NOTES

You should capitalize the first word of each subject heading, subfield heading, and proper nouns. Words after a comma are usually capitalized, as are the first letter of the first word of items inside a parenthetical phrase.

Librarians tend to utilize the same subject headings for similar items. This is good in that it provides users a single place to look for related items. It can be a hindrance if the librarian does not use new terms to describe new areas of knowledge and discovery. Also, having many items under broad headings alone can lead to frustration as the user will be forced to look at many records before they find an item that fits their needs.

Authority lists are something that are very useful when formulating subject headings. They are used by some automated systems to validate the correctness of new entries, while some systems will use them to generate cross-references.

EXAMPLES

Cars	*see* Automobiles
Negroes	*see* Blacks
Movies	*see* Motion pictures

PUNCTUATION

As a rule, you should not insert the dashes that you may see in the printed schedules or which you may have seen on cards. They should be system supplied. Consult your vendor for the particulars of your system.

$v, $x, $y, and **$z** generally come at the end of an entry.

Punctuation is the same as for the **1XX** tags. This usually is <u>not</u> system supplied and you will need to enter it. For assistance, consult the corresponding **1XX** tag information earlier in the book.

The tag ends with a terminal mark of punctuation.

600 SUBJECT ADDED ENTRY – PERSONAL NAME

REPEATABLE: YES
MANDATORY: NO
RELATES TO: 100, 245$c
AUTHORITY: YES

EXAMPLES

1st indicator

0	**Forename**	Madonna
1	**Single surname**	Black, Susan
2	**Multiple surname**	Watson-Bishop, Shirley

Note: The Library of Congress had planned to discontinue the use of this value, but has decided to wait until the implementation of their new online system.

3	**Family name**	Carnegie family

2nd indicator

0	**Library of Congress Subject Headings (LCSH)**
1	**LC Subject Headings for children's literature (LCAC)**
2	**Medical Subject Headings (MeSH)**
7	**Source specified in subfield 2** (Depending on source of records, may use **8** below)
8	**Sears Subject headings** (Depending on source of records, may use **7** above)

SUBFIELD CODES

a	**Personal name (NR)**
q	**Fuller form of name (NR)**
b	**Numeration associated with name (R)**
c	**Titles associated with name (R)**
d	**Dates associated with name (NR)**
v	**Form subdivision (R)**
x	**General subdivision (R)**
y	**Chronological subdivision (R)**
z	**Geographic subdivision (R)**

EXAMPLES

600 10	$aAdams, Henry,$d1938-1918$vBiography.
600 00	$aMadonna$vFilmography.
600 30	$aKennedy family.
600 00	$aJohn Paul$bII,$cPope,$d1920- $xQuotations$zPoland.
600 10	$aSeuss,$cDr.
600 30	$aClark family$vFiction.
600 10	$aKing, Martin Luther,$cJr.,$d1929-1968$xHomes and haunts.
600 20	$aSaint-Alary, Eric$xTravels.
600 10	$aFowler, T. M.$q(Thaddeus Mortimer),$d1842-1922 $xSpeeches$zEngland.

Note that the subfield values, except for **$v, $x, $y,** and **$z** are <u>identical</u> to those used in the **100** tag at the beginning of the record. Note that if you make a **600** tag, you will probably also need to enter a value into the *Biography* position in the **008** tag when you are cataloging bound printed material.

Usually, all names are capitalized.

For more information on Subject tags, refer to the **6XX   Subject Access Tags -- General Information.**

LOCATION

The information for this tag is only available upon direct investigation of the item. You will need to skim through it, as well as look at the table of contents, introduction, and index to determine if the book is about a person or persons. Note that all biographies do not have to be books. A videorecording or movie that describes the life of someone could be considered biographical.

FUNCTION

Record the name of a person who is the subject of an item (a biography), even if the person also wrote the book (autobiography). It is possible to have multiple people as the subject of a book, e.g. a biography of Hitler and Mussolini, or if the item is a collective biography, such as a famous NBA star or a criticism of various authors in literature. In some dictionary card catalogs, a separate entry was often not made for the subject of an autobiography, since it would appear under the author. This will not occur in an automated environment, so you will need to make as many **600** tags as necessary.

THE SUBFIELDS IN DETAIL

For information on subfields **$v, $x, $y,** and **$z,** consult the **6XX GENERAL OVERVIEW** at the beginning of the Subject tag area.

a   **Personal name (NR)**
This subfield contains a personal name. The name may be a surname and/or forename; letters, initials, abbreviations, phrases or numbers used in place of a name; or a family name. A parenthetical qualifying term associated with the name is contained in **$c**, and a fuller form of a name added as a qualifier is contained in **$q**. Names are usually entered in the form *Last name, First name* with the first letter in each name being capitalized. This subfield is <u>required</u> when the **600** tag is used.

*$aAudubon, John James,*$d1795-1851$xPoetry.

q   **Fuller form of name (NR)**
This subfield contains a more complete form of part of the name that is in **$a**. It is placed in parenthesis and is usually used if there are abbreviations or initials in the person's name as recorded in **$a**.

$aCummings, E. E.*$q(Edward Estlin),*$d1894-1962$xPhotograph collections.

b   **Numeration associated with name (R)**
This subfield contains a Roman numeral or a Roman numeral and a subsequent part of a forename. It is used <u>only</u> in a forename heading (*first indicator* value of **0**). This means that any name in the form *Last name, First name* <u>cannot</u> have a numeration associated with it.

$aJohn Paul*$bII,*$cPope,$d1920- $xQuotations.

600

c   **Titles associated with name (R)**

This subfield contains titles and other words associated with a name. These include qualifying information such as:

Titles designating rank, office or nobility.

        $a**Louis**$bXIV,**$c***King of France,***$d**1638-1715
        $xBibliography

Terms of address.

        $a**Lucas, Edgar,**$c*Mrs.***$x**Bonsai collections.

Other words or phrases associated with the name.

        $a**Moses,**$c*(Biblical leader)***$v**Diaries.

AACR2 discourages the use of titles except for royalty, nobility, or ranks of office. Thus, you would use terms like *king, queen, prince, pope,* or *marquee,* but not terms like *Dr., Jr., Sr.,* or *Mr.* They allow the use of terms of address or phrases needed to differentiate between two similar names or if the person is commonly known by their title or address, like *Dr. Seuss* or *Martin Luther King, Jr.*

Multiple adjacent titles or words associated with a name are contained in a single **$c**. The subfield is repeated only when words associated with a name are separated by subelements contained in other subfields.

d   **Dates associated with a name (NR)**

This subfield contains the dates of birth, death, or flourishing or any other date used with a name. A qualifier used with the date is also contained in **$d**. Some of these qualifiers and their meanings are:

b.	born	*b. 1965*
d.	died	*d. 1992*
ca.	circa or about	*ca. 1066*
fl.	flourished	*fl. 694-675 B.C.*
cent.	century	*fl. 9th cent. B.C.*
?	unknown or questionable	*1834?-1890*

Dates with a person are most commonly used if there are many people with the same name and some way is needed to differentiate between them.

PUNCTUATION

There is no punctuation before a **$b**

$c is preceded by a comma.

$d is preceded by a comma.

The information in **$q** is placed in parentheses.

$q is <u>usually</u> preceded by the period ending the abbreviation.

If the date of death in **$d** is open (the person is still alive), no punctuation follows the hyphen at the end of **$d**.

$e is preceded by a comma.

$v is preceded by no punctuation.

$x is preceded by no punctuation.

$y is preceded by no punctuation.

$z is preceded by no punctuation.

The **600** tag usually ends in a period. If **$d** is the last subfield, then the **600** tag ends with either a hyphen or a period. If **$q** is the last subfield, then the tag ends with the closing parentheses.

610 SUBJECT ADDED ENTRY -- CORPORATE NAME

REPEATABLE:	YES
MANDATORY:	NO
RELATES TO:	110, 245$c
AUTHORITY:	YES

1st indicator

1	**Jurisdiction name**	United States
2	**Name in direct order**	American Airlines

2nd indicator

0	**Library of Congress Subject Headings (LCSH)**	
1	**LC Subject Headings for children's literature (LCAC)**	
2	**Medical Subject Headings (MeSH)**	
7	**Source specified in subfield 2**	(Depending on source of records, may use **8** below)
8	**Sears Subject headings**	(Depending on source of records, may use **7** above)

1st indicator value **1** will usually be used for governmental entities, such as states, cities, countries, etc. Be careful when entering a corporate entity that has a jurisdictional name in it, but is not a governmental body, such as "United States Fidelity and Guarantee Insurance Company." While it may have the phrase *United States* in it, a governmental body does not own it. By the same token, not every governmental entity will have a jurisdiction name in it. Entries that are **not** part of a governmental agency will have a 1st indicator value of **2**.

SUBFIELD CODES

a	**Corporate name or jurisdiction name as entry element (NR)**	
b	**Subordinate unit (R)**	
t	**Title of a work (NR)**	
v	**Form subdivision (R)**	
x	**General subdivision (R)**	
y	**Chronological subdivision (R)**	
z	**Geographic subdivision (R)**	

EXAMPLES

610 20	$aBarr Films$xHistory$y20th century.
610 10	$aUnited States.$bCongress.$bHouse$vTelephone directories.
610 20	$aArmy Times Publishing Company$xPublishing$zVirginia.
610 10	$aUnited States.$tConstitution.
610 20	$aHarmony Railroad Corporation.$bTariffs Division$xMaps$xHistory.
610 20	$aUnited Nations$xEconomic assistance$vPeriodicals.

LOCATION

There is no specified location for this information. You will need to determine if the item is about a corporate entity based on a direct physical examination of the item.

610

This tag contains a corporate name used as a subject added entry. Subject added entries are assigned to a bibliographic record to provide additional access according to established subject cataloging principles and guidelines. You will use this tag most often when cataloging items that contain the history of a company or a political body. This would include military and regimental histories, as well as histories of particular legislative and judicial bodies such as histories of a state or country or perhaps a history of the US Supreme Court. This tag is also used when cataloging annual reports of companies.

Due to the nature of corporate bodies, you should consult your Authority List or system to verify the form of the name that is correct.

THE SUBFIELDS IN DETAIL

Information on subfields **$v, $x, $y,** and **$z** can be found in the introductory material to the **6XX** tags at the beginning of this chapter.

a   Corporate name or jurisdiction name (NR)

This subfield contains a name of a corporate body or the first entity when subordinate units are present, or a jurisdiction name under which a corporate body, city section, or title of a work are entered or a jurisdiction name that is also an ecclesiastical entity. A parenthetical qualifying term, jurisdiction name, or date is generally not separately subfield coded. This subfield is <u>required</u> when the **610** tag is used.

> *$aJohn F. Kennedy Space Center*$xHistory
>
> *$aUnited States.*$bNational Aeronautics and Space Administration$vTelephone directories

b   Subordinate unit (R)

This subfield contains a name of a subordinate corporate unit, a name of a city section, or a name of a meeting entered under a corporate or a jurisdiction name. You should enter corporate entities in a subordinate structure if there are several units that could be confused or have the same name. By showing the upward hierarchy of the organization, it will aid the user in determining which level of a particular organization the subordinate unit is placed, as well as serving to differentiate between several subordinate units that may have the same name. This is particularly true of governmental agencies.

> $aUnited States.*$bCongress.$bHouse*$xPublishing.
>
> $aConfederate States of America.*$bArmy*$xPersonnel.

t   Title of a work (NR)

This subfield contains a uniform title, a title page title of a work, or a series title used in a name/title field. They are most prominent when cataloging official documents of governmental agencies.

> $aUnited States.$bPresident (1861-1865 : Lincoln).*$tEmancipation Proclamation*$xManuscripts.

PUNCTUATION

Each **$b** is preceded by a period.
$t is preceded by a period.
$v is preceded by no punctuation.
$x is preceded by no punctuation.
$y is preceded by no punctuation.
$z is preceded by no punctuation.
The tag ends with a period or a terminal mark of punctuation.

611 SUBJECT ADDED ENTRY -- MEETING NAME

REPEATABLE: YES
MANDATORY: NO
RELATES TO: 111, 245$c
AUTHORITY: YES

INDICATOR CODES

1st indicator

1 **Jurisdiction name** Used only for governmental entities.
2 **Name in direct order** Use this value for most entries.

2nd indicator

0 **Library of Congress Subject Headings (LCSH)**
1 **LC Subject Headings for children's literature (LCAC)**
2 **Medical Subject Headings (MeSH)**
7 **Source specified in subfield 2** (Depending on source of records, may use **8** below)
8 **Sears Subject headings** (Depending on source of records, may use **7** above)

SUBFIELD CODES

a **Meeting name or jurisdiction name as entry element (NR)**
n **Number of part/section/meeting (R)**
d **Date of meeting (NR)**
c **Location of meeting (NR)**
v **Form subdivision (R)**
x **General subdivision (R)**
y **Chronological subdivision (R)**
z **Geographic subdivision (R)**

EXAMPLES

611 20 **$a**Lewis and Clark Expedition**$d**(1804-1806)**$x**Centennial celebrations, etc.
611 20 **$a**Olympic Games**$n**(25th :**$d**1996 :**$c**Atlanta, Ga.)**$x**Finance.
611 20 **$a**World Series (Baseball)**$x**History.
611 20 **$a**Olympic Games**$n**(23rd :**$d**1984 :**$c**Los Angeles, Calif.)**$v**Periodicals.
611 20 **$a**Vatican Council**$n**(1st :**$d**1869-1870)**$v**Reports.

LOCATION

There is no specified location to find this information. You will need to physically inspect the item to determine which subject headings are appropriate for the item.

This field contains a meeting, conference, expedition, or Olympic name used as a subject added entry.

611

For Olympic games, only the names of <u>specific</u> games should be entered here. Olympic games or Olympic in general should be entered in a **650** tag. Words that indicate you might have a **611** tag include *Congress on, Conference on, Expedition, Expo, Olympic games.*

For specific examples, consult your Name Authority reference source or The Library of Congress database. Because of their nature, you should maintain an authority list for these items, either utilizing the Authority Control module in your automation system, if so equipped; in some type of commercial database software; or in a manual card file.

THE SUBFIELDS IN DETAIL

For information on subfields **$v, $x, $y,** and **$z,** please refer to the introductory material on the **6XX General Overview** tags at the beginning of this chapter.

a   **Meeting name or jurisdiction name as entry element (NR)**
This subfield contains a name of a meeting or a jurisdiction name under which a meeting is entered. Parenthetical qualifying information is not separately subfield coded. Meeting names are not entered under jurisdiction names in AACR2 formulated **111** fields.

> *$aPan-American Exposition*$d(1901 :$cBuffalo, N.Y.)$xFinances.

n   **Number of part/section/meeting (R)**
This subfield contains the number of a meeting.

> $aVatican Council*$n(1st :*$d1869-1870)$xInfluence.

d   **Date of meeting (NR)**
This subfield contains the date a meeting or conference was held. A date added parenthetically to a meeting name to distinguish between identical names is not separately subfield coded.

> $aLouisiana Cancer Conference$n(2nd :*$d1958 :*$cNew Orleans, La.)
> $vReports.

c   **Location of meeting (NR)**
This subfield contains a place name or a name of an institution where a meeting was held. You should follow the same format for entering names here as you would for any other geographic location.

> $aConference on Cancer Public Education$d(1973 :*$cDulles Airport)*
> $vPeriodicals.

PUNCTUATION

$n is preceded by no punctuation.
$d is preceded by no punctuation unless it is preceded by **$n**, then it is preceded by a colon.
$c is preceded by a colon.
$n, $d, $c are enclosed in one set of parenthesis, which are expanded to include all of the subfields.
$v is preceded by no punctuation.
$x is preceded by no punctuation.
$x is preceded by no punctuation.
$z is preceded by no punctuation.
The tag ends with a period or a terminal mark of punctuation.

630   SUBJECT ADDED ENTRY -- UNIFORM TITLE

REPEATABLE:	YES
MANDATORY:	NO
RELATES TO:	130, 245$a, 630, 740
AUTHORITY:	YES

INDICATOR CODES

1st indicator

0-9   Nonfiling characters

As a rule, the Library of Congress drops all initial articles before entry, so you will usually have the value of zero in this position.

2nd indicator

0	**Library of Congress Subject Headings (LCSH)**	
1	**LC Subject Headings for children's literature (LCAC)**	
2	**Medical Subject Headings (MeSH)**	
7	**Source specified in subfield 2**	(Depending on source of records, may use **8** below)
8	**Sears Subject headings**	(Depending on source of records, may use **7** above)

SUBFIELD CODES

a	**Uniform title (NR)**
n	**Number of part/section of a work (R)**
p	**Name of part/section of a work (R)**
l	**Language of a work (NR)**
k	**Form subheading (R)**
s	**Version (NR)**
f	**Date of a work (NR)**
v	**Form subdivision (R)**
x	**General subdivision (R)**
y	**Chronological subdivision (R)**
z	**Geographic subdivision (R)**

EXAMPLES

630 00	$aBible.$lEnglish.$sAuthorized.$kSelections.$f1989 $xNumerical division.
630 00	$aBible.$pO.T.$pMalachi.$lEnglish.$sNew International.
630 00	$aArabian nights$vJuvenile sound recordings.
630 00	$aUkranian weekly$xIndexes$vPeriodicals.
630 00	$aUkranian weekly$xIndex$vPeriodicals.
630 00	$aSilent running (Motion picture)

LOCATION

Because of their nature, there is no specified location for this information. You will need to physically examine the item, along with consulting your title authority source.

630

NOTES

This tag is used only when the work is <u>about</u> the uniform title, not an adaptation or modification of it. This means that entries like *Bible stories* or titles used in phrase subject headings should be entered in a **650**, not a **630**. *USMARC Bibliographic 630 - p. 2 ; H1188 - p. 1.*

Every **630** must contain a **$a**. The **630** is similar in layout and coding to the **130** tag. You will use this tag most often when working on commentaries for the bible, evaluations of classical literature, or works that have been translated into numerous languages.

It is strongly recommended that you maintain an authority file for uniform titles with their attendant cross-references. This will enable your searchers to consistently find not only the main work, but also works that comment or discus that work.

THE SUBFIELDS IN DETAIL

Because of their nature, subfields **$v, $x, $y,** and **$z** are not covered here. For more information on these subfields, refer to the **6XX -- General Overview** at the beginning of this chapter.

a **Uniform title (NR)**
This is where the actual uniform title used as the main entry is entered. Parenthetical information added to make a title distinctive is not separately subfield coded except for treaties.

> *$aGenesis (Anglo-Saxon poem)$v*Translations.

n **Number of part/section of a work (R)**
This subfield contains a *number* designation for a part/section of a work used in a uniform title field. "Numbering" is defined as an indication of sequencing in any form. **$n** is often followed by **$p**.

> $aArabian nights.*$nBooks 1-4$v*Dictionaries.

p **Name of part/section of a work (R)**
This subfield contains a *name* designation of a part/section of a work used in a uniform title field. *$p* will often follow **$n**.

> $aBible.*$pO.T.$x*Natural history
> $aBible.*$pN.T.$p*Revelation$vCommentaries.

l **Language of a work (NR)**
This subfield contains the name of the language(s) used in a uniform title.

> $bBible.$pO.T.*$lEnglish$x*History, criticism, etc.

k **Form subheading (R)**
This subfield contains a form subheading used in a uniform title field. Some typical form subheadings are *Manuscript, Selections,* and *Protocols.*

> $aMother Goose.*$k*Selections*$vDictionaries.*

s   **Version**

This subfield contains version, edition, etc., information used in a uniform title field.

     $aBible.$lEnglish.*$sAuthorized*$xAntiquities.

f   **Date of a work (NR)**

This subfield contains the date of publication used in a uniform title field.

     $aBible.$lEnglish.$sRevised Standard.*$f1959*$xGeography.

PUNCTUATION

$n is preceded by a period.

$p is preceded by a comma if it follows a **$n**, otherwise it is preceded by a period.

$l is preceded by a period.

$k is preceded by a period.

$s is preceded by a period.

$f is preceded by a period.

$v is preceded by no punctuation.

$x is preceded by no punctuation.

$y is preceded by no punctuation.

$z is preceded by no punctuation.

If any subfield has parenthesis, the punctuation goes **outside** the parenthesis.

The tag ends with a period or a terminal mark of punctuation.

650 SUBJECT ADDED ENTRY - TOPICAL TERM

REPEATABLE: YES
MANDATORY: NO
RELATES TO: --
AUTHORITY: YES

1st indicator

blank   **No information available** (Use this value for most entries.)
0   **No level specified**
1   **Primary subject**
2   **Secondary subject**
        (Note that it is Library of Congress policy to always leave this value blank. You may wish to use the other values if you are attempting to create a hierarchy of subject values or if your system is able to manipulate the headings to create new subject strings.)

2nd indicator

0   **Library of Congress Subject Headings (LCSH)**
1   **Library of Congress Subject Headings for children's literature (LCAC)**
2   **Medical Subject Headings (MeSH)**
7   **Source specified in subfield 2**   (Depending on source of records, may use **8** below)
8   **Sears Subject headings**   (Depending on source of records, may use **7** above)

SUBFIELD CODES

a   **Topical term or geographic name used as entry element (NR)**
v   **Form subdivision (R)**
x   **General subdivision (R)**
y   **Chronological subdivision (R)**
z   **Geographic subdivision (R)**

EXAMPLES

650 0 $aAmish.
650 0 $aPiano music$zSpain$y19th century.
650 0 $aNational songs (Instrumental settings)
650 0 $aZoology$zCanada$vJuvenile films.
650 0 $aBible stories, English.
650 0 $aArt$vCatalogs.
650 0 $aMusic$y500-1400.
650 0 $aWorld War, 1939-1945$xCampaigns$zJapan.
650 0 $aReal property$zMinnesota$zHennepin County$vMaps.
650 0 $aGettysburg (Pa.), Battle of, 1863$vPictorial works.
650 0 $aArdennes, Battle of the, 1944-1945.
650 0 $aVideo recordings for the hearing impaired.

LOCATION

Because of their nature, you will need to physically inspect and review the publication to determine which subject headings are applicable for the work. Suggested places to look for ideas would be the table of contents, introduction, summaries, and dustjackets.

NOTES

Topical headings are what users are usually referring to when they think of subjects. These cover such concepts as concrete physical items, philosophical concepts, social groups, social issues, intellectual ideas, and historical time periods not associated with a particular country or region.

The **650** are the most often used subject area for bibliographic records. Here is where you will enter concepts, topics, and ideas covered in the item.

Topical subject added entries might consist of general subject terms including names of events or objects. Subject added entries are assigned to a bibliographic record to provide access according to generally accepted lists (e.g., *Library of Congress Subject Headings (LCSH), Sears List of Subject Headings.* A title (e.g., Bible and atheism), a geographic name (e.g., Iran in the Koran), or the name of a corporate body (e.g., Catholic Church in motion pictures) used in a phrase subject heading are also recorded in field **650**.

Traditional cataloging guidelines state that if you need more than three subject headings to accurately describe an item, you should choose a broader subject heading. While appropriate for card environments, this logic does not hold for automated environments. You should feel free to create as many subject headings as your users will require to gain access to the material. Feel free to add more subject headings to MARC records that you purchase from your jobbers or download off union databases. You are in the best position to know what your patrons want; feel free to enter those subject headings provided they conform to the subject authority scheme that you use in your library (*Sears* or *LC*).

It is important to differentiate between the two different types of subject headings. The first is *topic* subject headings. These are what most people think about when they think of subject headings. This would include terms like *Computers, Substance abuse, Automobiles,* and *Philosophy.* They are what the item is about, or its *topic.*

The second types of subject headings are known as *form* headings. They describe what physical form or attributes the item has. For example, the subject heading *Encyclopedias and dictionaries* doesn't mean that the item is about encyclopedias and dictionaries, instead it means that the item is an encyclopedia or dictionary. Another example of a form heading would be *Music videos.* The two types can be used in a single bibliographic record, but are usually contained in separate **650** tags.

Note that in the standard subdivisions, form and topical subdivisions used to be recorded in **$x**. With Format Integration, the **form** subdivisions have been moved to **$v** with the **general** subdivisions remaining in **$x**.

SUBFIELD CODES IN DETAIL

For more information on subfields **$v, $x, $y,** and **$z**, consult the information in the **6XX General Overview** area at the beginning of this chapter.

a   **Topical term or geographic name used as entry element (NR)**

650

This subfield contains a topical subject or a geographic name used as an entry element for a topical term. Parenthetical qualifying information associated with the term is not separately subfield coded. This subfield must be entered when using the **650** tag.

If you are converting your library from *Sears List of Subject Headings* to *Library of Congress Subject Headings*, you may wish to consult Joanna Fountain's book that is available from Libraries Unlimited.

> 650 0   *$aAmish.*
> 650 0   *$aBible Stories.*
> 650 8   *$aMiddle ages.*

v   **Form subdivision (R)**
> $aScuba diving*$vPeriodicals.*
> $aVomiting$xTreatment*$vHandbooks, manuals, etc.*

x   **General subdivision (R)**
> $aDentistry*$xHistory.*
> $aNumismatics*$xCollectors and collecting.*

y   **Chronological subdivision (R)**
> $aArt*$y500-1400.*
> $aReal property*$y1981-1990.*

z   **Geographic subdivision (R)**
> $aForeign relations*$zUnited States$zCanada.*
> $aWorld War, 1939-1945$xCampaigns*$zFrance.*

PUNCTUATION

There is no punctuation between subfields in the **650** tag.
The tag ends with a period unless another terminal mark of punctuation is present.

651 SUBJECT ADDED ENTRY - GEOGRAPHIC NAME

REPEATABLE: YES
MANDATORY: NO
RELATES TO: --
AUTHORITY: YES

1st indicator

The 1st indicator is always blank.

2nd indicator

0	**Library of Congress Subject Headings (LCSH)**
1	**LC Subject Headings for children's literature (LCAC)**
2	**Medical Subject Headings (MeSH)**
7	**Source specified in subfield 2** (Depending on source of records, may use **8** below)
8	**Sears Subject headings** (Depending on source of records, may use **7** above)

SUBFIELD CODES

a	**Geographic name**	**(NR)**
v	**Form subdivision**	**(R)**
x	**General subdivision**	**(R)**
y	**Chronological subdivision**	**(R)**
z	**Geographic subdivision**	**(R)**

EXAMPLES

651	0	$aKing Ranch (Tex.)
651	0	$aHusum-Schwesing (Germany : Concentration camp)
651	0	$aClear Lake (Iowa : Lake)
651	0	$aUruguay$xHistory$yGreat War, 1843-1852.
651	0	$aGreece$xHistory$yGeometric period, ca. 900-700 B.C.
651	0	$aUnited States$xForeign relations$zCanada.
651	0	$aCanada$xForeign relations$zUnited States.
651	0	$aAix-en-Provence (France)$xSocial life and customs$yEarly works to 1800.
651	0	$aUnited States$xHistory$yCivil War, 1861-1865$xPersonnal narratives.
651	0	$aSalem (Mass.)$vFiction.

LOCATION

Because of their nature, you will need to physically examine the item to determine if there are any geographical subject headings that should be assigned. Geographical subject headings appear most often in items on history, geography, and social issues confined to a particular place.

651

These subject headings will allow your patrons to access items that are about a particular place on the map, or in outer space. You should use them liberally. Note that some entries that cover shared items or topics between two countries, such as borders or foreign relations, will require two subject headings, inverted from each other, to provide proper access to the item.

This field contains a geographic name used as a subject added entry. This tag differs from the entries in the **610** in that these entries describe a **geographic** location or place, as opposed to a governmental or corporate entity. It is possible for a record to have both **610** and **651** entries that have an identical place in the **$a**. Generally, a **651** is used to describe a place, while a **610** would be used to identify a group of people who inhabit that place. A good rule of thumb to use is "if you can point to it on a map, it probably is a **651** tag," since groups of people cannot be located on a map. If there is a subordinate unit listed, like a committee or group below the entry in **$a**, then it is a **610,** not a **651** tag.

SUBFIELD CODES IN DETAIL

For more information on subfields **$v, $x, $y,** and **$z**, consult the information in the **6XX General Overview** area at the beginning of this chapter.

a **Geographic name (NR)**
   This subfield contains a geographic name. Parenthetical qualifying information is not separately subfield coded. This subfield must be used if you are entering information for this tag.

   > *$aLos Angeles (Calif.)*
   > *$aChicago (Ill.)*

v **Form subdivision (R)**
   $aRussia$xHistory*$vMaps.*
   $aChelsea (London, England)*$vIndexes.*

x **General subdivision (R)**
   $aUnited States*$xHistory.*
   $aCanada*$xPrime ministers$xStaff.*

y **Chronological subdivision (R)**
   $aGreece$xHistory*$yGeometric period, ca. 900-700 B.C.*
   $aGreat Britain$xHistory*$y0-1066.*

z **Geographic subdivision (R)**
   $aUnited States$xForeign Relations*$zCanada.*
   $aCanada$xBoundaries*$zUnited States.*

PUNCTUATION

The tag ends with a period unless a terminal mark of punctuation is present.
There is no punctuation between subfields **$v, $x, $y,** and **$z**.

7XX ADDED ENTRY TABS - GENERAL INFORMATION

Fields **700-740** contain added entries that provide additional access to a bibliographic record for names and/or titles having various relationships to a work. Added entries are made for persons, corporate bodies, and meetings having some form of responsibility for the creation of the work, including intellectual and publishing responsibilities. Field **740** contains titles for the work being cataloged. Added entries are assigned to records for persons, corporate bodies, meetings, and titles that are not given through subject or series entries. They are particularly useful when cataloging audio-visual materials as they can be used to provide direct access to producers, directors, actors, narrators, and the companies which created, sold and/or distributed the item.

Like the **6XX** tags, the structure for the **7XX** tags is based on the **1XX** tags.

INFORMATION

AACR2 only allows one name to be the main entry. If you recall some of the information from the **1XX** tags, it was discussed that multiple names or people who have non-authorship functions, such as editors, compilers, and illustrators should not be entered in the **1XX**, rather they should be entered in the **7XX** tags. Your automation system should search the **700, 710,** and **711** tags when doing author searches. It should search the **730** and **740** tags when doing title searches. You may wish to consult your particular vendor for more information.

The structure of the **7XX** tags is the same as the **1XX** tags, that is, the **700** contains a personal name, a **710** contains a corporate name, and a **711** contains a conference or meeting name. The **730** is similar in structure to the **130** tag and will be used most frequently when cataloging novelizations or adaptations of television programs and motion pictures. The **740** tag is designed to provide variant access to the **245** tag. You should use it when it would be possible to look for a title under variant forms.

The same authority guidelines that you utilize for the **1XX** tags should be utilized here.

While AACR2 does give us some guidance for added entries, you should feel free to enter those names and/or titles that you feel your users will try to access. Remember, it is not possible to have too much access.

The **7XX** tags described in the this book are:

700	**Added Entry - Personal Name**
710	**Added Entry - Corporate Name**
711	**Added Entry - Meeting Name**
730	**Added Entry - Uniform Title**
740	**Added Entry - Uncontrolled Related/Analytical Title**

2ND INDICATOR VALUES

The second indicator position was redefined as part of Format Integration. The value is left blank to indicate that the added entry is not for an analytic or when no information is provided whether the added entry is for an analytic. The latter will be the value you will use most often.

The value of **2** is used to indicate that the item in hand contains the word that is represented by the added entry. This would be the value you would use if you were to trace the authors of individual chapters or stories for an item.

The first indicator value will be determined by the type of name entered and which tag is being entered. For specific information, refer to the documentation for the particular **7XX** tag. It is usually the same as the corresponding **1XX** first indicator value.

700 ADDED ENTRY - PERSONAL NAME

REPEATABLE:	YES
MANDATORY:	NO
RELATES TO:	245$c
AUTHORITY:	YES

<u>1st indicator</u>

EXAMPLES

0 Forename   **Cher**

1 Single surname   **Walter, Johannes**

2 Multiple surname   **Saint-Alary, Eric**

At one time, the Library of Congress was going to eliminate this value and code all surnames with the value of 1, but since they are unable to globally change the information in their database, they have decided to retain the separate values of 1 and 2.

3 Family name   **Kennedy family**

These are the same as the 1st indicator in the **100** tag.

2nd indicator

blank No information provided

(Generally, this is the value you will use, particularly for added authors, editors, compilers, or illustrators.)

2 **Analytical entry**

SUBFIELD CODES

a	**Personal name (NR)**
q	**Fuller form of name (NR)**
b	**Numeration (R)**
c	**Titles and other words associated with name (R)**
d	**Dates associated with a name (NR)**
e	**Relator term (R)**
t	**Title of a work (NR)**

EXAMPLES

700 1 $aJung, C. G.$q(Carl Gustav),$d1875-1961.

700 1 $aWalter, Johannes,$eill.

700 1 $aBizet, Georges,$d1869-1951.$tCarmen.$kSelections.$f1983.

LOCATION

This information will usually be located on the chief source of information for the item. The tag is used to transcribe the name of any joint contributors to the publication. You must obtain this information from the chief source of information for the item.

AACR2 states that you should enter the person's name that appears first or most prominently on the chief source of information in the **100** tag. If there are more than three people, then do not enter anything in the **100** and enter the most prominent name listed on the chief source in the **700** tag. Generally, if a person's name does not appear on the chief source of information, you should not trace it in the record.

For *sound recordings*, you can enter the names of individual performers on the recording, or accompanying musicians of significance. For *videorecordings*, you can enter the names of the producers, directors, and actors if you feel they are important. What is most important is that you are consistent in your choice of entries.

NOTES

This field contains a personal name used as an added entry. This tag is used to record the personal names of people who are editors, compilers, transcribers, joint authors, illustrators, actors, narrators, producers, and directors, as well as the individual names of people in a musical group.

Examples include names like joint authors, since only one can be recorded in the **100** tag. This area would also be used to record editors and compilers, since they are not recorded in the **1XX** tags. Illustrators are also usually recorded here. Note that if an item has more than three people responsible for the creation of it, only the first one should be entered here. While AACR2 gives fairly rigid guidelines for this tag, you should feel free to trace any person whom you think your patrons might find useful. Of course, you should construct the names in the form that you have established in your authority file.

These names should be searchable in your system when doing an author search. Check with the vendor of your particular system for their specific guidelines and limitations.

THE SUBFIELDS IN DETAIL

a   **Personal name (NR)**   *(Rules 21.29 and 21.30 and Rule 22)*
This subfield contains a personal name. The name may be a surname and/or forename; letters, initials, abbreviations, phrases or numbers used in place of a name; or a family name. A parenthetical qualifying term associated with the name is contained in **$c**, and a fuller form of a name added as a qualifier is contained in **$q**. Names are usually entered in the form Last name, First name with the first letter in each name being capitalized. This subfield is required when the **700** tag is used.

> *$aCanby, Henry Seidel,$d1878-1961.*
> *$aFrost, Robert,$d1874-1963.*

q   **Fuller form of name (NR)**   *(Rule 22.18)*
This subfield contains a more complete form of part of the name that is in **$a**. It is placed in parenthesis and is usually used if there are abbreviations or initials in the person's name as recorded in **$a**.

> $aEliot, T. S.*$q(Thomas Sterns),*$d1888-1965.
> $aPritchett, V. S.*$q(Victor Sawdon),*$d1900-

b   **Numeration (R)**   *(Rule 22.16A)*
This subfield contains a roman numeral or a roman numeral and a subsequent part of a forename. It is used only in a forename heading (first indicator value of **0**). This means that any name in the form Last name, First name cannot have a numeration associated with it.

> $aPius*$bXII,*$cPope,$d1876-1958.
> $aWilliam*$bII*$cGerman Emperor,$d1859-1941.

c

Titles and other words associated with a name (R)

(Begin at Rule 22.6)

This subfield contains titles and other words associated with a name. These include qualifying information such as:

> Titles designating rank, office or nobility.
> $aLouis$bXIV,$cKing of France,$d1638-1715

> Terms of address.
> $aLucas, Edgar,$cMrs.

> Other words or phrases associated with the name.
> $aMoses,$c(Biblical leader)

AACR2 discourages the use of titles except for royalty, nobility, or ranks of office. Thus, you would use terms like king, queen, prince, pope, or marquee, but not terms like Dr., Jr., Sr., or Mr. They allow the use of terms of address or phrases needed to differentiate between two similar names or if the person is commonly known by their title or address, like Dr. Seuss or Martin Luther King, Jr.

Multiple adjacent titles or words associated names are contained in a single **$c**. The subfield is repeated only when words associated with a name are separated by subelements contained in other subfields.

d

Dates associated with a name (NR)   *(Rule 22.17)*

This subfield contains the dates of birth, death, flourishing or any other date used with a name. A qualifier used with the date is also contained in **$d**. Some of these qualifiers and their meanings are:

b.	born	b. 1965
d.	died	d. 1992
ca.	circa or about	ca. 1066
fl.	flourished	fl. 694-675 B.C.
cent.	century	fl. 9th cent. B.C.
?	unknown or questionable	1834?-1890

Dates with a person are most commonly used if there are many people with the same name and some way is needed to differentiate between them.

e

Relator term (R)   *(Rule 21.30D)*

This area is used to contain a relator term. A relator term is used to describe what function the name in the tag had to the entire work. A list of approved relators is available from the Library of Congress

The most commonly used relators in the **700** tag are *ill.* for *illustrator, ed.* for *editor, jt. auth.* for *joint author, comp.* for *compiler, jt. comp.* for *joint compiler* and *jt. ed.* for *joint editor.* Note that according to AACR2 you should not trace the translators of works. To simplify the screen displays on your catalog, you may choose to omit the relator terms. This will result in a particular name being listed only once, with many "hits" shown for it. On the other hand, this means that users will need to look at all the entries under that person's name to determine the role they played in each one. You will need to make the decision as to what is more important and useful to your users.

> $aAliki,$eill.
> $aAsimov, Isaac,$d1920- $ejt. auth.

Illustrators and selectors of illustrations are generally considered to be the most significant people involved in books, particularly in school libraries. As a rule, you will want to trace them whenever possible. You may choose to use the relator *ill.* only for the illustrators but no other relators. Sometimes it will be difficult to determine if a person should be traced or not. A good rule of thumb is, if you find yourself agonizing over the decision to trace or not, then you should err on the side of access and trace the name. Remember that the computer is better able to store and access these tracings than you were in a card environment. You need to make certain that you are not letting the old notion of having to file cards hinder your making access points for your users.

People who make the maps for a book and are not the main entry should be put in a **700** with a **$e** for *ill.*

Generally, illustrators are not included in lists of prominent people. They are often considered secondary and should usually be traced regardless. On the other hand, you may wish to never trace the illustrators. You will need to make these decisions on your own for your particular library. School libraries may wish to trace all illustrators, due to the unique nature of their collection. Public libraries may wish to trace illustrators only for juvenile books. You should always trace illustrators for art books, oversize books, and books where the illustrations are fundamentally important to the text. Remember that it's not as important if you trace someone, but that you are consistent in your policy. You will need to determine this for your library, and then consistently apply it. You may wish to record tracing information in your authority file in a non-public note (if you have an online system) so that you and your staff can accurately apply the rules and policies in effect in your library.

t   **Title of a work (NR)**   *(Rule 25.3A)*

This subfield contains a uniform title. It is often found in AV records when an author's work has been adapted for a movie or motion picture and the name of the movie bears a different name than the author's original work. The name of the original work would be entered in this subfield following the author's name.

> $aDahl, Roald.$tCharlie and the chocolate factory.
> This would be the entry for the movie *Willie Wonka and the chocolate factory.*

> $aDick, Philip K.$tDo androids dream of electric sheep?
> This would be the entry for the movie *Blade runner.*

> $aShakespeare, William,$d1564-1616.$tRomeo and Juliet.
> This would be the entry for the movie or the Broadway play *West Side story.*

700

<u>PUNCTUATION</u>

There is no punctuation before a **$b**.

$c is preceded by a comma.

$d is preceded by a comma.

The information in **$q** is placed in parentheses.

$q is usually preceded by the period ending the abbreviation.

If the date of death in **$d** is open (the person is still alive), no punctuation follows the hyphen at the end of **$d**.

$e is preceded by a comma.

<u>PUNCTUATION NOTE</u>

When creating a **700** tag with a **$d** and **$t**, apply the following guidelines:

If **$d** is an open date (1961-), leave a space after the dash, but do not place a period before **$t**.

If **$d** has a closing date (1961-1989), then there should be a period before **$t**.

If **$d** is the last subfield in the tag and it has an open date, the dash is the terminal mark of punctuation. If the date is closed, then place a period after the last date.

710 ADDED ENTRY - CORPORATE NAME

REPEATABLE: YES
MANDATORY: NO
RELATES TO: 245$c
AUTHORITY: YES

1st indicator

1	Jurisdiction name	United States
2	Name in direct order	American Airlines

These are the same as the 1st indicator in the **110** tag.

2nd indicator

blank   **No information provided** (Generally, this is the value you will use)
            Analytical information

Refer to the 2nd indicator table in the documentation for **7XX** Tags for the appropriate values.

SUBFIELD CODES

a   **Corporate name or jurisdiction name as entry element (NR)**
b   **Subordinate unit (R)**
e   **Relator term (R)**
t   **Title of a work (NR)**

EXAMPLES

710 2 $aWalt Disney Company,$eill.
720 2 $aWeston Woods, Inc.
710 1 $aUnited States.$aNational Aeronautics and Space Adminstration.
710 2 $aArmy Times Publishing Company,$ejt. ed.
710 1 $aUnited States.$bNational Park Service,$eill.
710 2 $aImage Entertainment (Firm)

LOCATION

This information will usually be located on the chief source of information, or it may be on some accompanying material, including the packaging container or box that the item came in.

NOTES

If you are cataloging corporate histories that are written by the company, or promotional material written and distributed by a company, you will put the company's name here. For books, do not enter the name of a publisher or distributor in this field. You should enter the names of production and distribution companies for visual items here, as well as the name of companies that create and distribute computer software. For *sound recordings*, you should not enter the name of the record label here.

$t is used when you have a work uses the work in **$t** as the foundation or starting point for its own work. It is often used when doing commentaries or adaptations of the original work. Note that Bibles do not apply to this, as they are entered in the **730** tag.

710

<u>THE SUBFIELDS IN DETAIL</u>

a   **Corporate name or jurisdiction name as entry element (NR)**
(Begin at Rule 24.1)

This subfield contains a name of a corporate body or the first entity when subordinate units are present, or a jurisdiction name under which a corporate body, city section, or title of a work is entered or a jurisdiction name that is also an ecclesiastical entity. A parenthetical qualifying term, jurisdiction name, or date is generally not separately subfield coded. This subfield is required when the **710** tag is used.

> *$aAssociated Press.*
> *$aGreen Bay Packers (Football team)*

b   **Subordinate unit (R)**   *(Begin at Rule 24.12)*

This subfield contains a name of a subordinate corporate unit, a name of a city section, or a name of a meeting entered under a corporate or a jurisdiction name. You should enter corporate entities in a subordinate structure if there are several units that could be confused or have the same name. By showing the upward hierarchy of the organization, it will aid the user in determining which level of a particular organization the subordinate unit is placed, as well as serving to differentiate between several subordinate units that may have the same name. This is particularly true of governmental agencies.

> $aUnited States.*$bCongress.*
> $aConsolidated Railroad Corporation.*$bRate and fares division.*

e   **Relator term (R)**   *(Rule 21.30D)*

This area is used to contain a relator term. A relator term is used to describe what function the name in the tag had to the entire work. A list of approved relators is available from the Library of Congress

> $aNational Geographic Society,*$e*ill.
> $aUnited States.$bBureau of Alcohol, Tobacco and firearms,*$e*jt. auth.

The most commonly used relators in the **710** tag *ill.* for *illustrator, ed.* for *editor, jt. auth.* for *joint author, comp.* for *compiler*, and *jt. comp.* for *joint compiler*. Note that according to AACR2 you should not trace the translators of works. To simplify the screen displays on your catalog, you may choose to omit the relator terms. This will result in a particular name being listed only once, with many "hits" shown for it. On the other hand, this means that users will need to look at all the entries under that corporation's name to determine the role they played in each one. You will need to make the decision as to that is more important and useful to your users.

 Illustrators and selectors of illustrations are generally considered to be the most significant entities involved in books, particularly in school libraries. As a rule, you will want to trace them whenever possible. You may choose to use the relator lll. only for the illustrators but no other relators. Sometimes it will be difficult to determine if a company should be traced or not. A good rule of thumb is, if you find yourself agonizing over the decision to trace or not, then you should err on the side of access and trace the name. Remember that the computer is better able to store and access these tracings than you were in a card environment. You need to make certain that you are not letting the old notion of having to file cards hinder your making access points for your users.

Institutions that make the maps for a book and are not the main entry should be put in a **710** with a **$e** for ill.

t   **Title of a work (NR)**   *(Begin at Rule 25)*

This subfield contains a uniform title, a title page title of a work, or a series title used in a name/title field. They are most prominent when cataloging official documents of governmental agencies.

> **$a**United States.**$b**President (1861-1856 : Lincoln).*$tEmancipation Proclamation.*

PUNCTUATION

Each **$b** is preceded by a period.
$e is preceded by a comma.
$t is preceded by a period.
The tag ends with a period or a terminal mark of punctuation.

711 ADDED ENTRY - MEETING NAME

REPEATABLE:	YES
MANDATORY:	NO
RELATES TO:	245$c
AUTHORITY:	YES

1st indicator

1	**Jurisdiction name**	Use when working with political jurisdictions.
2	**Name in direct order**	Use this value for most entries.

These are the same as the 1st indicator in the **111** tag.

2nd indicator

blank	**No information provided**	(Generally, this is the value you will use)
2	**Analytical entry**	

This field contains a meeting or conference name used as an added entry. Added entries are assigned according to various cataloging rules to give access to the bibliographic record from meeting or conference name headings that may not be more appropriately assigned as a **611** tag.

SUBFIELD CODES

a   **Meeting name or jurisdiction name as entry element (NR)**
n   **Number of part/section/meeting (R)**
d   **Date of meeting (NR)**
c   **Location of meeting (NR)**
e   **Subordinate unit (R)**

EXAMPLES

710 2 $aVan Cliburn International Piano Competition.
710 2 $aPan American Games$n(6th :$d1971 :$cCali, Columbia)
710 2 $aUnited Nations Conference on the Law of the Seas$n(1st :$d1958 :$cGeneva, Switzerland)

Usually, the **711** will not stand-alone. Rather, it will often also have an editor or committee named in either a **700** or **710** tag as the people who compiled or edited the proceedings.

LOCATION

This information will usually be located on the chief source of information. The tag is used to transcribe the name of any joint contributors to the publication.

AACR2 states that you should enter the author's name that appears first or most prominently on the chief source of information in the **1XX** tag. If there are more than three authors, then do not enter anything in the **1XX** and enter the first name listed on the title page in the **700** tag. Generally, if an author's name does not appear on the title page, you should not trace them in the record.

NOTES

This tag is usually used if you are entering a record for an item that contains conference proceedings, minutes, or reports of a particular meeting or session of a body. Specific Olympic games are recorded here (see the **111** tag for an example of the formulation) as are national association conferences (such as ALA) and religious body meetings.

<u>THE SUBFIELDS IN DETAIL</u>

a   **Meeting name or jurisdiction name as entry element (NR)**

(Begin at Rule 24 ; Check 24.3F1 and 24.7)

Record here the name of the meeting or conference. You may be able to obtain this information from the item itself. You should verify this information with your authority file. If there is no entry, or you do not maintain an authority file, then construct it to be consistent with other meetings or conferences by this particular organization. If a jurisdiction name, make certain it is consistent with previous entries, checking to see that it is consistent with any corporate entries of the particular jurisdiction.

$a*Pan-American Exposition*$d(1901 :$cBuffalo, N.Y.)

n   **Number of part/section/meeting (R)**   *(Rule 24.7B2)*

This subfield contains a number designation to designate which meeting of a particular organization is contained in this tag. "Numbering" is defined as an indication of sequencing in any form. This is not limited to numerical values, but can be anything that indicates an order, such as the numbers one, two, three or the letters *A, B, C* or an ordinal number, like *1st, 2nd, or 3rd.*

$aVatican Council$*n(1st :*$d1869-1870)

d   **Date of meeting (NR)**   *(Rule 24.7B3)*

Record here the date, or range of dates during which a meeting took place. You may be able to obtain this information from the item itself. Your should record this information in your authority file for future use.

$aLouisiana Cancer Conference$n(2nd :$*d1958 :*$cNew Orleans, La.)

c   **Location of meeting (NR)**   *(Rule 24.7B4)*

If an organization meets frequently, you may wish to note the location of the meeting, particularly if it is relevant to the topic of the conference or meeting. Generally, if you have used **$n** and **$d**, you will probably want to enter a value in **$c**.

$aConference on Cancer Public Education$d(1973 :$*cDulles Airport)*

e   **Subordinate unit (R)**

This subfield contains a subordinate unit entered under a meeting name.

$aMostly Mozart Festival. $eOrchestra.

PUNCTUATION

$n is preceded by no punctuation.
$d is preceded by no punctuation unless it is preceded by **$n**, then it is preceded by a colon.
$c is preceded by a colon.
$e is preceded by a period.
$n, d, and **c** are enclosed in 1 set of parenthesis, which are expanded to include all of the subfields. Note that the parenthesis follow the subfield indicator of the first subfield following **$a**. It is not entered in **$a** itself.

730 ADDED ENTRY - UNIFORM TITLE

REPEATABLE: YES
MANDATORY: NO
RELATES TO: 245 $a
AUTHORITY: YES

1st indicator

0-9 **Nonfiling characters**

As a matter of policy, the Library of Congress drops all initial articles on uniform titles before entering them, unless the title is commonly known with the inclusion of that title, but even then, it is not counted as a non-filing character. Therefore, as a matter of policy, this position should be zero.

2nd indicator

blank **No information provided** (Generally, this is the value you will use)
2 **Analytical entry**

SUBFIELD CODES

a **Uniform title (NR)**
n **Number of part/section of a work (R)**
p **Name of part/section of a work (R)**
l **Language of a work (NR)**
k **Form subheading (R)**
s **Version (NR)**
f **Date of a work (NR)**

EXAMPLES

730 0 $aAfrica (London, England : 1971)
730 0 $aPeople speak (Radio program)
730 0 $aUnplugged (Television program)
730 0 $aMother Goose.

LOCATION

This information will rarely be printed directly on the item.. Instead, you will usually need to consult your authority list to see if any of the titles on the chief source of information have a uniform title.

NOTES

This tag is designed to provide title access to a uniform title. It is used most frequently when cataloging books that are novelizations of television programs and movies, as well as books that are adaptations of other forms. In some circumstances, where a named publication has some creative input into the publication in hand, the title of that publication would be recorded here. It can also be used to record the title of an item which is in a different form or is a cutting of a larger form, for example the soundtrack of a motion picture would have the name of the motion picture entered here.

THE SUBFIELDS IN DETAIL

a **Uniform title (NR)** *(Begin at Rule 25)*

This is where the actual uniform title is entered. Parenthetical information added to make a title distinctive is not separately subfield coded except for treaties.

$aGenesis (Anglo-Saxon poem)

166

n   **Number of part/section of a work (R)**   *(Rule 25.6)*

This subfield contains a number designation for a part/section of a work used in a uniform title field. "Numbering" is defined as an indication of sequencing in any form. For music, the serial opus, or thematic index number, or a date used as a number is contained in this subfield. **$n** is often followed by **$p**.

      $aArabian nights.*$nBooks 1-4.*

p   **Name of part/section of a work (R)**   *(Rule 25.18)*

This subfield contains a name designation of a part/section of a work used in a uniform title field. **$p** will usually follow **$n**.

      $aBible.*$pO.T.*
      $aBible.*$pN.T.$pRevelation.*

l   **Language of a work (NR)**   *(Rule 25.18A10)*

This subfield contains the name of the language(s) used in a uniform title.

      $aBible.$pO.T.*$lEnglish.*

k   **Form subheading (R)**   *(Rule 25.9)*

This subfield contains a form subheading used in a uniform title field. Some typical form subheadings are Manuscript, Selections, and Protocols.

      $aMother Goose.*$kSelections.*

s   **Version (NR)**   *(Rule 25.18A11)*

This subfield contains version, edition, etc., information used in a uniform title field.

      $aBible.$lEnglish.*$sAuthorized.*

f   **Date of a work (NR)**   *(Rule 25, 18A13)*

This subfield contains the date of publication used in a uniform title field.

      $aBible.$lEnglish.$sRevised Standard.*$f1959.*

Note that not all uniform titles will have every one of these subfields. Uniform titles will occur most frequently in books about folklore and fairy tales, fables, literature, music, and holy writings (not limited to the bible), as well as for adaptations and novelizations of movies, television programs, and radio shows.

PUNCTUATION

$n is preceded by a period.
$p is preceded by a comma if it follows a **$n**, otherwise it is preceded by a period.
$l is preceded by a period.
$k is preceded by a period.
$s is preceded by a period.
$f is preceded by a period.
If any subfield has parenthesis, the punctuation goes outside the parenthesis.
The tag ends with a period or a terminal mark of punctuation.

740 ADDED ENTRY - UNCONTROLLED RELATED/ANALYTICAL TITLE

REPEATABLE:	YES
MANDATORY:	NO
RELATES TO:	245$a, 245$b, 246, 5XX
AUTHORITY:	NO

1st indicator

0-9 Number of nonfiling characters

These values are counted in the same manner as those for the **245** and **440** tags. AACR2 specifies that initial articles should be dropped, but you may wish to retain them to create grammatically correct titles.

2nd indicator

blank No information provided

2 Analytical entry

You will use this value if you are creating analytical entries based on information in the **505** tag. Do not enter variant forms of the title from the **245** tag here. These are more correctly entered in the **246** tag. Some older records may have variant forms of the title entered here. At the time those records were created, this was the correct tag to enter them in. As a general guideline, you should move them from the **740** to **246** only if you are editing the record for another purpose.

SUBFIELD CODES

a Uncontrolled related/analytical title (NR)
n Number of part/section of a work (R)
p Name of part/section of a work (R)
h Medium (GMD)(NR)

EXAMPLES

505 0 $aSuddenly human - Brothers.
740 02 $aSuddenly human$h[videorecording].
740 02 $aBrothers$h[videorecording].

505 0 $aOpening (6:18) -- Floe (5:32) -- Island (7:39) -- Rubric (6:04) -- Facades (7:19) -- Closing (5:56)
740 02 $aOpening$h[sound recording].
740 02 $aFloe$h[sound recording].
740 02 $aIsland$h[sound recording].
740 02 $aRubric$h[sound recording].
740 02 $aFacades$h[sound recording].
740 02 $aClosing$h[sound recording].

<u>LOCATION</u>

There is no specified location for this information. Usually, you will obtain it from the contents note, table of contents, item container, or accompanying material. Direct physical examination of the item is usually the best method to ensure the complete selection of entries.

<u>NOTES</u>

This tag is designed to provide variant access to titles not provided for elsewhere, most notably, as uniform titles. It is used to provide access to individual portions of a larger work that would not normally be accessible via a title search or would not be cataloged separately. You will need to use your own discretion when you should individually trace titles from an item to provide direct title access via keyword access. Your knowledge of your library's collection, as well as the needs and searching habits of your users can help guide you in this area.

<u>THE SUBFIELDS IN DETAIL</u>

a   **Uncontrolled related/analytical title (NR)**   *(Rule 13.5)*
This subfield contains the title proper exclusive of the designation of number or name of part and any alternative title. The first letter is capitalized. Generally, titles will be separated in the **505** by the space -- space punctuation. You should not enter running titles for AV items here.

       505 0 $aA tale of two cities -- A Christmas carol.
       740 02 *$aTale of two cities.*
       740 02 *$aChristmas carol.*

n   **Number of part/section of a work (R)**
This subfield contains a number designation for a part/section of a work used in a title. "Numbering" is defined as an indication of sequencing in any form. In music titles, the serial opus, or thematic index number are generally not contained in subfield **$n**. Note that it does not have to be numerical in nature, but could be alphabetic in nature, e.g., Part A. It is usually followed by **$p**.

       505 0 $aHow to read faster (part one) - How to read more accurately (part one)
       740 02 $aHow to read faster.*$nPart one.*
       740 02 $aHow to read more accurately.*$nPart one.*

p   **Name of part/section of a work (R)**
This subfield contains a name of a part/section of a work in a title. This subfield frequently follows a **$n**.

       505 0 $aThe book of North America (vegetation) - The book of North America (animals)
       740 02 $aBook of North America.*$pVegetation.*
       740 02 $aBook of North America.*$pAnimals.*

740

h   **Medium (GMD)(NR)**   *(Rule 1.1C1)*

This subfield contains the name of the type of media being cataloged. See rule 1.1C1 in the **245** tag for a list of media names that can be used.

505 0	$aShut up and kiss me (3:40) -- He thinks he'll keep her (4:16) -- Passionate kisses (3:20) -- I feel lucky (4:16) -- Down at the twist and shout (3:20) -- You win again (3:17) -- This shirt (3:57)
740 02	$aShut up and kiss me*$h[videorecording]*.
740 02	$aHe thinks he'll keep her*$h[videorecording]*.
740 02	$aPassionate kisses*$h[videorecording]*.
740 02	$aI feel lucky*$h[videorecording]*.
740 02	$aDown at the twist and shout*$h[videorecording]*.
740 02	$aYou win again*$h[videorecording]*.
740 02	$aThis shirt*$h[videorecording]*.

With time and experience you will learn when to make and not make **740**s. Be patient, it is a learning process. Much of the interpretation of the decision to make or not make a **740** is based on listening to feedback from your users, as well as paying attention to their searching patterns. As time goes along, you will get a better feel as to when to make and not to make a **740** tag. Remember that you are not hindered by a false limitation like typing and filing cards. If you think something is a reasonable access point, go ahead and enter it. The instructors, in a school library environment, can be a good resource to tap regarding which titles from an anthology to trace. Feel free to consult with them. Doing so makes your collection more relevant to the research needs of the students and other users.

PUNCTUATION

$n is preceded by a period.
$p is preceded by a comma **if** it follows a **$n**, otherwise it is preceded by a period.
$h is preceded by a period.

The tag ends with a period or other terminal mark of punctuation.

8XX TAGS -- GENERAL INFORMATION

These tags are used to form general linkages in your system. They can contain series related information, call number information, holding and location information, and other non-specified local information. Because most of the information in these tags, most notably call number information, is machine encoded, they are covered here mostly for your convenience, although the **800** tag can be used when making entries for non-traced or title traced differently series.

The **8XX** tags covered in this book are:

800   Series Added Entry -- Personal Name
852   Location/Call Number

800 -- SERIES ADDED ENTRY - PERSONAL NAME

REPEATABLE:	YES
MANDATORY:	NO
RELATES TO:	490
AUTHORITY:	YES

1st indicator

0	**Forename**	
1	**Single surname**	
2	**Multiple surname**	
3	**Family name**	

EXAMPLES

Howard *or* Jesus Christ
Fitzgerald, David
Rousseau-Darnell, Lyse
Dunlop family

2nd indicator

The 2nd indicator is always blank.

SUBFIELD CODES

a	**Personal name(NR)**
q	**Fuller form of name (NR)**
b	**Numeration associated with name (R)**
c	**Titles or other words associated with a name (R)**
d	**Dates associated with name (NR)**
t	**Title of a work (NR)**

Note that subfields are not entered in alphabetical order, rather, they are entered in the order for the information they contain. Not all subfields are required for a given tag. You should only enter those for which you have information. Except for **$t**, the remaining subfields are formulated very similar to the **100, 600,** and **700** tags.

EXAMPLES

490 1   **$a**Letters from China
800 1   **$a**Strong, Anna Louise,**$d**1885-1970.**$t**Letters from China.

490 1   **$a**Effective supervision series
800 1   **$a**Gellerman, Saul W.**$t**Gellerman effective supervision series.

<u>LOCATION</u>

Usually, you will be taking this information from the CIP data on the front of the book. For more information on how to interpret the CIP data information for entry into the **490** and **800** tags, please refer to the documentation for the **490** tag.

<u>NOTES</u>

This tag is used to record series information that is uniquely linked to a particular person's name. <u>Nancy Drew</u> and <u>Hardy boys books</u> often fall into this area since they are uniquely linked to Carolyn Keene and Franklin Dixon respectively.

<u>SUBFIELDS IN DETAIL</u>

a   **Personal name (NR)**

This subfield contains a personal name. The name may be a surname and/or forename; letters, initials, abbreviations, phrases or numbers used in place of a name; or a family name. A parenthetical qualifying term associated with the name is contained in **$c**, and a fuller form of a name added as a qualifier is contained in **$q**. Names are usually entered in the form *Last name, First name* with the first letter in each name being capitalized. This subfield is <u>required</u> when the **800** tag is used.

        490 1 $aNew dinosaur library
        800 1   *$aBurton, Jane.*$tNew dinosaur library.

q   **Fuller form of name (NR)**

This subfield contains a more complete form of part of the name that is in **$a**. It is placed in parenthesis and is usually used if there are abbreviations or initials in the person's name as recorded in **$a**.

b   **Numeration <u>associated with a name</u> (R)**

This subfield contains a roman numeral or a roman numeral and a subsequent part of a forename. It is used <u>only</u> in a forename heading (*first indicator* value of 0). This means that any name in the form *Last name, First name* <u>cannot</u> have a numeration associated with it.

c   **Titles associated with name (R)**

This subfield contains titles and other words associated with a name. These include qualifying information such as:

       Titles designating rank, office or nobility.
       Terms of address.
       Initials of an academic degree or denoting membership in an organization.
       Other words or phrases associated with the name.

Note that AACR2 tends to discourage the use of titles except for royalty, nobility, or ranks of office. They allow the use of terms of address or phrases associated in a name to the extent that they are needed to differentiate between two similar names or if the person is commonly known by their title or address.

Multiple adjacent titles or words associated with a name are contained in a single **$c**. The subfield is repeated only when words associated with a name are separated by subelements contained in other subfields.

800

d   **Dates associated with a name (NR)**

This subfield contains the dates of birth, death, flourishing or any other date used with a name. A qualifier used with the date is also contained in **$d**. Some of these qualifiers and their meanings are:

b.	born	*b. 1965*
d.	died	*d. 1992*
ca.	circa or *about*	*ca. 1066*
fl.	flourished	*fl. 694-675 B.C.*
cent.	century	*fl. 9th cent. B.C.*
?	unknown or questionable	*1834?-1890*

Dates with a person are most commonly used if there are many people with the same name and some way is needed to differentiate between them.

t   **Title of a work (NR)**

This is where the title of a work uniquely associated with a particular author is recorded. Capitalization rules are the same as the **245$a**, but you should never have any nonfiling words at the beginning of this subfield.

490 1 $aEnchantment of America
800 1 $aCarpenter, Alan,$d1917- $tEnchantment of America.

PUNCTUATION

There is no punctuation before a **$b**
$c is preceded by a comma.
$d is preceded by a comma.
The information inside **$q** is placed in parentheses, with the subfield <u>usually</u> being preceded by the period ending the abbreviation in the **$a**.
If the date of death in **$d** is open, meaning that the person is still alive or his death date has not yet been entered into your system, no punctuation follows the hyphen at the end of the subfield.
$t is preceded by a period, <u>unless</u> it follows **$d**, then it <u>can</u> either be followed by a period if there is an ending date in **$d** or a space following the dash if there is an open date in **$d.**

The **800** tag usually ends in a period.

852 -- LOCATION/CALL NUMBER

REPEATABLE:	YES
MANDATORY:	NO
RELATED TO:	--
AUTHORITY:	NO

1st indicator

0   Library of Congress Classification
1   Dewey Decimal Classification

2nd indicator

blank   No information provided
0   No enumeration
1   Primary enumeration (This will usually be the value you will use.)
2   Alternative enumeration

SUBFIELD CODES

a   Location (NR)
k   Call number prefix (NR)
h   Classification part (NR)
i   Item part (R)
p   Piece designation (NR)
t   Copy number (NR)
9   Purchase price (NR)

EXAMPLES

852      $aCTY$h339.2$iNEV
852      $aInU$kREF$h909iBor$p2347$t1
852      $kFIC$h813.54$iAsi$p33458898

This field contains the information required to locate an item. It may contain the name of the library or organization holding the item (the holding code), and it may also contain detailed information necessary to locate the item. This would include the call number, any necessary prefixes and suffixes, as well as copy and price information. Note that many automation systems do not allow you to enter information directly into this tag. Rather, they will often have a "window" or template to enter this information in, which the computer translates to the correct locations in the record.

852

LOCATION

On books with CIP information, this will usually be located in the lower right-hand corner of the CIP information. CIP information is information provided to the publisher by the Library of Congress when they catalog publisher's galleys so that cataloging information is available to libraries when books are published. CIP data is usually located on the verso of the title page. If there is no CIP data, you will need to assign a call number either using *Library of Congress Classification Tables* or the *Dewey Decimal Classification* scheme, depending on which you use in your library.

NOTES

This tag makes it possible for your automation system to display call number and copy information to the searcher. The library may use this information when doing inventory, or if it is contributing information to a shared database for a union catalog.

THE SUBFIELDS IN DETAIL

a   **Location (NR)**
This subfield contains the library's NUC symbol if it has one. If your library does not have a NUC code, one can be requested from the Library of Congress. This information is valuable if you are building a union catalog or database with other libraries. It is not required, but is highly recommended. Your automation system may automatically insert this value in the tag. Check with your particular vendor to be certain.

       *$aCTY*$h339.2

k   **Call number prefix (NR)**
This subfield contains a term that precedes a call number. This would include such things as *R* and *REF.* for Reference items, *F* and *FIC* for Fiction items, or *B* for *BIO* for biographical works. If you are entering standard non-fiction books, this subfield is not needed.

       $aTXdaS*$kFic*$hAsi

h   **Classification part/ (NR)**
This subfield contains the classification portion of the call number used as the shelving scheme for an item. It is in this subfield that you will record the actual Dewey or LC number.

       $aInU*$h873.4*$iLor

i   **Item part (R)**
This subfield contains a Cutter, date, or main entry information added to the call number. Many libraries will follow the Dewey number in their collection with the first three letters of the main entry. It is in this subfield that they should be recorded.

       $kRef$h303.0973*$iYur*

p   **Piece designation (NR)**
This subfield can contain the barcode for a particular item if the system does not store it elsewhere. It is very important to know where your system stores this information for possible exporting uses later.

$kBio$h921.92$iRoo$p33458898

t   **Copy number (NR)**
This subfield contains the particular copy number of an item. It is not mandatory to have an entry in this filed. Do not enter volume information into this tag.

$h973.04$iNev$t3

9   **Purchase price (NR)**
Use this subfield to record the price actually paid for the item. It will often be different from the list price of an item that is retained in the **020**.

$hDS838.7.H37$i1992$p29.95

PUNCTUATION

There is no punctuation between subfields in this tag. Nor does the tag end with any punctuation.

008/006

008/006 TAG

The **008** tag contains information that your system will use for routine processing of the records. Very rarely is it used directly by patrons or library staff. Rather, it is usually used during inventory, weeding, report generation, and re-ordering of replacement materials. This tag has been covered last since much of the material and information it contains has already been entered in the record, thereby allowing you to use it to "check" your work and to refer to those tags directly without having to go back to the item.

When cataloging, you should enter information into the appropriate **008** for the item that is most prominent in your record. If you are doing a book, then use the book form, if you are doing videorecordings, then you should use the videorecording form. If you have something that is mixed media (cassette and book), then you will need to select the **008** that you feel is most predominant. This decision will usually be based on local policy and will be influenced on how you created your **300** tag. After entering the most prominent item in the **008**, you should enter information for related items in the **006** tag. The information for all the **008** tag positions **11-17** and **35-39** are the same for all formats. The variant values are in positions **18-34**. The **006** tag is designed to accommodate that information which is different between the formats. This book presents the information for the similar positions, with specialized **008/006** sections for the unique areas for each format. The **008** tag position value is listed first, followed by that for the **006** tag.

008 FIXED LENGTH DATA ELEMENTS

REPEATABLE: NO
MANDATORY: YES
RELATES TO: --
AUTHORITY: NO

This tag contains coded information that is essentially a "summation" of the rest of the record. Even though it is at the beginning of the record, it is highly dependent on what you will later enter in the respective tags, so you may want to enter this tag after you have done the rest of the record.

1st Indicator
There is no 1st indicator for this tag.

2nd Indicator
There is no 2nd indicator for this tag.

SUBFIELD CODES

There are no subfield codes for this tag. Rather, there are data elements. There are 40 possible positions for this tag (**00-39**) that provide coded information about the record as a whole or about special elements of particular tags.

EXAMPLES

Due to the wide variety of possible ways of displaying this information among the various automation systems, no examples are given. You are encouraged to review the manual for your system regarding how the information for this tag is displayed.

NOTES

Because of the nature of the information in this tag, it is not possible to give a location to find each piece of necessary information. You will need to scan and review various areas of the item, as well as review what you have entered in the individual tags in the rest of the record so that this information can be correctly coded. The information you enter here should agree with what you enter in the individual tags in the record.

FUNCTION

Many systems will use the information in this tag in screen displays, sorting routines, limiting criteria, such as language, year of publication, juvenile, fiction, etc. While this information is contained in narrative form elsewhere in the record, here it is positionally defined. This makes it easier for programmers to write software to limit searches and reject or accept necessary pieces of data.

Because of their dependence on the information in this tag, both now and for the future, it is very important that you enter it correctly. While the particular automation system you are currently using may not use this information now, it may in the future. Also, you may migrate to another system that does use this information. If you have not entered it, you will need to go back and do so, a very costly and time-consuming proposition.

Please note that the values given here are only for those character positions that are common to all forms of materials. You should examine the **008** tag information for the specific materials listed as well as coding of the **006** tag.

008/006

DOCUMENTATION CONVENTIONS

Character positions are positionally defined. Character positions that are not defined contain a **blank [b]** or a **fill character [I]**. All defined character positions must contain either a defined *code* or a fill character. **Code [n] (not applicable)**, when it is defined for a data element, indicates that the character definition does not apply to the record.

Your particular system may automatically generate some values, while some are defaulted in by the designers. Anytime an alphabetic character is entered, it must be lowercase.

The character position(s) of each element will be listed first, followed by the element name. Below them will be a statement of Mandatory or Optional. Each element will also contain information regarding the acceptability of the use of the fill character and blank values. Depending on your system, you may only have the character position numbers displayed, or you may have a narrative phrase for a single position or group of positions.

Many vendors will use some type of editing aid, be it pop-up box(es), hot keys, or mnemonic aids. Again, check the manual that came with your system to determine how your particular editing aid is designed.

This first group covers positions **00-17** and **35-39** which are common to <u>all</u> the formats. Information for *item specific* positions are given after this section.

THE ELEMENTS IN DETAIL

008/00-05 **Date entered on file**
Mandatory These six numerical characters specify the date the record was first entered into machine-readable form, not when it was last accessed or any changes were made to it. The date is given in the pattern *yymmdd* (*yy* for the year, *mm* for the month, *dd* for the day).

Many automation systems will automatically enter this information based on the clock/calendar build into the computer. Make certain that your computer's clock and calendar accurately reflect the current date and time.

EXAMPLE
August 19, 1986 would be entered as *860819*
March 11, 1992 would be entered as *920311*

008/06 **Type of date/Publication status**
Mandatory This position contains a one-character alphabetic code indicating the type of dates given in **008/07-10** and **008/11-14** (Dates 1 and 2 respectively). This information will generally need to agree with what you enter in the **260$c** tag.

TYPE OF DATE CODES

s	**Single known date/probable date**
c	**Serial item currently published**
d	**Serial item ceased publication**
m	**Multiple dates (multipart items only)**
p	**Date of distribution/release/issue and production/recording session when different**
q	**Range of dates or a questionable date**
r	**Reprint/reissue date and original date**
t	**Publication date and copyright date**

s   Use this code when there is one, and only one, date on the book, even if it is the copyright date.

c   Use this value to indicate that the dates listed in *Date 1* and *Date 2* are for a serial currently being published.

d   Use this code for the dates for a serial which has ceased publication. The dates in Date 1 and Date 2 would reflect the starting and ending publication dates. Note that the date in Date 2 cannot be later than the current date of cataloging.

m   This code is used when *Date 1* and *Date 2* contain the range of years of publication of a multipart item. There must be multiple volumes listed in the **300$a** for this value to be used.

p   Use this code when a date of distribution/release/issue and a date of production/recording session are present because there is a difference between the two dates. This will be used most often in sound recordings and videorecordings.

q   Use this letter if entering a questionable range of dates, such as when you enter [19--] in the **260$c**. Also use this for a single monographic item when you are uncertain as to the exact date of publication (e.g., there is no date or LC number on the item). The earliest possible date is entered in *Date 1* and the latest or current date is entered in *Date 2*.

r   Use this to indicate that *Date 1* contains the date of reproduction or reissue and *Date 2* contains the date of the original, if known. If the date of the original is unknown, ***Date 2*** contains blanks. If multiple dates are available for the original publication, *Date 2* contains the earlier date.

t   Use this code if you have an actual date of publication as well as a copyright date. Copyright dates are preceded with a small "c" or a "c" inside of a circle. Enter the publication date in **Date 1** and the copyright date in *Date 2*. Also use this code if you have two dates for a single item that are linked by a comma, i.e., they do not cover a range of dates.

008/07-10
Mandatory

Date 1/Beginning date of publication

Enter the first year of publication that is shown. If you have no date but do have an LC Number, take the year from the LC number and enter it into this tag. If you have no date or LC number, you can enter the letter u for those portions of the date you do not know.

If you are doing multiple dates, enter the first date here. If you are doing a copyright date and publishing date, enter the publishing date here.

If entering a reprint date, enter the date of reprinting here.

008/11-14
Mandatory

Date 2/Ending date of publication

Enter the last year shown in the **260$c** if there are multiple dates.

If there is no date and no LC number and you have entered q for type of date, enter the letter u for those portions of the date that you do not know.

If you have a copyright date and a publishing date, enter the copyright date here.

If entering a reprint date, enter the date that the item was originally published here.

008/006

008/15-17
Mandatory

Place of publication, production, or execution

Enter a two or three character alphabetic code indicating the place of publication, production or execution. The place of publication code is an authoritative-agency data element. The Library of Congress maintains the *USMARC Code List for Countries* and is the authoritative agency for the United States. The value entered here should agree with what you enter in the **260$a**.

As a rule, places in the United States will be the postal abbreviation followed by the letter u, hence, *California* would be *cau*, *Florida* would be *flu*. Note that all letters are entered lowercase.

If you have a substantial quantity of publications from outside the United States, it is advisable that you purchase *USMARC Code Llist for Countries* from the Library of Congress. A complete, detailed listing of all codes is beyond the scope of this book.

If there is no place, enter **xx** in the first two positions.

008/35-37
Mandatory

Language code

This area contains a three-character alphabetic code indicating the language of the item. The language code is an authoritative-agency data element. The Library of Congress maintains the *USMARC Code List for Languages* and is the authoritative agency. You should choose a language code based on the predominant language of the item. If the item contains text in more than one language, or is a translation, textual information regarding the language is entered in the **500** tag. If more than one language code is appropriate to an item, enter the code for the language that predominates in the item. If none of the languages are dominant, then enter the one that comes first in the English alphabet here.

If you are doing *sound recordings*, enter the language of the vocals. If the sound recording has no vocals or singing, leave these three positions blank. For *Computer software*, enter the language used in the user interface on the computer, not the language the program is written in.

Note that the value or language you enter here should agree with the language in **$l** of the uniform title tags or any place else in the record a language is indicated.

Below are listed the most common language codes.

CODE VALUES

eng	**English**
fre	**French**
ger	**German**
ita	**Italian**
lat	**Latin**
spa	**Spanish**

008/38
Mandatory

Modified record

This position contains a one-character alphabetic code indicating whether any data on a bibliographic record is a modification of information that appeared on the item being cataloged or that was intended to be included in the machine-readable record. Generally, you will leave this value blank as it deals with dashed-on entries, shortened information, or romanization schemes. Unless you are in a large academic library, you will not usually encounter these situations.

008/39	Cataloging source
Mandatory	This element contains a one-character alphabetic code indicating the original cataloging source of the record. If the cataloging source is known, the NUC symbol or name of the organization may be carried in the **040** tag.

When you are creating original records for your library, you should use value d, which means that the record was created by a source other than a national library. When downloading records off other databases, you may find the following values in the record.

<u>CODE VALUES</u>

blank	**Library of Congress**
a	**National Agricultural Library**
b	**National Library of Medicine**
c	**Library of Congress cooperative cataloging program**
d	**Other Non National Library**

Very often, the value of **d** will automatically be inserted by the automation system.

008 FIXED LENGTH DATA ELEMENTS

Books and other bound printed materials (pamphlets, vertical files, etc.)

REPEATABLE:	NO
MANDATORY:	YES
RELATES TO:	--
AUTHORITY:	NO

This tag contains coded information that is essentially a "summation" of the rest of the record. Even though it is at the beginning of the record, it is highly dependent on what you will later enter in the respective tags, so you may want to enter this tag after you have done the rest of the record.

1st Indicator
There is no 1st indicator for this tag.

2nd Indicator
There is no 2nd indicator for this tag.

SUBFIELD CODES

There are no subfield codes for this tag. Rather, there are data elements. There are 40 possible positions for this tag (**00-39**) that provide coded information about the record as a whole or about special elements of particular tags.

EXAMPLES

Due to the wide variety of possible ways of displaying this information among the various automation systems, no examples are given. You are encouraged to review the manual for your system regarding how the information for this tag is displayed.

NOTES

Because of the nature of the information in this tag, it is not possible to give a location to find each piece of necessary information. You will need to scan and review various areas of the book, as well as review what you have entered in the individual tags in the rest of the record so that this information can be correctly coded. The information you enter here should agree with what you enter in the individual tags in the record.

DOCUMENTATION CONVENTIONS

Character positions are positionally defined. Character positions that are not defined contain a **blank [b]** or a **fill character [l]**. All defined character positions must contain either a defined code or a fill character. **Code [n] (not applicable)**, when it is defined for a data element, indicates that the character definition does not apply to the record.

Your particular system may automatically generate some values, while the designers default some in. Anytime an alphabetic character is entered, it must be lowercase.

The character position(s) of each element will be listed first, followed by the element name. Below them will be the tag positions for the **006** tag. Note that final tentative coding and determination of the **006** tag was accomplished in 1996. What is presented here is accurate as of the press date as presented in *USMARC Bibliographic*. Below the **006** value will be a statement of **Mandatory** or **Optional**. Each element will also contain information regarding the acceptability of the use of the fill character and blank values. Depending on your system, you may only have the character position numbers displayed, or you may have a narrative phrase for a single position or group of positions.

The positions covered here are those unique to books and other printed material. If another item in the record is predominant, then the information for the book would be coded in a **006** tag.

THE ELEMENTS IN DETAIL

008/18-21
006/01-04
Optional
    Illustrations

These four positions contain one-character alphabetic codes that indicate the presence of types of illustrations in the item represented by a book's record. Information for this character position is usually, but not always, derived from terms in the **300$b** tag.

Up to four codes may be recorded here, in alphabetical order. If fewer than four codes are assigned, the codes are left justified and unused positions are blank. If there are more than four possible codes, only the first four are entered.

CODE VALUES

a	**Illustrations**
b	**Maps**
c	**Portraits**
d	**Charts**
e	**Plans**
f	**Plates**
g	**Music**
h	**Facsimiles**
i	**Coats of arms**
j	**Genealogical tables**
k	**Forms**
l	**Samples**
o	**Photographs**
p	**Illuminations**

008/22
006/05
Mandatory
    Target audience

Enter a one-character alphabetic code describing the intellectual level of the target audience for which the material is intended.

CODE VALUES

blank	Indicates that the intellectual level of the target audience is unknown, or that the identification of the item as juvenile material is not applicable.
a	**Preschool**
b	**Primary**
c	**Elementary and junior high**
d	**Secondary (senior high)**
e	**Adult**
f	**Specialized**
g	**General**
j	**Juvenile** This means that the item is intended for use by children and young people through the age of 15 or the 9th grade.

Be aware of the fact that if you enter **a, b, c,** or **j** here, you may need to enter *Juvenile literature* in the subject headings.

The values other than **blank** and **j** were incorporated into USMARC specifications in February of 1995.

008/006

008/23 **006/06** **Mandatory**	**Form of item**

This position contains a one-letter alphabetic code that specifies the form of material for the item in hand.

CODE VALUES

blank None of the following
d   Large print
f   Braille

Note that if you use either one of these values, you will need to make the appropriate notation in the **300$a.**

008/24-27 **006/07-10** **Optional**	**Nature of contents**

This area contains up to four one-character alphabetic codes that indicate that an item contains certain types of materials. Generally, a specific code is used only if a significant part of the item is the type of material represented by the code. Note that if you enter a particular value here, such as b for bibliography, you may also have to have a **504** tag. If there are fewer than four codes, the codes are left justified and the unused positions contain blanks. If more than four codes are appropriate to an item, the four most significant codes are selected and recorded in alphabetical order. If no codes are applicable, all positions are left blank.

CODE VALUES

blank No specified nature of contents
a   Abstracts/summaries
b   Bibliographies
c   Catalogs
d   Dictionaries
e   Encyclopedias
f   Handbooks
g   Legal articles
i   Indexes
k   Discographies (lists of records, similar to a bibliography)
l   Legislation
n   Surveys of literature in a subject area
o   Reviews
p   Programmed texts
q   Filmographies (lists of films or movies, similar to a bibliography)
r   Directories
s   Statistics
t   Technical reports
v   Legal cases and case notes
w   Law reports and digests

CODE VALUES AND THEIR APPLICATIONS

008/28 **006/11** **Mandatory**	**Government publication code**

This position contains a one-character alphabetic code indicating whether or not the item is produced by or for an international, national, state or local **blank**   Not published by or for a governmental body, government agency, or by any subdivision of such a body.

CODE VALUES

a   Autonomous or semi-autonomous component.

c   Published by or for a multilocal jurisdiction that is defined as a regional combination of jurisdictions below the state level.

f   Federal or national. This value is also used for American Indian tribes and for the governments of England, Wales, Scotland, and Northern Ireland.

i   International intergovernmental body.

l   Local jurisdiction, such as a city.

m   Multistate, such as Midwest or organizations that cross state lines.

s   State (including state-owned or controlled universities).

z   Other types of government publications.

If an item is published or produced jointly by government agencies at two different levels, record the code for the higher government form.

Academic Publications are considered government publications if the institutions are created or controlled by a government.

University Publications are considered government publications if the presses are created or controlled by a government (e.g., state university presses in the United States.)

008/29
006/12
Optional   **Conference publication**

This position contains a one-character numeric code indicating whether a work consists of the proceedings, reports, or summaries of a conference.

CODE VALUES

0   Not a conference publication
This includes such publications as works composed of or based on a single paper; symposiums in print; hearings of legislative bodies; and courses given in a school.

1   Conference publication

008/30
006/13
Optional   **Festschrift**

This position contains a one-character numeric code indicating if the work is a festschrift.

A festschrift is defined as a complimentary or memorial publication usually in the form of a collection of essays, addresses, or biographical, bibliographic, scientific, or other contributions. It often embodies the results of research, issued in honor of a person, an institution, or a society, as a rule, on the occasion of an anniversary celebration.

A true festschrift generally mentions the person, institution, or society it commemorates on the title page. The title of the work may or may not use the word festschrift. Other indications that an item is a festschrift include phrases such as: papers in honor of, in memory of, commemorating, and their equivalents in foreign languages. As a rule, they are usually only found in academic and large research libraries.

CODE VALUES

0   Not a festschrift
1   Festschrift

008/006

008/31
006/14
Optional

Index

This position contains a one-character numeric code indicating whether or not an item includes an index to its own contents. Information for this data element is derived from mention of an index in another part of the bibliographic record.

If you enter a **1** here, you will need to have the word index either in the title or in a **500** or **504** tag.

CODE VALUES

0	**No index**
1	**Index present**

008/32
006/15
Optional

Undefined

This element used to contain a code indicating if the main entry was in the body of the entry. It was made obsolete in 1990. You should either leave this value blank or put the fill character in it. If you are editing older records, you should remove any other values that are here.

008/33
006/16
Optional

Literary form (Formerly *Fiction*)

A one-character code used to indicate the literary form of an item. Numeric codes **0** and **1** provide a generic identification of whether or not the item is a work of fiction. Alphabetic codes may be used to identify specific literary forms. Generally, if you state that the item is other than a work of non-fiction, your call number and subject headings should agree with that statement.

It is very important that you accurately code this area, since some systems utilize this to generate reports on all fiction items in your collection, including those that are shelved in the Dewey 800's.

CODE VALUES

0	**Not fiction (not further specified)**
c	**Comic strips**
d	**Dramas**
e	**Essays**
f	**Novels**
h	**Humor, satires, etc.**
i	**Letters**
j	**Short stories**
m	**Mixed forms**
p	**Poetry**
s	**Speeches**
u	**Unknown**
0	**Fiction (not further specified)**

008/34
006/17
Mandatory

Biography

This element contains a one-character alphabetic code indicating whether or not an item contains biographical material, and if so, what type of biography it is.

It is important that you code this area correctly, as some automation systems will use this information to generate reports on biographies. While it may seem obvious that all your biographies are together (if you maintain a separate biography section in your library), many books that contain biographical information will be inter-shelved with your regular non-fiction books. This code provides a way to access those titles.

<u>CODE VALUES</u>

blank   No biographical material
a   Autobiographies (biography written by the subject)
b   Standard biographies(individual biographies)
c   Collective biographies (biographies about more than one person)

008/006

008 FIXED LENGTH DATA ELEMENTS
[computer files] [interactive multimedia]

REPEATABLE: NO
MANDATORY: YES
RELATES TO: --
AUTHORITY: NO

This tag contains coded information that is essentially a "summation" of the rest of the record. Even though it is at the beginning of the record, it is highly dependent on what you will later enter in the respective tags, so you may want to enter this tag after you have done the rest of the record.

1st Indicator
There is no 1st indicator for this tag.

2nd Indicator
There is no 2nd indicator for this tag.

SUBFIELD CODES

There are no subfield codes for this tag. Rather, there are data elements. There are 40 possible positions for this tag (**00-39**) that provide coded information about the record as a whole or about special elements of particular tags.

EXAMPLES

Due to the wide variety of possible ways of displaying this information among the various automation systems, no examples are given. You are encouraged to review the manual for your system regarding how the information for this tag is displayed.

NOTES

Because of the nature of the information in this tag, it is not possible to give a location to find each piece of necessary information. You will need to scan and review various areas of the software, as well as review what you have entered in the individual tags in the rest of the record so that this information can be correctly coded. The information you enter here should agree with what you enter in the individual tags in the record.

DOCUMENTATION CONVENTIONS

Character positions are positionally defined. Character positions that are not defined contain a **blank [b]** or a **fill character [|]**. All defined character positions must contain either a defined code or a fill character. Code **[n] (not applicable)**, when it is defined for a data element, indicates that the character definition does not apply to the record.

Your particular system may automatically generate some values, while the designers default some in. Anytime an alphabetic character is entered, it must be lowercase.

The character position(s) of each element will be listed first, followed by the element name. Below them will be the tag positions for the **006** tag. The final coding of this tag was accomplished in 1996. What is presented here are the values as of date of publication. Below the **006** value will be a statement of Mandatory or Optional. Each element will also contain information regarding the acceptability of the use of the fill character and blank values. Depending on your system, you may only have the character position numbers displayed, or you may have a narrative phrase for a single position or group of positions.

The positions covered here are those unique to *computer software* and *interactive multimedia*. If another item in the record is predominant, then the information for the software would be coded in the **006** tag.

THE ELEMENTS IN DETAIL

008/18
006/01

Optional

Undefined

This character position used to contain a code denoting the frequency of a serially published computer file. It should be left blank in the **008** tag, but would be coded for the appropriate information according to the serial information for the **006** tag.

008/19
006/02

Optional

Undefined

This character position used to contain a code denoting the regularity of a serially published computer file. It should be left blank in the **008** tag, but would be coded for the appropriate information according to the serial information for the **006** tag.

008/20-21
006/03-04

Optional

Undefined

These two character positions are undefined. They should either be blank or contain the fill character.

008/22
006/05

Optional

Target audience

This area describes the target audience for which the material is intended. It is used primarily for educational computer file materials. When items with factual content are considered appropriate for more than one intellectual level, the code is recorded for the highest level.

CODE VALUES

blank Unknown or not applicable
a Preschool (up to, but not including, kindergarten)
b Primary (kindergarten through third grade)
c Elementary and junior high (grades 4-8)
d Secondary (senior high) (grades 9-12)
e Adult
f Specialized (e.g. handicapped, training films, etc.)
g General
j Juvenile

008/23-25
006/23-25

Optional

Undefined

These three character positions are undefined; each contains a blank or the fill character.

008/26
006/09

Mandatory

Type of computer file

This area is used to indicate the type of computer file being discussed. It is very closely related to the information in field **516** (Type of File or Data Note)

CODE VALUES

a Numeric
This value indicates a file that contains mostly numbers or representation by numbers, such as records containing all information on student test scores, all information on football team statistics, etc. It can generally be statistically manipulated.

b   Computer programs

This code indicates a file containing an ordered set of instructions directing the computer to perform basic operations and identifying the information and mechanism required. This is where most game and application software will be located.

c   Representational

This code indicates a file that contains pictorial or graphic information that can be manipulated in conjunction with other types of files to produce graphic patterns that can be used to interpret and give meaning to the information.

d   Text

This code indicates a file that contains mostly alphabetic information (words or sentences) converted into a coded format that can be processed, sorted and manipulated by machine, and then retrieved in many optional formats. This category includes such information as bibliographic files and records containing full text of documents.

m   Combination

This code is used when the item is a combination of two or more of the above types of files.

u   Unknown

This code indicates that the type of file is unknown.

z   Other

This code indicates that the type of file for which none of the other defined codes is appropriate.

008/27
006/10
Optional

Undefined

This character position is undefined; it contains either a blank or the fill character.

008/28
006/11
Mandatory

Government publication code

This position contains a one-character alphabetic code indicating whether or not the item is produced by or for an international, national, state or local government agency, or by any subdivision of such a body.

CODE VALUES

blank Not published by or for a governmental body

a   Autonomous or semi-autonomous component.

c   Published by or for a multilocal jurisdiction that is defined as a regional combination of jurisdictions below the state level.

f   Federal or national. This value is also used for American Indian tribes and for the governments of England, Wales, Scotland, and Northern Ireland.

i   International intergovernmental body.

l   Local jurisdiction, such as a city.

m   Multistate, such as Midwest or organizations that cross state lines.

s   State (including state-owned or controlled universities).

z   Other types of government publications.

If an item is published or produced jointly by government agencies at two different levels, record the code for the higher government form.

Academic Publications are considered government publications if the institutions are created or controlled by a government.

University Publications are considered government publications if the presses are created or controlled by a government (e.g., state university presses in the United States.)

008/29-34
006/12-17
Undefined

Undefined

These six character positions are undefined; each contains a blank or the fill character.

008   FIXED LENGTH DATA ELEMENTS
[maps] [globes]

REPEATABLE: NO
MANDATORY: YES
RELATES TO: --
AUTHORITY: NO

This tag contains coded information that is essentially a "summation" of the rest of the record. Even though it is at the beginning of the record, it is highly dependent on what you will later enter in the respective tags, so you may want to enter this tag after you have done the rest of the record.

1st Indicator
There is no 1st indicator for this tag.

2nd Indicator
There is no 2nd indicator for this tag.

SUBFIELD CODES

There are no subfield codes for this tag. Rather, there are data elements. There are 40 possible positions for this tag (**00-39**) that provide coded information about the record as a whole or about special elements of particular tags.

EXAMPLES

Due to the wide variety of possible ways of displaying this information among the various automation systems, no examples are given. You are encouraged to review the manual for your system regarding how the information for this tag is displayed.

NOTES

Because of the nature of the information in this tag, it is not possible to give a location to find each piece of necessary information. You will need to scan and review various areas of the map or globe, as well as review what you have entered in the individual tags in the rest of the record so that this information can be correctly coded. The information you enter here should agree with what you enter in the individual tags in the record.

DOCUMENTATION CONVENTIONS

Character positions are positionally defined. Character positions that are not defined contain a **blank [b]** or a **fill character** [l]. All defined character positions must contain either a defined code or a fill character. **Code [n] (not applicable)**, when it is defined for a data element, indicates that the character definition does not apply to the record.

Your particular system may automatically generate some values, while the designers default some in. Anytime an alphabetic character is entered, it must be lowercase.

The character position(s) of each element will be listed first, followed by the element name. Below them will be the tag positions for the **006** tag. The final coding and determination of this tag was accomplished in 1996. What is presented here are the values which were current as of date of publication. Below the **006** value will be a statement of **Mandatory** or **Optional**. Each element will also contain information regarding the acceptability of the use of the fill character and blank values. Depending on your system, you may only have the character position numbers displayed, or you may have a narrative phrase for a single position or group of positions.

008/006

The positions covered here are those unique to *maps* and *globes*. If another item in the record is predominant and you have coded the **008** for that information, than the information for the map or globe would be coded in the **006** tag.

THE ELEMENTS IN DETAIL

008/18-21
006/01-04
Optional

Relief

These four positions indicate the relief type specified on the item. The codes used in this field indicate only the relief forms most commonly found on maps and are usually derived from information given in field **500**. Up to four codes may be recorded, and are entered in order of their importance to the map being described.

CODE VALUES

blank	no relief shown
a	Contours
b	Shading
c	Gradient and bathymetric tints
d	Hachures
e	Bathymetry/soundings
f	Form lines
g	Spot heights
i	Pictorially
j	Land forms
k	Bathymetry/isolines
m	Rock drawings
z	Other

008/22-23
006/05-06
Optional

Projection

These two character positions are used to indicate the projection used in producing the item.

CODE VALUES

blank	Projection not specified
zz	Other projection
aa	Aitoff
ab	Gnomic
ac	Lambert's azimuthal equal area
ad	Orthographic
ae	Azimuthal equidistant
af	Stereographic
au	Azimuthal, specific type unknown
ba	Gall
bb	Goode's homolographic
bc	Lambert's cylindrical equal area
bd	Mercator
be	Miller
bf	Mollweide
bg	Sinusoidal
bh	Transverse Mercator
bi	Gauss-Kruger
bu	Cylindrical, specific type unknown

ca	Alber's equal area
cb	Bonne
cc	Lambert's conformal conic
cp	Polyconic
cu	Conic, specific type unknown
da	Armadillo
db	Butterfly
dc	Eckert
dd	Goode's homolosine
de	Miller's bipolar oblique conformal conic
df	Van Der Grinten
dg	Dimaxion
dh	Cordiform

008/24
006/07

Optional

Obsolete

Prior to 1997, this position was used to indicate the prime meridian that was named on a map. The defined codes were:

CODE VAL;UES

blank	Prime meridian not specified
e	Greenwich, England
f	Ferro (Hierro)
g	Paris, France
p	Philadelphia, Pennsylvania.
w	Washington, D.C.
z	Other prime meridian

008/25
006/08

Mandatory

Type of cartographic material

This position indicates the type of non-book cartographic item being described.

CODE VALUES

a	Single map
b	Map series
c	Map serial
d	Globe
e	Atlas

008/26-27
006/09-10

Optional

Undefined

These two character positions are undefined; each contains a blank or fill character.

008/28
006/11

Mandatory

Government publication code

This position contains a one-character alphabetic code indicating whether or not the item is produced by or for an international, national, state or local government agency, or by any subdivision of such a body.

CODE VALUES

blank	Not published by or for a governmental body
a	Autonomous or semi-autonomous component.
c	Published by or for a multilocal jurisdiction that is defined as a regional combination of jurisdictions below the state level.

f   Federal or national. This value is also used for American Indian tribes and for the governments of England, Wales, Scotland, and Northern Ireland.

i   International intergovernmental body.

l   Local jurisdiction, such as a city.

m   Multistate, such as Midwest or organizations that cross state lines.

s   State (including state-owned or controlled universities).

z   Other types of government publications.

If an item is published or produced jointly by government agencies at two different levels, record the code for the higher government form.

Academic Publications are considered government publications if the institutions are created or controlled by a government.

University Publications are considered government publications if the presses are created or controlled by a government (e.g., state university presses in the United States.)

008/29-30
006/12-13
Optional

Undefined

These two character positions are undefined; each contains a blank or fill character.

008/31
006/14
Optional

Index

This position contains a one-character numeric code indicating whether or not an item includes an index to its own contents. Information for this data element is derived from mention of an index in another part of the bibliographic record.

If you enter a **1** here, you will need to have the word index either in the title, or in a **500** or **504** tag.

CODE VALUES

0   **No index**

1   **Index present**

008/32
006/15
Optional

Undefined

This character position is undefined; it contains a blank or fill character.

008/33-34
006/16-17
Mandatory

Special format characteristics

These positions are used to identify some of the special format characteristics of a map. Up to two codes may be recorded. Codes are recorded in order of their importance to the map being described. If more than two characteristics are appropriate to an item, only the two most important are recorded.

CODE VALUES

blank **No specified special format characteristics**

e   **Manuscript**

j   **Picture card, post card**

k   **Calendar**

l   **Puzzle**

m   **Braille**

n   **Game**

o   **Wall map**

p   **Playing cards**

q   **Large print**

r   **Loose-leaf**

z   **Other special format characteristic**

008 FIXED LENGTH DATA ELEMENTS
[sound recordings] [music]

REPEATABLE: NO
MANDATORY: YES
RELATES TO: --
AUTHORITY: NO

This tag contains coded information that is essentially a "summation" of the rest of the record. Even though it is at the beginning of the record, it is highly dependent on what you will later enter in the respective tags, so you may want to enter this tag after you have done the rest of the record.

1st Indicator
There is no 1st indicator for this tag.

2nd Indicator
There is no 2nd indicator for this tag.

SUBFIELD CODES

There are no subfield codes for this tag. Rather, there are data elements. There are 40 possible positions for this tag (**00-39**) that provide coded information about the record as a whole or about special elements of particular tags.

EXAMPLES

Due to the wide variety of possible ways of displaying this information among the various automation systems, no examples are given. You are encouraged to review the manual for your system regarding how the information for this tag is displayed.

NOTES

Because of the nature of the information in this tag, it is not possible to give a location to find each piece of necessary information. You will need to scan and review various areas of the sound recording or printed music, as well as review what you have entered in the individual tags in the rest of the record so that this information can be correctly coded. The information you enter here should agree with what you enter in the individual tags in the record.

DOCUMENTATION CONVENTIONS

Character positions are positionally defined. Character positions that are not defined contain a **blank [b]** or a **fill character [|]**. All defined character positions must contain either a defined code or a fill character. **Code [n] (not applicable)**, when it is defined for a data element, indicates that the character definition does not apply to the record.

Your particular system may automatically generate some values, while the designers default some in. Anytime an alphabetic character is entered, it must be lowercase.

The character position(s) of each element will be listed first, followed by the element name. Below them will be the tag positions for the **006** tag. The values for this tag were finalized in 1996. What is presented here are the values which were accurate as of date of publication. Below the **006** value will be a statement of **Mandatory** or **Optional**. Each element will also contain information regarding the acceptability of the use of the fill character and blank values. Depending on your system, you may only have the character position numbers displayed, or you may have a narrative phrase for a single position or group of positions.

008/006

The positions covered here are those unique to *sound recordings*, both musical and nonmusical, as well as printed scores and sheet music. If another item in the record is predominant, then the information for that item is entered in the **008** tag, while the information for the music is entered in the **006** tag.

THE ELEMENTS IN DETAIL

008/18-19
006/01-02
Optional

Form of composition

A two character alphabetic code indicates the form of composition of printed and manuscript music, and musical sound recordings. The form of composition code is based on the terminology in the work itself and is intended to provide a coded approach to the content of the work. In addition to codes for forms, the list also includes codes for musical genres. The codes are based on LCSH.

Codes should be assigned when they apply to the item as a whole (e.g., if the item is a symphony and one of the movements is in sonata form, only the code for symphonies is recorded). If more than one code is appropriate, the code mu (Multiple forms) is used in this element.

an	Anthems
bt	Ballets
bg	Bluegrass music
bl	Blues
cn	Canons and rounds
ct	Cantatas
cz	Canzonas
cr	Carols
ca	Chaconnes
cs	Chance compositions
cp	Chansons, polyphonic
cc	Chant, Christian
cb	Chants, Other religious
cl	Chorale preludes
ch	Chorales
cg	Concerti grossi
co	Concertos
cy	Country music
df	Dance forms
dv	Divertimentos, serenades, cassations, divertissements, and notturni.
ft	Fantasias
fm	Folk music
fg	Fugures
gm	Gospel music
hy	Hymns
jz	Jazz
md	Madrigals
mr	Marches
ms	Masses
mz	Mazurkas
mi	Minuets
mo	Motets

mp	Moving picture music (soundtracks)
mc	Musical revues and comedies
mu	Multiple forms
nc	Nocturnes
nn	Not applicable
op	Operas
or	Oratorios
ov	Overtures
pt	Part-songs
pa	Passacaglias
pm	Passion music
pv	Pavans
po	Polonaises
pp	Popular music
pr	Preludes
pg	Program music
rg	Ragtime music
rq	Requiems
ri	Ricercars
rc	Rock music
rd	Rondos
sn	Sonatas
sg	Songs
st	Studies and exercises
su	Suites
sp	Symphonic poems
sy	Symphonies
tc	Toccatas
ts	Trio-sonatas
uu	Unknown
vr	Variations
wz	Waltzes
zz	Other forms of composition

008/20
006/03

Mandatory Format of music

This area contains a one-character alphabetic code which indicates the format of a musical composition. This character is used for printed or manuscript music only

Code values

a	Full score
b	Full score, miniature or study size
c	Accompaniment reduced for keyboard
d	Voice score
e	Condensed score or piano-conductor score
g	Close score
m	Multiple score formats
n	Not applicable
u	Unknown
z	Other score format

008/006

008/21
006/04
Optional | **Undefined**

This character position is undefined; it contains a blank or fill character.

008/22
006/05
Optional | **Target audience**

Enter a one-character alphabetic code describing the intellectual level of the target audience for which the material is intended.

CODE VALUES

blank Indicates that the intellectual level of the target audience is unknown, or that the identification of the item as juvenile material is not applicable.

a **Preschool**
b **Primary**
c **Elementary and junior high**
d **Secondary (senior high)**
e **Adult**
f **Specialized**
g **General**
j **Juvenile**

The values other than **blank** and **j** were made valid for use in February of 1995.

Be aware of the fact that if you enter *a, b, c* or *j* here, you may need to enter juvenile subject headings (LCAC).

008/23
006/06
Mandatory | **Form of item**

This area contains a single letter code which specifies the form of material for the item being described. This area is used only with printed or manuscript music.

CODE VALUES

blank **None of the following**
a **Microfilm**
b **Microfiche**
c **Microopaque**
d **Large print**
f **Braille**
r **Regular print reproduction**

008/24-29
006/07-12
Mandatory | **Accompanying matter**

Use up to six positions available here to indicate the contents of program notes and other accompanying material for sound recordings, music manuscripts, or printed music. Generally, a specific code is used only if a significant part of the accompanying material is the type of material represented by the code. Codes are recorded in alphabetical order. If fewer than six codes are assigned, the codes are left justified and the unused positions contain blanks.

Note that you may need to enter supporting information into the **300$e, 500**, or **504** fields.

blank **No accompanying matter**
a **Discography**
b **Bibliography**

c	Thematic index
d	Libretto or text
e	Biography of composer or author
f	Biography of performer or history of ensemble
g	Technical and/or historical information on instruments
h	Technical information on music
i	Historical information
k	Ethnological information
r	Instructional materials
s	Music
z	Other accompanying matter.

008/30-31
006/13-14
Mandatory

Literary text for sound recordings

This one-character alphabetic codes indicate the type of literary text contained in a nonmusical sound recording. Up to two codes may be recorded, and they are entered in the order given below. If more than two codes are appropriate to an item, only the two most significant are recorded.

CODE VALUES

blank	Item is a musical sound recording
p	Poetry
d	Drama
f	Fiction
k	Comedy
h	History
l	Lectures, speeches
o	Folktales
c	Conference proceedings
i	Instruction
j	Language instruction
s	Sounds
a	Autobiography
b	Biography
e	Essays
g	Reporting
m	Memoirs
r	Rehearsals
t	Interviews
n	Not applicable
z	Other types of literary text

008/32-34
006/15-17
Optional

Undefined

These three character positions are undefined; each contains a blank or fill character.

008 FIXED LENGTH DATA ELEMENTS
Visual materials
[motion pictures] [videorecordings] [slide] [transparency] [realia] [picture] [art original] [art reproduction]
[flash card]

REPEATABLE: NO
MANDATORY: YES
RELATES TO: --
AUTHORITY: NO

This tag contains coded information that is essentially a "summation" of the rest of the record. Even though it is at the beginning of the record, it is highly dependent on what you will later enter in the respective tags, so you may want to enter this tag after you have done the rest of the record.

1st Indicator
There is no 1st indicator for this tag.

2nd Indicator
There is no 2nd indicator for this tag.

SUBFIELD CODES

There are no subfield codes for this tag. Rather, there are data elements. There are 40 possible positions forthis tag (**00-39**) that provide coded information about the record as a whole or about special elements of particular tags.

EXAMPLES

Due to the wide variety of possible ways of displaying this information among the various automation systems, no examples are given. You are encouraged to review the manual for your system regarding how the information for this tag is displayed.

NOTES

Because of the nature of the information in this tag, it is not possible to give a location to find each piece of necessary information. You will need to scan and review various areas of the item, as well as review what you have entered in the individual tags in the rest of the record so that this information can be correctly coded. The information you enter here should agree with what you enter in the individual tags in the record.

DOCUMENTATION CONVENTIONS

Character positions are positionally defined. Character positions that are not defined contain a **blank [b]** or a **fill character [l]**. All defined character positions must contain either a defined code or a fill character. **Code [n] (not applicable)**, when it is defined for a data element, indicates that the character definition does not apply to the record.

Your particular system may automatically generate some values, while the designers default some in. Anytime an alphabetic character is entered, it must be lowercase.

The character position(s) of each element will be listed first, followed by the element name. Below them will be the tag positions for the **006** tag. Note that final coding and determination of the **006** tag was accomplished in 1996. What is presented here is accurate as of date of publication. Below the **006** value will be a statement of **Mandatory** or **Optional**. Each element will also contain information regarding the acceptability of the use of the fill character and blank values. Depending on your system, you may only have the character position numbers displayed, or you may have a narrative phrase for a single position or group of positions.

The positions covered here are those unique to visual materials. If another item in the record is predominant, then the information for the book would be coded in the **006** tag.

THE ELEMENTS IN DETAIL

008/18-20
006/01-03

Running time for motion pictures and videorecordings

Mandatory

Enter the running time, in minutes, of a motion picture or videorecording (including videocassettes and laserdiscs.) You should enter the value in minutes, rounding any fraction of a minute up. Use up to three character positions. This means that 52 min. becomes *052* and 2 hrs., 7 min. becomes *127*. If more than three characters are needed, enter *000* here.

If the running time is unknown, enter three dashes [---]

For slides, filmstrips, transparencies, etc., you should always enter *nnn* in these three positions.

008/21
006/04

Undefined

Optional

This character position is undefined; it is either blank or contains the fill character.

008/22
006/05

Target audience

Optional

This area contains a one-character code describing the target audience for which the material is intended. When items with factual content are considered appropriate for more than one intellectual level, the code is recorded for the highest level appropriate.

CODE VALUES

blank **Unknown or not applicable**
a   **Preschool (up to, but not including, kindergarten)**
b   **Primary (kindergarten through third grade)**
c   **Elementary and junior high (grades 4-8)**
d   **Secondary (senior high) (grades 9-12)**
e   **Adult**
f   **Specialized (e.g. handicapped, training films, etc.)**
g   **General**
j   **Juvenile**

008/23-27
006/06-10

Undefined (Formerly *Accompanying matter*)

Optional

These five positions used to indicate the type of accompanying production and publicity material. These values were:

CODE VALUES

blank **No accompanying matter**
l   **Stills**
m   **Script material**
o   **Posters**
p   **Pressbooks**
q   **Lobby cards**

r   Instructional materials (Use this if the item contains tests, quizzes,etc.)

s   Music

z   Other accompanying matter (Such as teacher's guides, sound recordings, study guides, and media-grams.)

008/28
006/11
Mandatory   **Government publication code**

This position contains a one-character alphabetic code indicating whether or not the item is produced by or for an international, national, state or local government agency, or by any subdivision of such a body.

CODE VALUES

blank   Not published by or for a governmental body

a   Autonomous or semi-autonomous component.

c   Published by or for a multilocal jurisdiction that is defined as a regional combination of jurisdictions below the state level.

f   Federal or national. This value is also used for American Indian tribes and for the governments of England, Wales, Scotland, and Northern Ireland.

i   International intergovernmental body.

l   Local jurisdiction, such as a city.

m   Multistate, such as Midwest or organizations that cross state lines.

s   State (including state-owned or controlled universities).

z   Other types of government publications.

If an item is published or produced jointly by government agencies at two different levels, record the code for the higher government form.

Academic Publications are considered government publications if the institutions are created or controlled by a government.

University Publications are considered government publications if the presses are created or controlled by a government (e.g., state university presses in the United States.)

008/29-32
006/12-15
Optional   **Undefined**

These four character positions should be left blank or contain the fill character.

008/33
006/16
Mandatory   **Type of material**

The value you enter here should agree with what you entered in the **300$a**.

CODE VALUES

a   Art original

b   Kit

c   Art reproduction

d   Diorama

f   Filmstrip

g   Game

i   Picture

k   Graphic

l   Technical drawing

m   Motion picture

n   Chart

o   Flash card

p	Microscope slide
q	Model
r	Realia
s	Slide
t	Transparency
v	Videorecording
w	Toy
z	Other type of material

008/34
006/17
Mandatory   Technique

This position indicates the technique used in creating motion in motion pictures or videorecordings.

<u>CODE VALUES</u>

a   **Animation** (including puppets, graphic film, model, clay or puppet animation and other techniques.)

c   **Animation and live action**

l   **Live action**

n   **Not applicable**

u   **Unknown**

z   **Other technique** (including microcinematography, time lapse cinematography, trick cinematography, and videorecordings and motion pictures made from still image slide sets or filmstrips without adding animation to the images.)

008   FIXED LENGTH DATA ELEMENTS
Serials

REPEATABLE: NO
MANDATORY: YES
RELATES TO: --
AUTHORITY: NO

This tag contains coded information that is essentially a "summation" of the rest of the record. Even though it is at the beginning of the record, it is highly dependent on what you will later enter in the respective tags, so you may want to enter this tag after you have done the rest of the record.

1st Indicator
There is no 1st indicator for this tag.

2nd Indicator
There is no 2nd indicator for this tag.

SUBFIELD CODES

There are no subfield codes for this tag. Rather, there are data elements. There are 40 possible positions for this tag (**00-39**) that provide coded information about the record as a whole or about special elements of particular tags.

EXAMPLES

Due to the wide variety of possible ways of displaying this information among the various automation systems, no examples are given. You are encouraged to review the manual for your system regarding how the information for this tag is displayed.

NOTES

Because of the nature of the information in this tag, it is not possible to give a location to find each piece of necessary information. You will need to scan and review various areas of the periodical, as well as review what you have entered in the individual tags in the rest of the record so that this information can be correctly coded. The information you enter here should agree with what you enter in the individual tags in the record. You may need to consult an outside source, like your subscription service company, *Ebsco's Serials Directory* or *Ulrich's* for more information.

DOCUMENTATION CONVENTIONS

Character positions are positionally defined. Character positions that are not defined contain a **blank [b]** or a **fill character** [l]. All defined character positions must contain either a defined code or a fill character. Code **[n] (not applicable)**, when it is defined for a data element, indicates that the character definition does not apply to the record.

Your particular system may automatically generate some values, while the designers default some in. Anytime an alphabetic character is entered, it must be lowercase.

The character position(s) of each element will be listed first, followed by the element name. Below them will be the tag positions for the **006** tag. The final coding of this tag was accomplished in 1996. What is presented here are the values which were current as of date of publication. Below the **006** value will be a statement of **Mandatory** or **Optional**. Each element will also contain information regarding the acceptability of the use of the fill character and blank values. Depending on your system, you may only have the character position numbers displayed, or you may have a narrative phrase for a single position or group of positions.

The positions covered here are those unique to serials. If you are cataloging a non-print item which is serially issued, (a CD-ROM disc that comes quarterly), you should enter the serial aspect in the **008** tag and the computer file aspect in the **006** tag.

THE ELEMENTS IN DETAIL

008/18
006/01

Frequency

Mandatory

This one-character code indicates the frequency of a serial. It is used in conjunction with **008/19** (regularity).

CODE VALUES

blank	**No determinable frequency**
a	**Annual**
b	**Bimonthly**
c	**Semiweekly**
d	**Daily**
e	**Biweekly**
f	**Semiannual**
g	**Biennial**
h	**Triennial**
i	**Three times a week**
j	**Three times a month**
m	**Monthly**
q	**Quarterly**
s	**Semimonthly**
t	**Three times a year**
u	**Unknown**
w	**Weekly**
z	**Other frequencies**

008/19
006/02

Regularity

Mandatory

This position contains a one-character code indicating the intended regularity of a serial. It is used in conjunction with the **008/18** (frequency) position.

CODE VALUES

n   **Normalized irregular** -- (not completely regular, but irregular in a predictable pattern).

r   **Regular** -- (serial has an intended regular publishing pattern).

u   **Unknown** -- (the regularity of the serial is unknown. If code u is used here, it must also be used in the Frequency position above).

x   **Completely irregular** -- (when the frequency is known to be intentionally irregular and the Frequency position is coded as blank or when the frequency in the **310** is expressed in numbers per year.

008/20
006/03

ISSN Center

Optional

This area contains a one-character code indicating the ISSN Network center responsible for assigning and maintaining certain data related to a serial item.

blank **No ISSN center code assigned** -- This indicates that no data has been assigned to the serial item by an ISSN Network center. This will be the value you will usually use.

0 **International center** -- The data has been assigned or maintained by the international Center of the ISSN Network, in Paris, France.

1 **United States** -- This value indicates that the ISSN Network data has been assigned or maintained by the United States National Serials Data Program (NSDP).

4 **Canada** -- The ISSN Network data has been assigned or are maintained by ISSN Network/ Canada.

z **Other** -- The ISSN Network data has been assigned or are maintained by an ISSN Network center other than the ones for which codes are defined.

008/21
006/04
Mandatory

Type of serial

A one-character alphabetic code indicating the type of serial item.

blank This code indicates that the serial does not fit one of the other types for which codes are defined. Yearbooks and annual reports are in this category.

m **Monographic series**
This code indicates that the item is a monographic series and is used for any title that is a series, regardless of its treatment. A monographic series is a group of analyzable items (i.e., each piece has a distinctive title) that are related to one another by a collective title. You should check with a cataloger before assigning code m.

n **Newspaper**
This code is used for a serial publication that is mainly designed to be a primary source of written information on current events connected with public affairs, either local, national and/or international in scope. It contains a broad range of news on all subjects and activities and is not limited to any specific subject matter. The *Wall Street Journal* and the *Chicago Tribune* are examples of newspapers.

p **Periodical**
This code is used for a serial appearing or intended to appear indefinitely at regular or stated intervals, generally more frequently than annually, each issue of which normally contains separate articles, stories, or other writings. *Stereo Review* and *US News & World Report* are examples of periodicals.

008/22
006/05
Optional

Form of original item

A one-character code specifying the form of material in which a serial was originally published.

CODE VALUES
blank None of the following
a   Microfilm
b   Microfiche
c   Microopaque

d	Large print	
f	Braille	
r	Regular print (standard eye-readable print)	

008/23
006/06

Mandatory

Form of item

This position contains a one-character code specifing the form of material for the serial item being described in this particular record.

<u>CODE VALUES</u>

blank	None of the following
a	Microfilm
b	Microfiche
c	Microopaque
d	Large print
f	Braille
r	Regular print (standard eye-readable print)

008/24
006/07

Optional

Nature of entire work

This position indicates the nature of a serial if it consists entirely of a certain type of material. It is used to specify what type of publication the item is as opposed to what it contains.

If the item can be considered more than one type of material, the types are recorded in **008/25-27** and this position is left blank.

<u>CODE VALUES</u>

blank	not specified
a	Abstracts/summaries
b	Bibliographies
c	Catalogs
d	Dictionaries
e	Encyclopedias
f	Handbooks
g	Legal articles
i	Indexes
k	Discographies
l	Legislation
n	Surveys of literature in a subject area
o	Reviews
p	Programmed texts
q	Filmographies
r	Directories
s	Statistics
t	Technical reports
v	Legal cases and case notes
w	Law reports and digests

008/006

Optional

Nature of contents

Use this area of the nature of the entire work cannot be described with a single character in the **008/24** position. Enter up to three codes in alphabetical order.

CODE VALUES

blank not specified
a   Abstracts/summaries
b   Bibliographies
c   Catalogs
d   Dictionaries
e   Encyclopedias
f   Handbooks
g   Legal articles
i   Indexes
k   Discographies
l   Legislation
n   Surveys of literature in a subject area
o   Reviews
p   Programmed texts
q   Filmographies
r   Directories
s   Statistics
t   Technical reports
v   Legal cases and case notes
w   Law reports and digests

008/28
006/11

Mandatory

Government publication

This position contains a one-character alphabetic code indicating whether or not the item is produced by or for an international, national, state or local government agency, or by any subdivision of such a body.

CODE VALUES

blank Not published by or for a governmental body
a   Autonomous or semi-autonomous component.
c   Published by or for a multilocal jurisdiction that is defined as a regional combination of jurisdictions below the state level.
f   Federal or national. This value is also used for American Indian tribes and for the governments of England, Wales, Scotland, and Northern Ireland.
i   International intergovernmental body.
l   Local jurisdiction, such as a city.
m   Multistate, such as Midwest or organizations that cross state lines.
s   State (including state-owned or controlled universities).
z   Other types of government publications.

If an item is published or produced jointly by government agencies at two different levels, record the code for the higher government form.

Academic Publications are considered government publications if the institutions are created or controlled by a government.

University Publications are considered government publications if the presses are created or controlled by a government (e.g., state university presses in the United States.)

008/29	**Conference publication**
006/12	
Optional	This position contains a one-character numeric code indicating whether a work consists of the proceedings, reports, or summaries of a conference.

CODE VALUES

0   **Not a conference publication**
This includes such publications as works composed of or based on a single paper; symposiums in print; hearings of legislative bodies; and courses given in a school.

1   **Conference publication**

008/30-32	**Undefined**
006/13-15	
Optional	These three character positions are undefined. They should be blank or contain the fill character. Some older serial records may have information in one of these three positions indicating the availability of a title page for cataloging (**008/30**), index availability (**008/31**) or cumulative index availability (**008/32**).

008/33	**Original alphabet or script of title**
006/16	
Optional	This position indicates the original alphabet or script of the title on the source item on which the key title (field **222**) is based.

blank   **no alphabet or script given**
a   **Basic roman** (Use this value for English items)
b   **Extended roman** (Use this value for most European, non-English language materials. Also use this if the title has diacritics in it.)
c   **Cyrillic**
d   **Japanese**
e   **Chinese**
f   **Arabic**
g   **Greek**
h   **Hebrew**
i   **Thai**
j   **Devanagari**
k   **Korean**
l   **Tamil**
u   **Unknown**
z   **Other**

008/34	**Successive/latest entry**
006/17	
Mandatory	This position indicates if the serial was cataloged according to successive entry or latest entry cataloging conventions.

0   **Successive entry** (this is used if the item is cataloged according to AACR2).

1   **Latest entry** (the practice of latest entry cataloging was abandoned with the introduction of AACR2.)

EVALUATING MARC RECORDS

The librarian today is faced with an array of cataloging sources. These include the vendor of the material itself, CD-ROM and network products, as well as shared union database products. While it is relatively easy to create a "basic" MARC records (one which contains the **001, 008, 040, 245, 260, 300** and *holding information), these are usually not adequate to provide the desired access in an automated system. According to *USMARC Bibliographic*, the inclusion of the above tags allows the vendor to say that the record is a "full" MARC record, yet it has no notes or summaries, no table of contents information and, most importantly, no subject entries.

The following records are designed to aid the user in evaluating records. Note that many of the tags listed are covered here, but very detailed tags, like the **007**, are beyond the scope of this publication. Suffice to say, when evaluating AV records, the **007** should be correctly entered by the cataloging source. Also, there are many areas of cataloging and the MARC record which are at the cataloger's discretion in accordance with *AACR2, USMARC Bibliographic*, and the library's own policies. The information presented here should be evaluated in light of that information. Also, the library should query its vendor about how these records will be accessed and which tags are indexed under the different search options.

This list is not intended to be all-inclusive. Rather, it is designed to be a starting point for further evaluation and study. Many automation vendors and retrospective conversion services provide forms and guidelines for evaluating (many designed to highlight the quality of their work.) The user should also search the relevant literature and publications on library automation for more guidance.